HEIDEGGER'S PHILOSOPHY AND THEORIES OF THE SELF

Explaining and defending a Heideggarian account of the self and our knowledge of the world, this book addresses the fundamental issues of selfhood and the elemental question of what it means to be human. Mitchell critically examines theories of the self derived from two distinct schools of thought: Descartes, Hume, Kant, Sartre and Stirner, representing a tradition which has dominated Western philosophy since Descartes, and who share a dualism which critically influences their theories of self; and Heidegger and Laing, representing a radical departure from the tradition and consequently a very different understanding of selfhood. Mitchell focuses on two key philosophical problems throughout: the problem of knowledge to explore the relation between the self and the world that is not-self, and the problem of identity to explore the relation between the self and itself over time.

Mitchell concludes that Heidegger provides a more adequate notion of selfhood than those from other philosophical traditions but argues that ultimately Heidegger does no more than echo Stirner's empty egoism and provides a bleak, inescapable heroism for the individual.

ASHGATE NEW CRITICAL THINKING IN PHILOSOPHY

The *Ashgate New Critical Thinking in Philosophy* series aims to bring high quality research monograph publishing back into focus for authors, the international library market, and student, academic and research readers. Headed by an international editorial advisory board of acclaimed scholars from across the philosophical spectrum, this new monograph series presents cutting-edge research from established as well as exciting new authors in the field; spans the breadth of philosophy and related disciplinary and interdisciplinary perspectives; and takes contemporary philosophical research into new directions and debate.

Series Editorial Board:

David Cooper, University of Durham, UK
Peter Lipton, University of Cambridge, UK
Sean Sayers, University of Kent at Canterbury, UK
Simon Critchley, University of Essex, UK
Simon Glendinning, University of Reading, UK
Paul Helm, King's College London, UK
David Lamb, University of Birmingham, UK
Stephen Mulhall, University of Oxford, UK
Greg McCulloch, University of Birmingham, UK
Ernest Sosa, Brown University, Rhode Island, USA
John Post, Vanderbilt University, Nashville, USA
Alan Goldman, University of Miami, Florida, USA
Joseph Friggieri, University of Malta, Malta
Graham Priest, University of Queensland, Brisbane, Australia
Moira Gatens, University of Sydney, Australia
Alan Musgrave, University of Otago, New Zealand

Heidegger's Philosophy and Theories of the Self

DEREK ROBERT MITCHELL

Routledge
Taylor & Francis Group

LONDON AND NEW YORK

First published 2001 by Ashgate Publishing

Reissued 2019 by Routledge
2 Park Square, Milton Park, Abingdon, Oxon, OX14 4RN
605 Third Avenue, New York, NY 10017

First issued in paperback 2021

Routledge is an imprint of the Taylor & Francis Group, an informa business

Copyright © 2001, Derek Robert Mitchell

All rights reserved. No part of this book may be reprinted or reproduced or utilised in any form or by any electronic, mechanical, or other means, now known or hereafter invented, including photocopying and recording, or in any information storage or retrieval system, without permission in writing from the publishers.

Notice:
Product or corporate names may be trademarks or registered trademarks, and are used only for identification and explanation without intent to infringe.

Publisher's Note
The publisher has gone to great lengths to ensure the quality of this reprint but points out that some imperfections in the original copies may be apparent.

Disclaimer
The publisher has made every effort to trace copyright holders and welcomes correspondence from those they have been unable to contact.

A Library of Congress record exists under LC control number:

ISBN 13: 978-1-138-72766-3 (hbk)
ISBN 13: 978-1-315-19078-5 (ebk)
ISBN 13: 978-1-138-72764-9 (pbk)

*This book is dedicated to the memory of my grandmother.
Eliza Ann Davis (1899-1976)*

Contents

Acknowledgements		*viii*
1	Theories of the Self	1
2	Max Stirner - The Tyranny of Pure Theory	12
3	R.D. Laing - All Together Now	23
4	Descartes, Locke and Hume - Self and World	43
5	Kant - Let Sleeping Dogma Awake!	60
6	Sartre - Goldilocks Uncovered	91
7	Heidegger - An Everyday Story of Beings-in-the-World	114
8	Heidegger - Goldilocks Divined	146
9	Conclusion - How to Argue with an Egoist	176
Bibliography		195
Index		201

Acknowledgements

I would like to acknowledge the support and assistance of Sean Sayers my PhD. Supervisor who directed my work over a long period and then assisted me in finding a publisher. I would also like to thank Sean for his patience. I would like to thank Simon Glendinning, Sue Wiseman and Megan Stern who all provided inspiration and constructive criticism when it was most needed. Most of all I would like to thank Gilda, who has put up with my philosophy and me for the best part of twenty-five years and without whom none of this would have been possible.

1

Theories of the Self

The aim of this book is to examine a number of different theories of the self explicitly set out in, or implied by, the work of Descartes, Hume, Kant, Max Stirner, Heidegger, Sartre, and R.D. Laing. These seven are divided into two camps representing two distinctly different schools of thought. The first group, which includes Descartes, Hume, Kant, Sartre and Stirner, represents a tradition that has dominated western philosophy since Descartes, and, although these five differ in many ways, I will argue that they share certain approaches and a dualism that critically influences their theories of the self. The second group, which comprises Heidegger and Laing, represents a radical departure from the tradition and a rejection of the approach shared by its members, and consequently a very different understanding of selfhood.

Two philosophical problems are used to focus the discussion of the works of these philosophers. The problem of knowledge, exemplified by the "veil of the senses" argument, is used to examine the relation between the self and the world that is not-self, and to address the question of the spatiality of the self. The problem of the continuity of the identity of the self over time, the problem of personal identity, is used to examine the relation between the self and itself at different times, and to address the question of the temporality of the self. The work of each of the philosophers cited is examined in respect of the way in which these problems are set out, and the questions they raise addressed.

Chapter Two sets out the position of Max Stirner.[1] Stirner's egoism provides the initial point of reference for the following discussion of theories of the self. Stirner gives us the ultimately subjective individual in "the Owner". His egoism is uncompromising and, although his work appears to be, and often is, disorganised and chaotic, it becomes clear throughout the book that, not only is his position more resilient than is at first apparent, but he poses questions about selfhood and individuality which those who would reject his egoism must answer if they are to be successful in developing alternative notions of the self. Crucial to the understanding of the strength of Stirner's position is the way in which he rejects the ground on which most criticism of his egoism is based. What is sometimes seen as Stirner's paranoia must be overcome by means other than taking up a position based either on faith, or the kind of normative positions which are precisely the target of Stirner's fiercest condemnation. This is the challenge of Stirner's egoism, which must be met.[2]

Chapter Three sets out the position of R.D. Laing, which differs from that of Stirner both in terms of its perspective, since Laing was a practising Psychiatrist, and also in its conclusions about the self. Laing, largely through a description of case histories of his patients, provides a picture of the self as essentially relational and only isolated and singular when dysfunctional. Laing gives us the essentially social individual. The contrast between these two views of the self is explicit, but in neither is there sufficient to decide the case one way or the other. While Laing's case histories seem to indicate that Stirner's position is not tenable, there are signs in Laing's work of the kinds of norms of behaviour and self conception that Stirner wishes to reject. The project of examining the philosophical underpinnings of both these positions is thereby set in motion as a means of determining which of these diametrically opposed views provides the most adequate understanding of selfhood.

Chapter Four begins the setting out of the way in which the work of Descartes, Hume, Kant and Sartre will be examined and used to support a Stirnerian view of the self. The two philosophical problems (the problems of knowledge and personal identity)[3] which will be used to focus the discussion of the works of these philosophers are introduced and explained. Specifically in this Chapter the works of Descartes and Hume are examined, in particular Descartes' *Meditations* with reference to the existence of a world external to the self and the mind/body problem, and Hume's discussion of personal identity in the *Treatise of Human Nature*. The ways in which these two fail, and succeed, in their solutions to the two problems, and the theories of the self, which are thereby implied, are given in the conclusion of this Chapter.[4]

In Chapter Five the contribution of Kant is set out and examined, in particular his theory of knowledge and his discussion of the self in the *Critique of Pure Reason*. The advances made by Kant are discussed and his development of the Cartesian position, in particular his retrieval of the sceptical position bequeathed by Hume, is recognised.[5] However Kant's work retains certain of the limitations found in Descartes and Hume and is ultimately found to have failed to solve either the problem of knowledge or the problem of personal identity. Despite the fact that Kant's work represents a significant advance on the work of both Descartes and Hume, I will argue that this advance does not move away from the structural dualism of Descartes and Hume and in this respect is only incremental to the tradition. Kant incorporates this inherited dualism firmly into his systems to the extent that it is both essential to the maintenance of the structure of his argument and equally fatal to his efforts to solve the problems. It becomes clear that this kind of approach will never succeed in answering the questions it raises. Some initial pointers towards the link between Kant's epistemology and the later work of Heidegger are given in the commentary on Kant in this Chapter.[6]

Chapter Six looks at Sartre's existentialism and examines the theory of the self put forward in his *Being and Nothingness*, including Sartre's attempt to re-interpret the Cartesian *cogito*.[7] Sartre's notion of human freedom is explored and its deficiencies exposed. His discussion of the Other in Part Three of *Being and Nothingness* is used as a means of looking at how he approaches the problems of knowledge and identity. In the conclusion of this Chapter it becomes clear that, although Sartre is an avowed Cartesian, the conclusions he reaches with regard to the nature of the self violate his Cartesian premise, the *cogito*. While Sartre brings some powerful insights, and an effective methodology, to discussions about the nature of the self, he fails to re-interpret the *cogito* to the degree required to generate the intensely relational view of the self finally presented in *Being and Nothingness*. Again, as with Kant, the dualism, which Sartre inherited from Descartes, proves fatal to his enterprise. In spite of this failure, and because of his conclusions about relation to the Other, Sartre represents an important bridge between the tradition represented by Descartes, Hume and Kant and the rejection of this tradition given in Heidegger's early work (1926-1929).

At the beginning of Chapter Seven the respective and relative failures and contributions of Descartes, Hume, Kant and Sartre, with regard to the questions raised by the problems of knowledge and identity, are summarised and a judgement made that this collective failure brings into question the founding premises of the tradition and its entire approach to questions regarding the self. As an alternative to this the early work of Heidegger is presented to provide the basis for a different understanding of the spatiality and temporality of selfhood. In this Chapter Heidegger's interpretation of the Being of everyday Dasein is set out, taken from the first Division of his *Being and Time*, Part One of *The Basic Problems of Phenomenology*, and his work on Kant in *Kant and the Problem of Metaphysics*.[8] In the conclusion of this Chapter it is argued that Heidegger has dissolved the problem of knowledge, undermined the position taken by Descartes, Hume, Kant and Sartre and established a new understanding of the spatiality of selfhood. Heidegger has also begun to explain the genesis of this position as a deficient mode of the understanding of Being.

In Chapter Eight Heidegger's interpretation of authentic Dasein is made explicit, including the analyses of death and conscience. The temporality of the self is described using Division Two of *Being and Time*, Part Two of *The Basic Problems of Phenomenology*, and his work on Kant in *Kant and the Problem of Metaphysics*. Heidegger's debt to Kant is acknowledged and the genesis of the positions taken by Descartes, Hume, Kant and Sartre is fully explained. By the end of this Chapter it appears that Heidegger has dissolved the problem of identity and established a radically new notion of selfhood, which does not set the apparently intractable problems encountered within the tradition he rejects. The notions of self, space and time are re-interpreted by Heidegger into a coherent and integrated whole which is neither solipsistic nor dualistic,[9] and which confirms rather than denies the conclusions we draw from everyday experience. Some criticism of the formalism of Heidegger's position is now developed and it is recognised that formalism is central to Heidegger's method and his rejection of the problems posed by the tradition.[10]

In the concluding chapter the contributions made by Descartes, Hume, Kant, Sartre, and Heidegger are summarised and placed in context. The discussion then returns to the original dispute between Stirner and Laing and, on the basis of Heidegger's success, Laing's position is vindicated and Stirner's position is shown to be self destructive and self contradictory. Heidegger provides the ground from which Stirner's egoism can be rejected, ground which is not subject to destruction from Stirner's criticism. However, further criticism of Heidegger, based on the now complete exposition of his work of this period can now finally be advanced and it is shown how the formalism, which is central to his approach and method, has damaging consequences for his notion of selfhood. I will argue that Heidegger avoids the questions posed by the problems within the tradition only by holding to a strict distinction between the forms of Being and its contents. By refusing to answer questions about the latter, Heidegger avoids the pitfalls of his predecessors but pays the penalty of being able to say nothing about how Being is to be filled up. It becomes clear that the cost to Heidegger of his manoeuvres, in avoiding the questions raised by the tradition, is an empty formalism in his conclusions about selfhood, an heroic formalism which in the end can do no more than echo Stirner's empty egoism, "Be yourself", "Be an Owner".[11] The book concludes ironically with the re-emergence of Stirner's egoism alongside Heidegger's notion of authentic Dasein.

Theories of the Self

Having set out clearly my own objectives for this book it is clear that many others have written on the same subject, in many different ways. In order in part to distinguish my approach from these, and to set my own argument in some sort of context, I will now briefly survey some of the other recent, and less recent work, on the Self which I have not used and which, in varying degrees, takes a different approach and reaches different conclusions to those I will arrive at. This is by no means intended to provide a comprehensive lexicon of work on this wide and much studied subject but may point the reader towards some other interesting and illuminating work on aspects of the Self which I will not be addressing.

In the tradition of Continental philosophy since the the eighteenth century much attention has been paid to the question of selfhood. Solomon in his book *Continental Philosophy Since 1750 - The Rise and Fall of the Self* provides a most useful historical survey tracing the development of the notion of the self, which he says was "discovered" in the mid-eighteenth century, to what he contends is the end of the notion with structuralism and post-modernism. Solomon parallels the development of the notion of the self in European (Continental) Philosophy with the development of European self-image. He describes the notion of self as the "transcendental pretence" and traces its development through the luminaries of Continental philosophy beginning with Rousseau and Kant, moving through the Romantics, Fichte, Schelling and Schiller, on through Hegel, Schopenauer, Feuerbach, Marx, Nietzsche, into phenomenology with Husserl and on to the Existentialists, Kierkegaard, Sartre, Heidegger, Camus, De Beauvoir and Merleau-Ponty, and finally to the structuralist and post-modern conclusion in Foucault and Derrida. This wide ranging enquiry is an excellent starting point for anyone interested in these issues.

Charles Taylor in his extensive book *Source of the Self* again traces the historical development of the notion of the self in an attempt to define modern identity through a description of its genesis. Taylor looks at three facets of identity. The first is what he calls the modern inwardness, the sense we have of ourselves as beings with inner depths, in short our sense of personal self. The second is what he refers to as the affirmation of ordinary life, in which he places great store and which bears some relation to Heidegger's notion of everydayness. The third facet is the expressivist notion of nature as an inner moral source. Taylor takes a much more specifically moral philsophical approach than I will be taking as he seeks to investigate the apparent conflict between identity and modernity. In view of his starting point it is perhaps not surprising that he comes to the conclusion that modern subjectivity has its roots in ideas of the human good and a rejection of the presumption that subjectivity leads to subjectivism or even nihilism. I find that I am much less optimistic about this by the end of my own investigation.

Parfit also provides a very extensive ethical and moral philosophical approach to the whole question of personal identity in *Reasons and Persons* and addresses vital questions about personal identity, and rationality and identity and morality, in looking at our beliefs about our own identity, what is wrong with these beliefs and why this matters. While I cannot but accept the importance of the moral dimension to the study of the self I am not primarily concerned with these aspects of the question in this book, although I will make some concluding references at the end of my investigation. Parfit provides an in-depth discussion of all of these issues and readers interested in these questions should not fail to read his book.

There has been a considerable amount of work on the self under the heading of Philosophy of Mind in the Analytic tradition. Gilbert Ryle's seminal work, *The Concept of Mind,* and work by Searle in this field are essential reading for those interested in the mind/brain argument.

Ryle attacks Cartesianism from within the analytical tradition and without any recourse to Heidegger, Sartre or Kant, which makes his approach very different from my own. He will have no truck with the bifurcation of lives into private and public, corporeal and non-corporeal, body and soul. For Ryle the myth of the "ghost in the machine" is no kind of explanation of the self. However, without the insights provided by the Existential School and by Heidegger's work it is hard to see how this kind of approach can really successfully escape from the confines of the tradition without finding itself with nowhere to go.

In the same vein Searle's work in books like *The Rediscovery of the Mind* presents another very different approach to the one I am taking. Searle, from within the analytical tradition, seeks to criticise both the materialist and dualist ideas of selfhood and to begin a serious examination of consciousness in its own terms. He firmly rejects the idea that the mind is like some sort of computer programme and wishes to reform the study of mental phenomena and thereby rediscover the mind. Searle provides a study of selfood from the point of view of the philosophy of language which locates consciousness within our general conception of the world and the rest of our mental life, in an attempt to go beyond what he sees as the sterility of the materialist and dualist approach in the Analytic tradition. Although I have sympathy with Searle's aims my own work will seek to criticise this same sterility from the Existential tradition and I will not enter the mind/brain debate in this way, nor am I interested in discussions as to whether the mind is some sort of computer programme or the brain a machine for thinking. My own work is primarily concerned with our knowing and how we can know about the self and about anything else for that matter. This means that my work takes a more unashamedly metaphysical approach than either Ryle or Searle.

There are inevitably many works, which take a psychoanalytical approach to the notion of the self. I will not attempt to provide even a summary list of this work since most of it is located well outside the path I have chosen and much of it is not even slightly connected to the ways in which the questions are addressed in philosophy. However of these kinds of works it is worth mentioning a few, if only in passing, as they can provide an interesting and sometimes informative perspective to philosophical enquiry. Modell in *The Private Self* considers what he calls "the unavoidable epistemological dilemma posed by an outside observer, observing the private self".[12] This is a question that is central to the epistemological debate that I will set out, and it is a dilemma to which I will return in some detail, particularly when considering the way that it is elegantly described by Hume. Modell also says that, "The self is paradoxical: it is an enduring structure and at the same time nearly co-terminous with an ever-changing consciousness" (Modell, 1993, p.3). This succinctly expresses the problem of the continuity of personal identity and I will use it later to focus the discussion on the temporality of the self. Modell is concerned with the balance between autonomy and dependence in the self and, using observations marshalled from psychoanalysis, infant research and neurobiology, he strives to correct the balance, or imbalance as he sees it, in work in this area. Modell believes that the self is something more than simply the socially constructed self and has an inbuilt capacity to start itself. However he is a firm believer in psychology as rooted in biology, and in brain as the source of self, in this he is some way from my own approach which, as I have said, is not concerned with the mind/brain problem in this way. In some ways this short work by Modell is reminiscent, as a mirror image, of Descartes in the *Meditations*. In the same way that Descartes wished to confirm the spirituality of the soul as the received wisdom and then struggles with the notion of a connected corporeality. Modell wants to remain a scientist, with a firmly materialist point of view, and yet to recognise an inner, perhaps more spiritual dimension to the self.

Jonathan Glover in his book, *The Philosophy and Psychology of Personal Identity* addresses more explicitly philosophical questions in a more philosophical way when he asks, in the first part of the book, "What is it to be a person?" in an attempt to show how work in philosophy and science converge. This is followed, in Part Two, by, "How are we able to create ourselves?". Glover usefully examines three important claims about selfhood, these are; that our natural belief that a person has indivisible unity is mistaken, that being a person requires self consciousness, and that our natural beliefs about what our own unity consists in are mistaken. All of these claims will be, at least indirectly, addressed in this book but specifically the first and third are of particular interest to my own discussion in that they are both highly relevant to the question of the continuity of personal identity over time and therefore to the relation of the self to itself at another time, and therefore to temporality itself. I will later show how this question is raised by Hume and how, successively, Kant and Sartre fail to answer it satisfactorily before showing how Heidegger reinterprets the question and demonstrates not only how it is answered but how and why it arises. The second part of Glover's work is concerned with self creation, and, by the end Glover, in some ways like Modell, ends with a slightly uneasy compromise between a socially created a self capable of, if not its own creation, contributing a unique character to its own particular development. My own work, though not primarily concerned with the source of the self, will, I am sure, touch on these important questions on the boundaries between philosophy and psychology.

Garrett in his book, *Personal Identity and Self Consciousness*, gives a good modern overview account of the issues in the philosophy of persons and personal identity, which does not make reference to the works of either Heidegger or Sartre. His aims are to give a new theory of personal identity over time, to defend the importance of personal identity from sceptical attack, and to explore the nature of self consciousness. To achieve this he uses a variety of sometimes ingenious thought experiments. After giving an account of the metaphysics of persons and of personal identity in the first five chapters he goes on in chapter six to explore whether the value we attach to persons and personal identity is justified, and in the final two chapters looks at self consciousness. While Garrett is interested in some of the same questions that interest me, like, "What is a person?" and "What is it for the same person to persist over time?" He also wants to look at questions like, "What happens if my brain is split in two?" and "Is personal identity all or nothing?" which are of less interest to my enquiry. He is however interested to consider whether the first person singular (I) is a device of reference to an object. I will consider this question at some length in discussing the work of Hume, Kant and Sartre, under the heading of the "Goldilocks Problem". This question, the ways that the Cartesian tradition fail to answer it, and ultimately the reasons why it can be posed in that tradition, will form a central part of my own argument against Cartesianism.

Nowhere in this book will I give an account of the work of Foucault, such an enterprise would be well beyond the scope of this work. However I must recognise his seminal influence on the philosophy of the self, particularly in looking at how the self constitutes itself and in the tracing of the techniques of self-formation from the early Greeks to the Christian age. Foucault wrote on many topics including, sexuality, punishment and discipline, and notions of illness, health and madness and sanity. However, as I have already said, I am not seeking to approach the question of the self from a psychoanalytical position and to attempt to combine my own examination of the development of epistemology and ontology as they affect ideas of the self with such work as produced by Foucault would only serve to confuse the reader in what is already a complex and difficult area.

Paul Ricouer in his book, *Oneself as Another*, addresses most of the main questions addressed by my book albeit from a somewhat different perspective. Ricoeur's book is made up of a series of ten studies and he sets out three intentions, which are addressed in the course of the book. First, to indicate the primacy of reflective meditation over the immediate positing of the subject, as this is expressed in the first person singular: "I think, I am" (this straight away constitutes a rejection of the Cartesian position and opens up a wide new field of investigation), second, to distinguish two major meanings of "identity" and to thereby explore the relation of self to temporality, and third, to examine the dialectic of self and other self. This third intention is perhaps the most central to the study and, as he indicates, implies a very specific kind of otherness and relation of self to other,

> A kind of otherness that is not the result of comparison is suggested by our title, otherness of a kind that can be constitutive of selfhood as such.

And,

> *Oneself as Another* suggests from the outset that the selfhood of oneself implies otherness to such an intimate degree that one cannot be thought of without the other. (Ricoeur, 1992, p.3)

These are notions, which clearly come down from not only from Heidegger but also from the work of Hegel. Ricoeur is contrasting distinct schools of thought on the self and attempting to show the gap between what he terms the hermeneutics of the self and philosophies of the *cogito*. As I will set out later the latter of these two approaches is characterised by the certainty of the *cogito* while the hermeneutic approach looks for the ground of selfhood in a form of attestation and is closely allied to Heidegger's use of the notion of conscience. While the Cartesian approach may be more familiar I will hope to show, as does Ricoeur, that the alternative is more fruitful. Ricoeur's studies cover several areas: Philosophy of language (Studies One and Two), philosophy of action, (Studies Three and Four), the question of identity at the point of intersection between hermeneutic and analytic philosophy (Studies Five and Six), the ethical and moral determinations of action (Studies Seven, Eight and Nine), and finally a tenth study which looks at the ontology of the Self. In particular Ricoeur addresses what he calls the crisis of the *cogito* and the way that this affects notion of the self in the Cartesian tradition, he equates what he calls philosophies of the subject inextricably with philosophies of the *cogito* and says,

> I hold here as paradigmatic of philosophies of the subject that the subject is formulated in the first person – *ego cogito*. (Ricoeur, 1992, p. 4)

He then proposes a mid-course between what he sees as this mistaken certainty and the polar alternative of Nietzschean nihilism. Hermeneutics provides the way to this alternative.

> It challenges the thesis of the indecomposable simplicity of the *cogito*, which is joined, to that of its immediacy. We shall see that it challenges the hypothesis of

> reflective simplicity without thereby giving in to the vertigo of the disintegration of the self pursued mercilessly by Nietzschean deconstruction. (Ricoeur, 1992, p.19)

And therefore

> To say *self* is not to say I. The *I* is posited – or is deposed. The self is implied reflectively in the operation, the analysis of which precedes the return toward this self. (Ricoeur, 1992, p. 18)

Finally,

> As credence without any guarantee, but also as trust greater than any suspicion, the hermeneutics of the self can claim to hold itself at an equal distance from the *cogito* exalted by Descartes and from the *cogito* that Nietzsche proclaimed forfeit. (Ricoeur, 1992, p. 23)

In the final study, in which he summarises the implications for the ontology of the self of what has been said in the first nine studies, Ricoeur examines Heidegger's re-appropriation of Aristotle in *Being and Time* but eventually turns to Spinoza for what he feels is a more successful attempt at this re-appropriation. Ricoeur also provides a critical examination of Heidegger's use of the notion of conscience as the attestation of Dasein's being-guilty. While Heidegger insists that the call of conscience is the call of lost Dasein to itself, Ricoeur interprets conscience as the call of the other from within Dasein and thereby uses this notion to unite self and other in a way that Heidegger either would not, or could not. I hope that this book will make it clear that Heidegger was unable rather than unwilling in this respect. Ricoeur's work is wide ranging and uses work from many sources including, Aristotle, Plato, Descartes, Kant, Hegel, Nietzsche, Husserl, Heidegger and Wittgenstein and provides an interesting and useful means of addressing the fundamental question, "What sort of being is the Self?" By the end of the book he hopes to have shown that,

> The *autonomy* of the self will appear to be tightly bound up with *solicitude* for ones neighbour and with justice for each individual. (Ricoeur, 1992, p.18)

I am doubtful as to whether this entirely laudable aim is within our grasp and by the end of this book I think that I will have successfully argued the case for a somewhat less optimistic and less ambitious conclusion.

Notes

1. Given in Stirner's only significant and enduring work *The Ego and Its Own* which is a testament to individualist anarchism and has achieved cult status in anarchist circles.
2. Stirner's Egoism will provide an analytic focus at one extreme end of the continuum between individual and community. I will not seek to defend his egoism as an ethical position.
3. The formulation of these problems is taken directly from the tradition. For the "veil of the senses" I have used Descartes in *Meditations* and *Discourse on the Method*. For the discussion of the problem of identity Locke's *Essay Concerning Human Understanding* and Hume's *Treatise of Human Nature* provide the clearest setting out of the problem.
4. This failure is elegantly outlined by Richardson, *Existential Epistemology* which argues that the tradition fails to ground scientific knowledge to the extent required by science.
5. As given most notably by Strawson, *The Bounds of Sense*, in which the traditionally understood shortcomings of Kant's position are clearly set out. Scruton gives a shorter more concise exposition of the whole of Kant's work in his slim volume *Kant*.
6. Heidegger's work in both *The Basic Problems of Phenomenology* and *Kant and the Problem with Metaphysics* provides a radically different reading of Kant, which opens the way to an escape from the dualism of the Cartesian tradition.
7. The discussion of Sartre's existentialism precedes the exposition of Heidegger's chronologically earlier work because although Sartre's *Being and Nothingness* is considerably derivative of Heidegger's *Being and Time*, following Sartre's time in Berlin in 1934, Sartre's most significant contribution to the debate at this stage is his attempt to rework the *cogito* and to solve the problems of the tradition from within. *Being and Nothingness* may therefore be reasonably held to be methodologically prior to *Being and Time*.
8. Interpretations of Heidegger's difficult texts vary in consistency, clarity and usefulness. While some offer excellent guidance through Heideggerian byways (Mulhall, Guignon), others direct the reader into distinctly un-Heideggerian modes of thought (Gelven, Zimmerman). Commentaries on Heidegger's work should be read and used with caution and Heidegger's text must be allowed to speak for itself.
9. Nor mystical, another common error committed by aspiring Heideggerians, notably Zimmerman in *Eclipse of the Self*.
10. Waterhouse, 1981, pp. 179-192, gives a stark if somewhat exaggerated argument for this interpretation in which he is perhaps less than fair as to what Heidegger might be expected to have achieved.
11. Ridley Scott's film *Blade Runner* provides a perfect description of the heroic position as the replicant Roy Batty learns to be human through a process of heroic self definition and self possession which is completed shortly before his "death".
12. Modell, 1993, p.1.

2

Max Stirner - The Tyranny of Pure Theory

To begin with I will set out a position which rejects every article of faith imaginable, Max Stirner's egoism. This will provide a starting point for the analysis from the point of view of the ultimate individual. Stirner sets out his startling views in his only significant work *The Ego and Its Own*.[1] To anyone who has not read the book it is difficult to describe. On the face of it the seemingly unorganised "stream of consciousness" of *The Ego and Its Own* suggests naivety in the extreme. It also makes the book difficult to read. It seems that Stirner has simply written down the first words that came into his head in a sort of philosophical word association game. Much of the book thus resembles what might be termed saloon bar philosophy. However a sympathetic interpretation, which is what I shall begin with, draws the conclusion that, Stirner, the individualist, has written about the individual in a highly idiosyncratic and individual manner in order to make his point about the unique individual, and, although his method sometimes seems confused to the point of absence, his conclusions have an almost hypnotic persuasiveness.

Before setting out the ideas he expresses in *The Ego and Its Own* it must be said that any attempt to judge the book by traditional standards of academic scholarship is pointless. The book describes the development of an individual psyche (Stirner's) in the process of coming to terms with the world. The "stream of consciousness" represents a real, though probably not intentional, description of the individual's perspective of himself and society, and it is as this that Stirner's work must be assessed.[2] It is not an attempt, in the traditional sense, to describe the world; it is a work of psycho-philosophy or even philosophical literature.

The Unique One - The Unmoved Mover

Max Stirner, the egoist *par excellence*, comes in a line of philosophers following and feeding upon Hegel's method.[3] In Stirner, the individual is broken free from the totality of the Hegelian Absolute and made the centre and end of all attention. For Stirner only the self is real, anything else, community, society, God, and even "Man" and "the individual" are an abstraction. Stirner's egoism is nihilistic and atheistic; Paterson expresses this succinctly when he says,

> His [Stirner's] symbolic act of self-assertion in *The Ego and Its Own* takes the form of a systematic and absolute denial of every principle by which the hearts and minds of men have been moved. At the end of his metaphysical rebellion he alone remains, the unmoved mover who has revealed himself by destroying everything that might have muffled or confined him. (Paterson, 1971, p.197)

He rejects the kind of uncompromising surrender demanded of the individual by Christianity and all other religions, including those political and philosophical trends that have assumed quasi-religious form. As Clark says, "he proposes a total reabsorption of the Absolute or Spirit in any form into the individual ego, its original creator" (Clark, 1976, p.11).

Stirner says it for himself, unequivocally, when he announces, "Away, then, with every concern that is not altogether my concern!"(Stirner, 1982, p.5). Stirner's intentions are made clear from the very beginning of his book, but the first substantive part of *The Ego and Its Own* is taken up with a setting out of the intellectual progress of mankind through the ages from "The Ancients" to "The Moderns" and on to "The Free". This is similar, in some ways, to Hegel's progress in his *Phenomenology of Spirit* (Hegel, 1977) when he describes the individual consciousness coming to full self-consciousness, and Stirner's description, in Part One of *The Ego and Its Own*, can best be seen as his exposition of man, as the individual consciousness, coming to himself, rather than as a simple historical dissertation on civilisation. We may even surmise that this is the route taken by the individual egoist Max Stirner in the process of his own self development. Wherever it came from, this part of *The Ego and Its Own* has little to tell us about Stirner's thought except that we must not expect his arguments to develop evenly or systematically, because they do not.

It is in Part Two of this strange book that Stirner really sets out the substance of his case in all its appalling clarity. Stirner assesses and dismisses transcendental values, which might be said to subsist beyond the individual and be worthy of his striving. In simple terms he points out that all of these values are given meaning, by his own self. Their attainment is irrelevant outside the context of this self. His argument against the primacy of freedom is a case in point.

> I have no objection to freedom but I wish more than freedom for you: you should not merely *be rid* of what you do not want; you should not only be a "freeman" you should be an "owner" too. (Stirner, 1982, p.156)

Freedom, like all the other values men pursue, is merely a means to an end, and that end is themselves, therefore,

> Now why, if freedom is striven for after love of the I after all - why not choose the I himself as the beginning, middle, and end? Am I not worth more than freedom? Is it not I that make myself free, am I not the first? Even unfree, even laid in a thousand fetters, I yet am. (Ibid, p.163)

Within a few short pages of admittedly flowery and unusual prose Stirner advances and dismisses freedom as an end worthy of his efforts, he contends that it is a value contingent merely upon our circumstances at a given moment and therefore always particular in content. For example,

> What the craving for freedom has always come to has been the desire for a *particular* freedom, such as freedom of faith; the believing man wanted to be free and independent; of what? of faith perhaps? no! but of the inquisitors of faith. (Ibid, p.159)

Furthermore Stirner recognises that new freedom from old constraints brings with it more new constraints, and this devalues the worth of the new freedom.[4] "The craving for a *particular* freedom always includes the purpose of a new dominion" (Ibid, p. 160). However, Stirner's response to this necessity is novel in the extreme. Instead of recognising and becoming reconciled to the constrained nature of any freedom which might be striven for or attained, Stirner affirms his belief in a kind of freedom which has an absolute character. He therefore rejects contingent and conditional freedom and tries to go beyond freedom.

> Freedom you all want, you want *freedom*. Why then do you higgle over more or less? *Freedom* can only be the whole of freedom; a piece of freedom is not *freedom*. You despair of the possibility of obtaining the whole of freedom, freedom from everything - yes, you consider it insanity even to wish this? - Well, then leave off chasing after the phantom and spend your pains on something better than the - *unattainable*. (Ibid, p.160)

To those who say that there is still nothing better than freedom Stirner points them towards themselves. "Why will you not take courage now to really make *yourselves* the central point and the main thing altogether?" (Ibid, p.161). It is as if absolute freedom, makes freedom into something else altogether, or at least points the way towards the ultimate reality and value of the individual ego.

Stirner has undermined the basis of conventional values and made values necessarily embodied in the individual if they are to be anything at all. In Stirner's terms the world and the individual have been progressively recovered, first from God by Feuerbach, from Hegel's Absolute by Marx, and now from abstract notions of Man and the individual, a God on earth, by Stirner. He exhorts us to see the true nature of things when he says,

> Therefore turn to yourselves rather than to your gods or idols. Bring out from yourselves what is in you, bring it to the light, bring yourselves to revelation. (Ibid, p.161)

The use of the language of illumination and revelation is a feature of Stirner's work. He uses it in the manner of one who has *seen the light* and simply wishes to show others the wonder he has encountered, this gives the individual in *The Ego and Its Own* a strong aura of the "born again". Stirner's egoist is as absolute as Dostoyevsky's Raskolnikov,[5] as detached as Camus' Mersault,[6] and as cold as Sartre's Roquentin.[7] Having established his initial position Stirner sets out his view of the self using two important terms of his own invention. These are "the unique one" and "ownness".

The unique one is the basis of Stirner's egoism. Essentially, and quite simply, all that Stirner does is to stress the difference between individuals to the point at which the difference becomes constitutive of their individuality.

> I am the *owner* of my might, and I am so when I know myself as *unique*. In the *unique one* the owner himself returns into his creative nothing, of which he is born. Every higher essence above me, be it God, be it man, weakens the feeling of my uniqueness and pales only before the sun of this consciousness. (Ibid, p.366)

Furthermore, difference comes down to nothing more than the difference between "I" and "not I", so that, "As Tom you would not be his equal, because he is Jim, therefore not Tom; as man you are the same that he is" (Ibid, p.173). "Man" for Stirner becomes, "but an unreal thing, the spook"(Ibid, p.174).

The essence of what Stirner is driving at is clear to see, and our cultural and linguistic disposition is equally clearly in his direction. The term "individual" brings to mind separation and difference. We see ourselves primarily as different from the next person. Apart from this difference, a sense of not-being the Other, it is hard to conceive of our individuality at all. In this sense everything is *outside* us. Stirner directly translates the spatial metaphor of our apparent day-to-day existence in the material world, to the ontological level. He clearly feels himself to be individuated in the context of the world, particularly in the context of the world of other egos, which he sees as threatening, and he wishes to preserve this individuality by elevating it to supreme ontological prominence.

It could be, and is, said that this is a crude and unsophisticated approach to a complex reality, and that Stirner is attempting to avoid his responsibility to express what we see as a much more subtle relation between ourselves and the world. But it is Stirner's primary contention that sophisticated understandings of our relations with the world are intended to deceive us as to the real, and underlying simplicity, of those relations. In Stirner's either/or world the onus is on the sophisticate to show the necessity of their analysis. Moreover, this must be achieved without a hint of suspicion that the deities, which Stirner has swept away, are not being revived or replaced in any way. Such appeal would only raise further cries of objection from the Stirnerian. In this way the Stirnerian position can only be overturned in its own terms and not simply by a re-assertion of the value systems it rejects. The defences raised by Stirner, even when they appear solipsistic, must be made ineffective at a much more fundamental level than that at which the simple consequences of thoroughgoing egoism become apparent. A rejection based solely on a preference for existing assumptions about value and the basis of social mores will not persuade the committed Stirnerian. It is central to Stirner's egoism that it is fatal to the kind or modern liberalism, which comes down from Mill,[8] and on which twentieth century western society is built.

If it is to be refuted Stirner's position must be shown to be dysfunctional in terms of the egoist's own declared aims, Stirner's egoism must be shown to be operating to the detriment of the egoist, despite its avowed aim only to do that which the egoist chooses and which benefits the egoist. This will require an investigation into the Stirnerian theory of the self, explicit and implied, and a look at what we mean by choice and possibility in terms of their practical everyday applications.

In support of the obstinacy of the Stirnerian position we can only say that there seems to be something in what Stirner says about individuality, a sense in which we wish to feel ourselves separated from Others and material things in the world. Stirner's psychological and ontological egoism is simply an expression of the clearly apparent "mineness"[9] of the world, derived from the articulation of the world around the perspective of the individual consciousness. It is a way of expressing the individual location of everyone who is in the world. Stirner insists that this is the only meaningful perspective and although this may seem to press the point too far, it is surely never completely escapable. Stirner brings forward a powerful feeling individuality, by so doing he strikes a chord that it will be hard, if not impossible, not to hear.

The ego, for Stirner, is prior to everything, prior to all presumption, reflection or mediation. In Stirner's very immediate writing, the ego, the individual, is immediate, born with hair and teeth complete. It is posited by its very existence.[10] Stirner even rejects any transcendental notion of "the ego" and fixes only on the primacy of "my ego". This gives the whole work some of the peculiarity of style that makes it so distinctive. *The Ego and Its Own* must remain a very personal statement both in the conventional sense that it describes his own conceptions and analysis, but also in that it must attempt to phrase its truths as its own, with no presumption of their necessary universalisation. For Stirner there can be no reason why, apart from himself. The ego is not to be a thing or an idea but a process, a creative nothing out of which all things, including itself, are created. This self-subsisting self is also self-renewing and self-creating, so that,

> over each minute of your existence a fresh minute of the future beckons to you, and, developing yourself, you get away "from yourself", that is, from the self that was at that moment. (Ibid, p.37) [11]

In this way the self is not only responsible for its own origins but for its constant re-origination from moment to moment. The continual self-surpassing, the new creation of the ego each day/hour/minute constitutes the ego as creator and created. This provides the ontological basis for the simple freedom to change our minds, the freedom we feel we have to deny what we did yesterday, and do differently today. By so doing we confirm the ego as primordial creator. The consequences of this for any assignment of personal responsibility, or even for the formulation of such a notion as responsibility are profound. Responsibility is annihilated by Stirner's nihilism. It is Stirner's nihilism, arrived at after his iconoclastic progress through man's deities, that is the challenge thrown down by *The Ego and Its Own*.

However the position taken by Stirner does bequeath itself some complimentary problems; with regard to the continuation of the personal identity of the ego through time, and the connectedness of individual experience, (how, precisely, can we *change our mind?*), and these will become apparent as the examination of this kind of ontology is developed. For Stirner, because I am unique, the world, and, in particular, value, is my creature. Stirner does not go so far as to deny existence to other selves, he has no necessity to do so, he represents their significance as qualitatively different from the status of his own ego.[12] The "unique one" is the Stirnerian self, self-subsistent, self-supporting, self-certain and complete, and its formulation constitutes the ontological basis of Stirner's egoism.

The Owner

Ownness is the manifestation of this self in the world. It is the alternative object, given by Stirner, to his ego, for its striving. Ownness, says Stirner, "is my whole being and existence, it is I myself. I am free from what I am *rid* of, owner of what I have in my *power* and what I *control*" (Ibid, p.157). Ownness is the only true manner of being available to the unique one, all others are characterised by self-deceit or ignorance. In fact ownness appears in contradistinction to the negative notion of freedom outlined by Stirner in the sections of Part Two of *The Ego and Its Own*. By taking the abstraction out of the pursuit of freedom it becomes ownness. "My freedom becomes complete only when it is my - *might*; by this I cease to be merely a free man, and become an own man"(Ibid, p.166). Stirner closely identifies *ownness* and the constitution of his own selfhood with notions of being in control, and power over the world. It is as if Stirner only feels himself to be truly alive and fulfilled through the forced objectification of the world around him, a world of objects subjected to his whim. A being recognising no right but his own, no values but his own, is an *own* man and, even though it may appear that he is materially affected by forces in the world outside, he says, "The fetters of reality cut the sharpest welts in my flesh every moment. But *my own* I remain" (Ibid, p.157), and..."even as the most abject of slaves I am - present"(Ibid, p.63).[13]

Stirner believes that the enduring presence of his individuality (the unique one) is inviolable and an acceptance of this leads straight to ownness, an attitude of mind which concentrates attention upon his essential individuality.[14] The idea of Being as presence is an unquestioned assumption in Stirner's work, not surprising, considering the immediacy of what he is trying to portray, but probably a significant weakness in his overall theory, particularly if it can be shown, in the light of the work of later thinkers, that *Being* is not even that sort of thing.

Stirner and Philosophy

Stirner's position is obviously overladen with theoretical considerations, of the very worst kind. He begins and ends the analysis with self-consciousness, decrying the efforts of every post-Cartesian to proceed beyond the *cogito*. Paradoxically, though Stirner's position seems to begin with simple everyday assumptions about experience, self-evident individuality, essential separation and the immediacy of presence, his subsequent analysis leads him to a position of complete isolation from aspects of our everyday lives which we would surely hold most dear, like our experience of the things we encounter and our human relationships, many of which he proclaims groundless.

The theoretical process adopted by Stirner, the requirements of proof he places on those who would dispute his case, the obstinacy of his egoism, and his blatant and unashamed use of solipsism, lead him to disregard the world in favour of the tyranny of pure theory, he destroys philosophy by solving the problem. Stirner divorces his philosophy from the kind of world we all suppose that we experience, and, once divorced, the activity of philosophy has no point and must cease. For it is Stirner's contention that the problem of behaviour towards Others, and the often confused conception of self which this engenders, is an illusion. Egoism is inescapable; we may either be honest about it or suffer the accusation of hypocrisy. Everything we do, we do for ourselves. Even avowed altruism, says Stirner, has its reward, and therefore its roots, in the individual self. It is the realisation of the goal of a particular individual and therefore egoistic in origin. However solipsistic this is, its untruth must be demonstrated by more than simple assertion of its meaninglessness, its failure, apparently, to say anything at all. We must address the problem as to how it comes about that such a defence can be mounted by Stirner at all and see what, if any, truth it may contain.

Although much of what Stirner appears to be saying is as much self-defeating as self-supporting, a mere conjuring trick with the meaning of the words, which makes every motivation egoistic and meaningless at the same time, it illustrates the fact that Stirner's egoism is primarily ontological and not simply a brand of ethical selfishness. Stirner does not proclaim the ascendancy of his own ego out of simple greed, or a will to power, but out of an inability, given the facts as he sees them, to proclaim anything else. He can only express himself as ego, simple existence. Thus Stirner's work in *The Ego and Its Own* articulates an ontological view of the self, that is, a view at the most fundamental level and this means that it contains much more substance than most of his critics would lead us to believe. Stirner makes so much smoke that it is impossible to believe that there is not a fire somewhere. If we accept Stirner's premises and conclusions as complete and unanswerable then we admit the futility of philosophy. We must reject both, not to preserve the academic discipline, but to give philosophers, and non-philosophers, the chance to make their own decisions about actions and their worth.

Stirner is saying something, even if something very crude, about what it is like to be an individual, he is talking about what it is like to live in the world. He is expressing the sheer primordiality of the isolation of the individual self, arrived at from a crude, but engagingly simple, analysis of a very everyday and immediate perception of individuality. He is left with what appears to him to be a glorious liberation from ideas that have oppressed him and stultified the opportunity for complete self-expression which is now made available to him. This is a powerful foundation for Stirner's ideas, it is either a fundamental and unshakeable libertarian position which Stirner will never give up and which we discard at our own greatest peril, or it is less of a liberation, and more of a hopeless state of isolated despair.[15] Significantly, to both parties, the facets of existence that Stirner highlights will provide the ground upon which notions of freedom will be based[16] and whether this kind of freedom prompts rejoicing (Stirner) or despair seems, at first, to be only a matter of taste.

Stirner and Ethics

The ontological character of what Stirner says is important because the most common reason for rejecting Stirner's philosophy is its manifestation as the ethics of "dog eat dog". It is a terrible prospect that all the constraints on the behaviour of others are imaginary, liable to be torn aside as soon as they impede the will of the individual ego. These ethical conclusions of Stirner's ontological individualism are actually of secondary importance when it comes to the evaluation of Stirner's egoism, since they are only derived from the underlying ontology which Stirner has mapped out. Stirner will say that we may not like the idea that morals have no real basis but if we wish to argue then it is incumbent upon us to show that such foundations actually exist. An isolated, self-subsistent individual will never be persuaded to act in a way which restricts itself in order to benefit others. To do so would be a denial of its very selfhood. Even more, a Stirnerian individual can make no sense of a theory which demands concern for the behaviour of human beings towards one another, such concerns can only be part of a smoke screen of deceit thrown up by other self seeking egoists. If as Warnock says,

> There can be no ethical theory which does not have as its first concern the behaviour of human beings towards one another; for morality consists in the regulation of this behaviour (Warnock,1966, p.129)

then morality must be inexplicable to the egoist, who sees no reason to regulate his behaviour except out of self preservation and self interest. However we may not judge Stirner's approach to be sterile because it fails to address problems which we, but not Stirner, see as significant. We cannot criticise Stirner for not providing a basis for morality as the result of his analysis of individuality. If that is the way it is, then we must put up with it, and not attempt to subvert the clarity of Stirner's theorising for the sake of the restoration of deities for which he has found no foundation, but which we find convenient, if fictional. If we are to find Stirner's position sterile then the argument with the egoist must be rooted in the view of the self which Stirner provides. His implied ontology must be found at fault, and not simply its ethical consequences. If the selfhood of the egoist is the stumbling block in the way of other regarding behaviour it is to the nature of this self that investigation must turn.

The Ego and Its Own is a cry from the loneliness of being, something which we all feel. For Stirner no other feeling has the same strength and clarity, and therefore, like Descartes, he builds on what he takes to be clear and distinct,[17] unlike Descartes, he seeks no escape from the logical stricture of the self certain existence of self. He admits no pre-conceived moral order which his ontology must support. If we wish to escape the awful inevitability of Stirner's progress from the self-evident existence of the individual to bleak egoism, we must be prepared to formulate an alternative notion of the self which should both retain the clarity and self-supporting strength of the Stirnerian ego, while at the same time provide more fertile ground for the accommodation and explanation of human experience. If we find that no such notion of the self is available then Stirner's conclusions cannot be avoided.

Notes

1. Little useful or constructive discussion and criticism of Stirner's work is available. Most notably Paterson, *The Nihilistic Egoist* (1971) and Clark, *Max Stirner's Egoism* (1976) are useful in elaborating and extrapolating Stirner's work. Marx's diatribe against Stirner in the final and usually unread section of *The German Ideology* (Marx and Engels, 1965, pp.123-510) is of little value.
2. To this extent *The Ego and Its Own* can be seen as a precursor to much later Existentialist work, like that of Sartre, which requires engagement at a personal level to facilitate its understanding.
3. Stirner was member of the group of left wing interpreters of Hegel, The Young Hegelians, which included Moses Hess, Bruno Bauer, Ludwig Feuerbach, Marx and Engels. Clark says Hegel's influence on Stirner was considerable (Clark, 1976, pp.10-12).
4. Recognising almost incidentally the necessity of pairing freedom with responsibility.
5. In Dostoyevsky's novel *Crime and Punishment* (1973) Raskolnikov is driven by the belief that he is a man privileged with the right to mete out justice by any means, and acting on this belief he murders the old pawnbroker.
6. In Camus' *The Outsider* (1983) Mersault achieves sufficient disconnection or desocialisation to allow him to shoot an Arab on the beach without motive. This kind of character type re-appears chillingly in Laing's description of his cases of schizophrenia in *The Divided Self*.
7. Sartre's character Roquentin in *Nausea* (Sartre, 1965) becomes detached from the world to the extent that he is able to stand apart from Being as an ontological outsider.
8. See *On Liberty* and *Utilitarianism* (Mill, 1965).
9. This is Heidegger's term; see *Being and Time*, H. 42 (Heidegger, 1987).
10. Resonant of Descartes "I think, therefore I am" in the Second Meditation.
11. Once again Stirner's language pre-echoes twentieth-century Existentialism, see especially Sartre's discussion of freedom in *Being and Nothingness*, Part Four (Sartre, 1956).
12. Stirner's rather crude form of expression clearly conflates ontological and ethical questions. For the purposes of this discussion I am using the ontological output of Stirner's theories about the self.
13. See also Sartre's discussion of sadism, masochism and indifference in *Being and Nothingness* (Sartre, 1956, pp.361-433).

14. This can easily be read as a forerunner of Heidegger's notion of *authenticity* as interpreted in Division Two of *Being and Time* however this glosses over significant differences between these two and it is doubtful that Stirner's work had much influence, if any, over Heidegger's thinking.
15. In particular Laing, *The Divided Self*, as discussed in Chapter Three.
16. Sartre, *Being and Nothingness*, Part Four (Sartre, 1956).
17. Descartes, Third Meditation, "clear and distinct perceptions".

3

R.D. Laing - All Together Now

In his short book *The Divided Self* R.D.Laing puts forward a view of the self, which is integrated into its environment.[1] From the clinical psychiatric point of view Laing describes the structures of the self in a way that explains the kinds of things that his patients say to him. That is, he describes the histories of actual people who have been diagnosed as in some way ill, malfunctioning in the terms not only of those around them, but also in the terms of their own aspirations and needs. Laing's perspective is essentially pragmatic; he is seeking to help those who come to him.[2] Laing says that he sets out attempting to leave behind pre-conceived ideas of madness and sanity, in order to be better able to understand the plight of his patients, such that,

> it is of considerable practical importance that one should be able to see that the concept and/or experience that a man may have of his being may be very different to one's own concept or experience of his being. In these cases one has to be able to orientate oneself as a person in the other's scheme of things rather than only to see the other as an object in one's own world....One must be able to effect this reorienatation without prejudging who is right and who is wrong. (Laing, 1965, p.26)

Entertaining the possibility of an alternative viewpoint, or view of the self, is critical to understanding the Other,[3] an importance brought out before Laing most notably by Sartre in "The Look".[4] Whether or not Laing succeeds in doing this with regard to a theory of the self provides a stern test of his thesis.

In *The Divided Self* Laing is discussing schizophrenia in existential terms and at the outset he rejects the way that individuals are described by the current terminology.

> The most serious objection to the technical vocabulary currently used to describe psychiatric patients is that it consists of words which split man up verbally in a way which is analogous to the existential splits we have to describe here. (Ibid, p.19)

> An example being when man is described in isolation, "as an entity not *essentially* "in relation to" the other and in a world". (Ibid, p. 19)

Thus

> Unless we begin with the concept of man in relation to other men and from the beginning "in" a world, and unless we realise that man does not exist without "his" world, nor can his world exist without him, we are condemned to start our study of schizoid and schizophrenic people with a verbal and conceptual splitting that matches the split up of the totality of the schizoid being-in-the world. (Ibid, p.19-20)

Laing wants to take for granted a view of our existence as beings in the world and rejects the kind of dualism and subjectivism espoused by Stirner.

> We all know from our personal experience that we can be ourselves only in and through our world and there is a sense in which "our" world will die with us, although "the world" will go on without us. (Ibid, p.19)

Philosophically speaking what Laing is saying is radical, sidestepping in one movement problems that have entertained philosophers for many years. Old epistemological chestnuts, like the problem of our knowledge of the "external" world, mind/body dualism,[5] and the asking of questions like, how do we know that we know? are themselves called into question by Laing's starting point in personal *everyday*[6] experience. Laing, in the course of seeking solutions to the problems posed by his patients, will challenge Cartesian metaphysics and post-Cartesian epistemology, and notions of selfhood derived from this tradition, by bringing a new perspective to bear on the problems of traditional epistemology.[7]

This challenge arises from the practical requirement for personally applicable results for real human individuals, and this benefit accrues whatever the fate of Laing's psychological theory and practice. Laing rejects the Cartesian *cogito* as a starting point and dualism as the structural context, as the practical clinician he dives straight into the human problem. Laing will characterise the Stirnerian ego, and by association the Cartesian subject, as an incomplete and consequently mistaken representation. Laing holds to the view that *being-with* is the fundamental way of being in the world.[8] It is his position, in clear distinction to Stirner, that, *being-with* is constitutive of individuality. He states the contention simply.

> The experience of oneself and others as persons is primary and self-validating. It exists prior to the scientific or philosophical difficulties about how such experience is possible or how it is to be explained. (Ibid, p.23)

Philosophically this is an extraordinary and dynamic statement. In this short sentence Laing begins to undermine the foundation of the Cartesian edifice, short circuiting the problem of dualism at one bold stroke and opening the way to a theory of the self which will not only accommodate but also welcome the Other. Laing's work represents a turning away from traditional empirical methods and proofs[9] as the starting point for the investigation into the nature of the self and a recognition that these methods and proofs depend themselves on an understanding which is prior to all empirical experience. Laing's clinical imperative to find a way of assisting his patients re-appears as the practical imperative for a human ethic to facilitate co-existence in the world. In rejecting the *cogito* as a starting point for his treatment of schizophrenia he rejects the Cartesian subject and the Stirnerian Ego outright. He also implies the rejection of a view of the world and the self which makes commonsensical everyday judgements about the world and Others problematic. It remains to be seen if Laing's justification for this is adequate.

True and False Self

Laing analyses schizophrenia using a twofold structure of true and false self.[10] Laing's believes that the schizophrenic is afraid that their individuality is threatened and will be destroyed by others. Without the option of simply not appearing in the world at all, the schizophrenic develops a strategy, and contingent structure of the self, to defend itself against this perceived threat. The false self is the self the schizophrenic parades in the world as a defence to shield the true self which is kept sacrosanct and never revealed. Laing's thesis will be that this split is unstable and will precipitate the schizophrenic into a series of ever more self destructive crises, in which the true self is gradually reduced and more and more is given up to the false self in desperate attempts to protect the diminishing core of selfhood to which the schizophrenic clings. This destructive bifurcation of the self is fundamental to Laing's criticism of theories of the self and the fact that it is a defining characteristic of the aberrant self, signals Laing's rejection of all dualistic theories of the self. It is a twofold structure that will be re-presented at different levels, and from varying perspectives, throughout the succeeding chapters of this book.[11] Its failure to provide an adequate notion of the self will lead ultimately, not only to a rejection of this structure, but also the rejection of the philosophical tradition to which it owes its origin.

On the face of it Laing has considerable "success" in treating his patients. The examples he uses to illustrate his thesis in *The Divided Self* show how those who have, for one reason or another, developed an entirely self-referenced being, not only find the position unsatisfactory, and hence seek help from such as Laing, but also find that their actions based on the premise of singularity, are ultimately destructive of the selves they seek to fortify and protect. This is a crucial point because, from what Laing says, it seems to be that an entirely self-referenced being not only malfunctions in terms of any pre-conceived norm which we may apply, but also in terms of its own ends and aspirations. Laing seeks to show that a self referenced individual will turn progressively in on itself towards its own destruction. Furthermore he contends that this conclusion applies quite apart from any medical, or psychological, notion of madness. A brief examination of the facts of one or two of Laing's cases should be sufficient to set out some of the clear structures of the self implied by Laing.

Case Studies

In "The Case of Peter"[12] Laing describes the case of a young man, Peter, who seeks his help because of an apparent delusion that he carries with him a constant smell, offensive to himself and to others. Laing's investigation of this case reveals the fact that, as a child, Peter was emotionally ignored by his parents, and consequently developed feelings of guilt about his "being there". He never became fully integrated into the world into which he had been born. Laing describes two techniques which Peter developed to cope with his state, "uncoupling" and "disconnection".

> By disconnexion, he meant widening the existential distance between his own self and the world. By uncoupling he meant the severance of any relationship between his "true" self and his repudiated false self. (Ibid, p. 127)

In this way Peter could feel safe from the world because he made himself apart from it. Having never felt at home in the world of Others, its occupants represented a constant threat, who must continually be fobbed off, and provided with a false self to aim at. However, as Laing goes on to explain, these activities on the part of Peter only made matters worse with regard to his original problem, the problem of not really having any right to be there in the first place. The more barriers Peter erected between himself and the world, the more pre-occupied he became with himself, or with that part of his consciousness which he had not yet chosen to disown, as Laing puts it,

> The world came to lose what reality it had for him and he had difficulty in imagining that he had any existence for others. Worst of all, he began to feel "dead". From his subsequent description of this feeling of being "dead", it was possible to see that it involved a loss of the feeling of realness and aliveness of his body. The core of this feeling was the *absence* of the experience of his body as a real object-for-others. He was coming to exist for himself (intolerably), and ceasing to feel that he had any existence in the eyes of the world. (Ibid, p. 130)

At the same time as feeling this lack of being Peter was also engaged in an attempt to protect himself from others, by uncoupling, "Now he tried to say,

'All of me that can be an object-for-the-other is not me'".[13] He made every effort to remain anonymous in his life, travelling from place to place, never settling anywhere, never forming close relationships, keeping on the move, and preventing himself from congealing into the reality which surrounded him.[14] Laing clearly sees the mess that Peter is in as a function of his inability to be at home in the world of Others, an inability derived from his never having been truly initiated into human society. The result of this was the slow but sure, break up of his psyche. As the patient himself put it to Laing,

> I've been sort of dead in a way. I cut myself off from other people and became shut up in myself. And I can see that you become dead in a way when you do this. You have to live in the world *with* other people. If you don't something dies inside. It sounds silly. I don't really understand it, but something like that seems to happen. It's funny. (Ibid, p. 133)

A more graphic statement of the necessary interdependence of being, straight from the horse's mouth, would be difficult to imagine. In this example Peter is not "mad", but Laing gives a chilling hint at what might happen if Peter continues on his self-contradictory course. Although the crux of the problem is that Peter feels himself to be no one, his inner self, the one he protects, retains a twisted kind of certainty. "At the same time he felt he was someone very special with a special mission and purpose sent by God to this earth."[15] Echoes of Dostoyevsky's Raskolnikov,[16] Camus' Outsider,[17] and countless other psychotic criminals, detached individuals outwardly parading a "normal" existence, which, from their own perspective, is nothing more than a cunning charade played out for a world of Others, seen as constantly threatening. Protection by isolation eventually bequeathing an invincibility which can excuse, and enables, horrific anti-social action.

In the case of Mrs R, Laing describes a woman who presents with the problem of agoraphobia, and who he diagnoses as lacking *ontological autonomy*,[18] that is, she only has a sense of being, through Others, and no sense of her self as individuated. The patient's agoraphobia, says Laing, is a function of this, a fear of being, or feeling to be, alone. In essence this woman has only one half of her being, being-for-others, consequently she rushes through her life clinging to a succession of "Others", parents, father, husband, lover, as Laing explains,

> If she is not in the actual presence of another person, who knows her, or, if she cannot succeed in evoking this person's presence in his absence, her sense of her own identity drains away from her. Her panic is at the fading away of her being. She is like Tinker Bell. In order to exist she needs someone else to believe in her existence. (Ibid, p. 56)

If Peter was a case of not being able to be-for-others, then, in the case of Mrs R, the reverse is true, she can *only* be-for-others and cannot be herself by herself. Laing says that this means that she cannot be herself at all. She has no freedom and must continually fill a role prepared for her in the lives of Others.

Whether or not Laing was able to help either Peter or Mrs R, it is clear that both needed help, both are aberrant, though different, and their aberration is explicable in terms of Laing's idea of the individual interdependent being. The implication of what Laing, and Peter, says is that individuality is simply not sustainable in isolation, and the attempt to create, or maintain, a subject consciousness, which is no more than that, is a serious malfunction, which will conclude in self destruction. Similarly, exclusive being-for-others is not enough and leaves a void at the centre. Individuality appears to be a balanced state of self consciousness and being-for-others. Peter, Mrs R, and others like them amongst Laing's patients, are out of balance, and seeking to maintain what is, in truth, a decaying position. Laing's explanations in these cases seem to be the "best fit" to the perceived phenomena. He is convincing because, from the descriptions he provides, even when he is not able to effect a "cure", he is able to explain consistently and, through a variety of different cases, exactly how the aberration may have come about. His theory thus allows a certain amount of prediction about the outcome of certain actions and events affecting the individual.

In complete opposition to Stirner Laing is able to sketch pictures of real solitary individuals who, from a position of profound ontological insecurity, constantly seek to reinforce their frail sense of being, while at the same time defending what they see as their vulnerable selves. This process takes the form of the construction of a false self which Laing's patients parade in the world in order to try to participate in reality, and to avoid having to risk their real selves, in what seems to them to be the most dangerous of environments. As Laing says;

> It is the thesis of this study that schizophrenia is a possible outcome of a more than usual difficulty in being a whole person with the other, and with not sharing the common sense way of experiencing oneself in the world. (Ibid, p. 189)

In case after case Laing describes people who are attempting to live only as beings-for-themselves, or only as beings-for-Others, the fact that all of those he describes are patients, that is people who have voluntarily sought his assistance, because they themselves are unable to continue functioning, is at least the beginning of evidence of the inadequacy of the notion of the solitary self. Laing's conviction that a notion of the self must include a constitutive relation to others as well as self-consciousness is repeated time and time again through *The Divided Self*. The dilemma is summed up succinctly, thus;

> The self can be "real" only in relation to real people and things. But it fears that it will become engulfed, swallowed up in any relationships. If the "I" only comes into play *vis-à-vis* objects of fantasy, while a false self manages dealings with the world, various profound phenomenological changes occur in all elements of experience (Ibid, p. 142)

and,

> the self, being transcendent, empty, omnipotent, free in its own way, comes to be anybody in fantasy, and nobody in reality. (Ibid, p. 142)

Where might this leave Stirner's "Owner"?

Which One of You is the Madman?

From the contrasting views that I have set out above it looks as if Laing has put forward the more acceptable and familiar way of understanding individuality, a being-with-Others as opposed to the stark portrait of the individual ego, provided by Stirner.

Most prominently Stirner takes no account of the formative influences acting on the self at work in the world, and in particular of Others.[19] The concept of relation has no part to play in Stirner's individual. The "Owner" is isolated beyond the scope of any outside power to affect him, fundamentally *not* related.[20] All significance, all value, emanates from the individual ego, which appears to exist in self affirming transcendence of the rest of the world, seeking only to realise itself as "unique" and as "owner". The consequence for Stirner's position of the uncompromising nature of his egoism is a profound dualism in his view of the world. The ego transcendental, isolated and inviolate, contrasting starkly with the rest of the world, which paradoxically includes the appearance of that same ego as an object in the world. The relation between these two apparently separate worlds remains unexplained, and hence highly problematic.

Laing on the other hand deals precisely with relation. He looks at how the individuals before him have been formed by the influences acting upon them and enables himself to unravel the complex route by which his patients arrived at their present "out-of-synch" state, as a prelude to pointing them in the direction of an alternative conception of themselves. Laing sees the sense of self as being built up through experience in the world, and as derived from its developing relation with the world, to the extent that relation with the world is constitutive of individuality. Laing's position avoids the explicit structural dualism of Stirner although perhaps at the potential cost of losing the individual as singularly defined.

In fact Laing and Stirner provide two very contrasting descriptions of the same kind of individual; in the case of Stirner; "the Unique One" the all powerful, the omnipotent, the Owner, destroyer and creator of his world, and inviolable in his tremendous singular individuality; in Laing's work the schizophrenic patient, alone, frightened, both confused and confusing, seemingly lost in a void from which they can see no escape - both isolated individuals, one celebrating, one in despair, one a superman, the other a madman. From all of this it is no surprise to find that both Laing and Stirner are closely connected with Existential schools of thought, Laing directly, by involvement and inheritance, and Stirner as a clear precursor. Stirner's theme of the free individual returns through Sartre's existentialism, and Laing explicitly draws on existential terminology and methods in his work with schizophrenia. It is not coincidental therefore that both can be understood as describing the same existential encounter with the sheer contingency of existence, what the Existentialists call the nothingness at the heart of Being.[21]

Stirner mercilessly cuts away all the supports available to him. For Stirner nothing is sacred, nothing is worth giving himself up for, he is alone and dependent wholly upon himself. This choice, which he makes freely for himself, places him in a position of total control and total isolation, he understands the arbitrary nature of his existence and chooses and lives it willingly. Laing describes the patients who come to see him. They are floundering at exactly the point at which Stirner rejoices. They have nothing to live for, no meaning, no purpose, their lives have become almost complete fantasy, having encountered the arbitrary nature of their existence they "go mad". Given this compelling conjunction between the descriptions of the self put forward by Laing and Stirner it is interesting and revealing to compare some of the self evident truths which Stirner sets out, in *The Ego and Its Own*, about his own view of the ego and his own self, with some of the things Laing has to say about his patients and his explanations for their predicaments. First from Stirner;

> I am the *owner* of my might and I am so when I know myself as *unique*. In the *unique one* the owner himself returns into his creative nothing, of which he is born. Every higher essence above me, be it God, be it man, weakens the feeling of my uniqueness and pales only before the sun of this consciousness. (Stirner, 1982, p.366)

> Ownness ... is my whole being and existence, it is I myself. I am free from what I am *rid* of, owner of what I have in my *power* and what I *control*. (Ibid, p.157)

> My freedom becomes complete only when it is my - *might*; by this I cease to be merely a free man, and become an own man. (Ibid, p.166)

> The fetters of reality cut the sharpest welts in my flesh every moment. But *my own* I remain. (Ibid, p.157)

> ...even as the most abject of slaves I am - present. (Ibid, p.163)

> ...nothing that is designated as my essence exhausts me; they are only names. (Ibid, p.366)

> I secure my freedom with regard to the world in the degree that I make the world my own, "gain it, and take possession of it" for myself (Ibid, p.165)

and finally, pregnant with sinister meaning, "All things are nothing to me" (Ibid, p.366).

Then from Laing and his patients we have...

> ever since I can remember I was sort of aware of myself, a sort of self-conscious - obvious in a way you know. (Laing, 1965, p.122)

> He was able to carry on in an outwardly normal way the deliberate employment of two techniques which he called "disconnexion" and "uncoupling". By disconnexion he meant widening the existential distance between himself and the world. By uncoupling he meant the severance of any relationship between his "true" self and his repudiated false self. (Ibid, p.127)

> ...he felt he had *no right to occupy space.* (Ibid, p.129)

In fact Laing's patient, Peter, contrasts with Stirner sharply in that he has a sense of himself as of no importance as opposed to Stirner's view of himself as the only one of any importance. Peter feels he has no right to occupy space, Stirner feels he has an absolute right to do so. Their obsessions mirror one another and in essence are identical. The question about our right to be in the world with others is no question at all. As Laing points out in a way that could be a direct commentary on Stirner's "Unique One",

> It is not possible to go on living indefinitely in a sane way if one tries to be a man disconnected from all others and uncoupled even from a large part of one's own being (Ibid, p.139)

because

> Such a mode of being-with-others would pre-suppose the capacity to maintain one's reality by means of a basically autistic identity (Ibid, p.139)

so,

> the schizoid individual characteristically seeks to make his awareness of himself as intensive and extensive as possible (Ibid, p.112)

and,

> the man who is frightened of his own subjectivity being swamped, impinged upon...is frequently to be found attempting to swamp, impinge upon, or to kill the other person's subjectivity (Ibid, p.52)

finally,

> The self, as long as it is "uncommitted to the objective element", is free to dream and imagine anything. Without reference to the objective element it can be all things to itself - it has unconditional freedom, power, creativity. But its freedom and its omnipotence are exercised in a vacuum and its creativity is only the power to produce phantoms. (Ibid, p.89) [22]

It is my contention that the individual as described by Stirner, the Unique One, is an example of the kind of "self" described by Laing in *The Divided Self* and elsewhere. Whether or not this judgement can be extended to incorporate a judgement of Stirner himself may seem doubtful, but, because of the way that Stirner has constructed the argument in *The Ego and Its Own*, it is difficult to divorce conclusions about "the Unique One" from conclusions about the author himself. Stirner's Unique One exhibits characteristics in common with Laing's patients. He has a strong belief in his own destructiveness, Stirner's whole approach is iconoclastic, he establishes the ego as all powerful, all creating, omnipotent and inviolable. He is overly self-conscious and self aware, and, as Laing points out, this is a common feature in individuals who see themselves as threatened. Stirner is totally preoccupied with his own sense of self. *The Ego and Its Own* is a totally self-centred work. The Unique One feels a profound mind/body split. The quote given above, "even as the most abject of slaves I am present", comes in a section of *The Ego and Its Own* which describes a master/slave relation in which Stirner is able to divorce his bodily suffering as a slave, from his intact ego (or true self). This is the same as the way that Laing's patient Peter tries to separate himself from the world. The Unique One objectifies others completely; they are nothing more than objects for his advancement. In Laing's terms this is the device of the ontologically insecure to protect their own fragile sense of self from engulfment by others. Stirner's seeming aggressive act of the appropriation of the world and others is simply a defence to protect himself, dead Others cannot harm him.

Stirner's Unique One is isolated, separate from the world outside, in fact a true self withdrawn from the danger that the world presents. Because of the dualism of the divided self of the Stirnerian individual it is unable to accommodate the possibility of reciprocal relations with others. The solution is to withdraw. Stirner's Unique One is uniquely placed to operate under a false self in the world. Separated from his body and withdrawn to the inner sanctum of his own true self, the Unique One must appear in the world as a pretence, a slave who, though he endures his masters beatings, remains "own", an individual who can behave as if he were free without regard to "external" considerations. Stirner's Unique One is one dimensional, and as, Laing says,

> if a man is not two-dimensional, having a two dimensional identity established by a conjunction of identity-for-others, and identity-for-oneself, if he does not exist objectively as well as subjectively, but has only a subjective identity, an identity-for-himself, he cannot be *real*. (Laing, 1965, p 95)

Laing's evidence for what he says are the descriptions he provides of the patients he sees, many of these sad, confused and distressed people embody the Unique One. Their paradox is their constant striving to be real in the real world, set against their overwhelming fear of the engulfing power of others. They desire, above all things, that which they fear will destroy them.

The notion of the self implied in *The Ego and Its Own*, by Stirner, seems to be incomplete and potentially self-destructive. It cannot support any form of relation between Others and the true self of the Stirnerian ego, indeed it must reject any such relation. Furthermore Stirner's egoism appears to be founded on a dualism between self and world which renders the relationship between these two highly problematic. Laing's descriptions seem to show that anyone who attempts to conceive of themselves in this way is well on the way to mental breakdown. The salvation of Laing's patients is not for them to affirm their own power over the world and Others, not to attempt to realise themselves as solitary in glorious isolation, but to come to an acceptance of themselves as existing in a world of other subjects, like themselves, to reinforce their own fragile sense of self through relation with the world. To help them to understand the blind alley they have gone down, and to help them back into the world as it really is and not as they have come to imagine it.

If Laing's position has a weakness it is in the potential lack of focus for individuality. If relation is made constitutive of self, how is individuality to be understood and in what sense is it individual? What Stirner's egoism lacks in relation to Others and a world beyond the ego, Laing's position may lack in room for singular individuality. These are clearly issues that will need to be addressed in some depth as the discussion between these two positions is developed.

As I suggested, it is difficult, because of the way he has styled The *Ego and Its Own*, to divorce any conclusions about the Unique One from probable conclusions about Stirner himself.[23] Even at such a distance in time Stirner's *The Ego and Its Own* is persuasive evidence of Stirner's own ontological insecurity, at least in terms of Laing's analysis. The autonomy, which Stirner so vehemently proclaims, betrays his underlying insecurity. He puts forward his own power to objectify, choose, control, and decide because he is afraid that someone else will exercise power over him. He has a fragile sense of self and wants to defend himself from a hostile world, so he creates the Unique One and shuts it off from the world of Other relation. He petrifies Others lest they do it to him. Why, we may now ask, did this inconsequential schoolteacher write under an assumed name? How is it that after this one great iconoclastic burst onto the philosophical scene of his time, did he fall back into obscurity? Furthermore, with regard to the eccentric style of *The Ego and Its Own* there is Laing's comment that,

> One of the greatest barriers against getting to know a schizophrenic is his sheer incomprehensibility: the oddity, bizarreness, obscurity in all that we can perceive of him (Laing, 1965, p.163)

and,

> A good deal of schizophrenia is simply nonsense, red herring speech, prolonged filibustering to throw dangerous people off the scent, to create boredom and futility in others. The schizophrenic is often making a fool of himself and the doctor. (Ibid, p.164)

This will strike a chord in anyone who has read *The Ego and Its Own*. On the other hand, on behalf of Stirner, we might respond that this is exactly the kind of social deception that will be presented in order to rob the sovereign ego of its freedom and to subsume the individual into the anonymous and amorphous "society" and to deny the ego the possibility of ever standing out and individuating itself.

It is obvious by now that further and deeper investigation into the underpinnings of both of these positions will be required to see if the *prima facie* confidence in Laing's position is justified. It seems unlikely that the question can be determined simply.

"Give me madness"[24]

It appears, following the unfavourable comparison of Stirner's Unique One with Laing's patients, that Laing's view of the self, as essentially relational, is the more plausible option. I will argue that the kind of isolate portrayed by Stirner in *The Ego and Its Own*,[25] is derived from the Cartesian affirmation of the immediate self-evident awareness of the self, "I think therefore I am".[26] I will further argue that writers like Stirner and Sartre have in effect presented this position stripped of the accretions that have been variously applied to it in order to avoid the unpalatable conclusions of individual isolation, nothingness, arbitrary existence, dualism, and eventually egoism.

Laing derives his notion of the self from a radically different premise, the idea of relation, "being-with", as the fundamental constitution of being. The strength of this premise is very different from the self justifying strength of "I think therefore I am". It is based on the contention that the view of the self presented by Stirner, and later by Sartre, is a description of a self which cannot function in the world, and consequently a view which is not as fundamental as it is made to appear. The *prima facie* plausibility of Laing's position calls into question the premise used by those presenting the isolated view of the self, and points towards a more primordial understanding of the self and the world which underlies the very possibility of Cartesian theories of the subject self. Laing is not only convincingly able to explain the difficulties his patients have, using his alternative premise, he is able to go on from this to set out a way of being, an idea of a self, which does appear to be able to function in the world. In short the strength of Laing's view of the self and by implication his premise is that it appears to help people to live with themselves and others and does not contradict or render problematic common sense assumptions we have about ourselves, Others, and the world in which we live.

Before going deeper into the implications of this kind of strength it is worthwhile to note that one result of accepting Laing's premise would be to reject ethical, as well as ontological, egoism. Stirner's "Unique One" could find no reason for other-regarding behaviour, his kind of egoistic individualism is amoral. Laing by demonstrating that, psychologically, the individual is dependent not only on himself but on his relations with others, may provide for the possibility of ethics. Once we have to accept that we are in a world with others, like ourselves, and that we need them in order to realise ourselves, the question of our behaviour towards them can begin to be discussed. Whether or not this is "ethics" remains an open question but there is clearly more potential here than there is in Stirner's work.

To return now to Laing's premise. Post-Cartesians, like Stirner, could never admit to the strength of Laing's proposition as an alternative to the *cogito*, and the reasons for this are obvious. While Descartes famous statement, arrived at after the dogged application of sceptical doubt, is finally without doubt, the first term giving the last out of itself, Laing's statement appears to be no more than a presumption, and to simply say that our understanding of selfhood and the world is beyond validation or prior to any difficulties encountered looks like an attempt to shift the point at issue somewhere we cannot get at it. It is not to prove it, at least not in a sense acceptable to the Cartesian school. Descartes' premise is entirely self-referenced and looks only within itself for its support. In other words it says that, for the proof of my existence I need look no further than within my own self and that the degree of certainty that I derive from this, of my own existence, is absolute, and not available to me with regard to any other question. Laing's premise does not appear to work in this way and to accept it is therefore to abandon the Cartesian kind of certainty and to attempt to formulate another starting point. Whether or not it involves the abandonment of anything we understand as individuality remains to be seen.

Despite the *prima facie* case in favour of Laing and against Stirner even Laing's position shows some signs of weakness. Laing recognises at the outset that he must not approach his patients with the notions of madness and sanity traditionally accepted in his discipline.[27] Obviously Laing clearly sees the danger in his enterprise of the normative approach. He is entering the world of his patients with an open mind. In fact he is seeking to escape the strictures and presumptions of the doctor/patient relationship in order to better understand the schizophrenia of his patients. This creditable attempt to reassess the notions of madness and sanity creates its own difficulties, and, apart from these, I will argue that even Laing fails to avoid some degree of prejudgment, and cannot wholly escape the constraints of the doctor/patient relationship. In *The Divided Self* Laing says, "the cracked mind of the schizophrenic may *let in* light which does not enter the intact minds of many sane people whose minds are closed",[28] and then, "*sanity or psychosis is tested by the degree of conjunction or disjunction between two persons where the one is sane by common consent*".[29] These two statements certainly point to an attempt by Laing to avoid a strictly normative position, but they also, by throwing doubt on conventional distinctions between the mad and the sane, make it more difficult to see what Laing is trying to say about his patients and the consequences of this for notions of the self. If Laing is not fitting his patients back into a mad society, because they have no choice but to go back or be put away, then what is he doing? From some of Laing's later work (*The Politics of Experience* and *The Ten Day Voyage*) it seems that it may amount to nothing more than describing a process, which has previously been misunderstood, and which marks the coming to true selfhood of the individual.[30] In fact Laing is trying to provide much more of the beginning of a criticism of the understanding society has of the individual than a judgement of the insane as mad and bad. However there is insufficient in his work alone to carry this through to a thoroughgoing criticism of traditional (Cartesian) notions of selfhood, still less for the setting out of a complete alternative. It remains the case that even if Laing is not making a presumption in favour of what constitutes sanity, then he is at least gesturing in the direction of an idea of authentic selfhood, which could amount to the same thing.[31] Laing may not take a normative position but he is pointing towards one. Laing is much more successful in avoiding the accusation of taking a normative position in his later work *The Politics of Experience* in which the schizophrenic experience is portrayed as a "normal" part of psychological development. Laing is very critical of our notion of the normal.

> What we call "normal" is a product of repression, denial, splitting, projection, introjection, and other forms of destructive action or experience. It is radically estranged from the structure of being. (Laing, 1967, p.23-4)

He goes on to describe our "normal" way of being as alienated, and schizophrenia as "a successful attempt not to adapt to pseudo social relations" (Ibid, p.57). By now Laing is even undermining his own position as a psychiatrist treating patients. He admits ironically that,

> The psychiatrist, as *ipso facto* sane, shows that the patient is out of contact with him. The fact that he *is* out of contact with the patient shows that there is something wrong with the patient, but not with the psychiatrist. (Ibid, p.90)

Interestingly this echoes what Laing says about the nineteenth century doctor Kraepelin[32] and, more surprisingly, a comment made by Paterson about Stirner,

> Written into the ostensibly medical concepts of mental health and mental hygiene are certain definite norms reflecting the ethical standards of the medical profession or of society at large

and

> Maturity, like virtue, turns out to mean conformity. (Paterson, 1971, p.262)

In effect Stirner is protesting his right to determine his own sanity, rejecting the existing structures by which madness and sanity are judged, a right which Laing would surely defend. For Stirner, notions of madness and sanity would be part of the wholesale deceit of the sovereign individual by those wishing to aggrandise their own position through his suppression. It is hard not to sympathise with Stirner on this point. Insanity is sometimes seen merely as social or political inconvenience, the response of a frightened or vindictive majority against those who dare to speak out their individuality. Witches were burned and political dissidents are consigned to psychiatric institutions.[33] Although this is the very opposite of what Laing would support it may be that he has only succeeded in offering to replace one norm, sanity, with another, self realisation.

By the end of *The Politics of Experience* Laing seems to have succeeded in reassessing the notions of sanity and madness. He re-affirms the adaptive nature of schizophrenic behaviour as

> The experience and behaviour that gets labelled as schizophrenic is a *special strategy that a person invents in order to live in an unliveable situation.* (Laing, 1967, p.95)

Following his account of *The Ten-Day Voyage*, it is clear that Laing regards this kind of experience, (of the arbitrary nature of being), as an essential formative experience for the balanced self. It is as if we cannot fully appreciate ourselves and acquire a proper perspective on life without facing up to its ultimate meaninglessness. Laing goes even further in the section on "Transcendental Experience" when he says,

> When the ultimate basis of our world is in question, we run to different holes in the ground, we scurry into roles, statuses, identities, interpersonal relations. We attempt to live in castles which can only be in the air. (Ibid, p. 108)

It looks as if we are sane in the world, as it is today, only if we are, by its terms, at least sometimes, insane. Stirner would certainly be in a position to agree with this. However, although an appreciation of the arbitrary nature of our existence may lead to a richer more self aware existence, the continued conduct of our lives along these lines is a non-starter if we are, in any way, to accept the co-existence of ourselves with Others in the world. We cannot live our lives like the patients described by Laing in *The Divided Self*, they could not and turned to Laing for help. Laing's efforts to break the strict dichotomy between sanity and madness are commendable and important but they do not adequately reflect the complexity of the situation with regard to notions of self and world which will require further and extensive discussion. They also confuse and blur a line of demarcation that remains necessary to human co-existence. If Laing were to succeed completely even his own position would be undermined, the curative nature of his therapy would be altered, and it would not be unreasonable to say that curative necessarily equals normative. We would be left with a facilitative process which would be unable to make judgements about its own efficacy, a kind of psychological relativism in which sanity and madness lose all meaning. This is an ever present danger in the territory inhabited by Laing and there is not enough explicit ontology in his work to ensure that this danger is permanently avoided.

It is to Laing's own position that we can now turn. Despite his efforts to avoid normative judgements and pre-judgements, and his own oft-repeated awareness of the dangers of taking a position on the sanity or madness of a patient, Laing's view is (and must remain) normative to some degree. His analysis operates on the assumption that, whatever his patients say and do, it is to protect themselves from fear of the opposite. Hence, a simple analysis of what Stirner says would be like this; Stirner seeks to put forward his own power, to objectify, choose, control, decide, and so on, because he is afraid of someone else doing it to him. He is afraid that someone else will make him "object" and choose and decide for him, he is afraid he will lose control. Analysed in Laing's terms, he has a fragile sense of self and seeks to defend himself against a hostile world. He creates the "Unique One" and shuts it off from the world of Other relation, by a negative self-affirmation. This analysis is plausible but by no means conclusive. In particular its validity outside the presumption of the doctor/patient relationship is questionable, and this relationship is essentially normative. It contains a powerful pre-judgement, which no amount of awareness can dispel. If Laing is not the doctor and those he describes are not patients then what are they up to? Even if we accept that they are simply two people talking together the object of their conversation remains the solution, or attempt at solution, of the problems of one of them, usually the one who seeks out the other. "Problems" are defined by the social environment and this embodies explicit norms. For Laing's activity to have any meaning at all he requires a distinction between those who need his help, and those who do not, without this he would not know when to start or stop treatment, or who to treat. However, as we have seen the only criterion that we are able to deduce from Laing for making any such distinction is the ability to be in a world with Others, and to gain their approval for, or at least their acquiescence to, our behaviour. This is precisely the kind of criterion that Stirner so vigorously rejects in terms which brook no argument.

From what Laing says, Stirner's notion of the isolated, independent, and fiercely individual self can only be rejected in terms which Stirner himself rejects. There is no way in which Stirner could be made to accept the kind of selfhood that Laing seems to help his patients towards. Stirner's "Unique One" as a resilience which cannot be dented simply by what Laing says about madness and sanity or self realisation. This is an indication of a potential weakness in Laing's case in its potential failure to provide sufficient ground for the individuation of the self from the premise of the fundamentally relational constitution of selfhood. It is already obvious that an adequate theory of the self must provide not only for links to Others but also sufficient room for individual affirmation as unique. A rejection of Stirner's egoism, if there is to be one, must therefore proceed, at a deeper level, from a premise, which is different, in kind, from the Cartesian *cogito*. This will require an examination and comparison of the fundamental ontology underlying both Stirner's and Laing's positions. Neither Laing nor Stirner are explicit about ontology, although it is clear that Stirner is basically a Cartesian dualist and that Laing is not.

In order to bring out the underlying differences between these two I will set out two traditional problems of philosophy which I take to be central to theories about the nature of the self, these are, the problem of knowledge of the external world including the existence of Others like ourselves; and, the problem of the continuity of personal identity through time. Comparison of some of the solutions to these problems, provided by philosophical positions which support either Stirner or Laing, will throw light on the ontological issues between Stirner and Laing with regard to their respective theories of the self and help to decide the issue between them.

Notes

1. Also see Laing's *Self and Others*, and *The Politics of Experience* and *The Bird of Paradise*, and for a discussion of the development of Laing's work in this area and its philosophical relevance, Kirsner, *The Schizoid World of Jean-Paul Sartre and R.D. Laing*, Part II.
2. Although Laing's work is written from a completely different perspective than that of Stirner and over a century later both are attempts at self definition, or drawing out the parameters of selfhood. In Stirner for himself, and in Laing through the proxy of his patients.
3. "Other" is a term taken directly from the Existential School and I will consistently use this term to denote those beings like me which are not-me.
4. Sartre, *Being and Nothingness*, pp. 252-302.
5. Discussed fully in Chapter Four.
6. This is Heidegger's term and is used by him to denote the starting point for all phenomenological enquiry. It is fully explained in Chapter Seven.
7. See, Richardson, *Existential Epistemology*, Chapter Two for a discussion of the way in which the Cartesian tradition is subverted.
8. This indicates Laing's close conceptual alliance with Heidegger who emphasises being-with (*Mitsein*) as a fundamental structure of being.
9. Methods and approaches exemplified by Descartes, Locke, and Hume.
10. Laing, *The Divided Self*, Part Two, pp. 65-133.
11. Chapters Four, Five, and Six.
12. Laing, *The Divided Self*, pp. 120-133.
13. Ibid, p. 131.
14. Closely reminiscent to the experience of Roquentin as described by Sartre in *Nausea*.

15. Laing, *The Divided Self*, p. 133.
16. Dostoyevsky, *Crime and Punishment* in which Raskolnikov determines himself as a special being destined to kill the old pawnbroker to release others from her power.
17. Camus, *The Outsider*, in which Mersault is able to detach himself sufficiently to kill, without apparent motive.
18. Laing, *The Divided Self*, pp. 39-61.
19. Laing explicitly recognises this influence, see *Self and Others* Chapter Six, "Complementary Identity", and Chapter Seven, "Confirmation and Disconfirmation".
20. Not even not-related as a form of relation. Stirner refuses any dialectic between self and not-self and celebrates isolation and singularity.
21. Most vividly portrayed by Sartre in both *Nausea* and *Being and Nothingness*.
22. Also see my discussion of Sartre's notion of freedom in Chapter Six.
23. It is not my intention to provide an in depth psychiatric assessment of Max Stirner, such an exercise would be beyond validation and, in any case, would not make significant contribution to the emerging debate about the self. However because of the way in which Stirner has phrased his work in *The Ego and Its Own* it is almost impossible to engage in any criticism of his work without at least some discussion of the psyche behind the book.
24. Nietzsche, *Daybreak*, p. 16. The quote in full reads, "Ah, give me madness, you heavenly powers! Madness that I may at last believe in myself", as Nietzsche sets out the thesis that in madness there is a grain of genius and that by this mean does society progress.
25. And later by Sartre in *Nausea* and *Being and Nothingness*.
26. Descartes, Second Meditation. Also see Chapter Four.
27. Laing clearly recognises this danger and the potency of the language which structures the discussion when he says, "The most serious objection to the technical vocabulary used to describe psychiatric patients is that it consists of words which split man up verbally in a way which is analogous to the existential splits we have to describe here" (Laing, 1965, p. 19).
28. Ibid, p. 27.
29. Ibid, p. 36.
30. Kirsner says, "In *The Divided Self* the schizophrenic does not see it and the Psychiatrist does: and in *The Politics of Experience* the schizophrenic can see it and the Psychiatrist cannot" (Kirsner, 1976, p. 153).
31. There is a similar gesture in Heidegger's work towards a similar presumption, which Heidegger too seeks to strenuously deny. See the discussion of authentic Dasein in *Being and Time*, Division Two, Sections II and III in which Heidegger repeatedly refuse the accretion of moral weight to his terminology of the self.
32. Laing, *The Divided Self*, p. 29.

33. Nietzsche could been seen to be defending Stirner's position when he says, "all superior men who were irresistibly drawn to throw off the yoke of any kind of morality and to frame new laws had, *if they were not actually mad,* no alternative but to make themselves or pretend to be mad" (Nietzsche, 1982, p. 14).

4

Descartes, Locke and Hume - Self and World

> Man is to himself the most miraculous object in Nature. For he cannot conceive what matter is, still less what is mind, and least of all how a body can be joined to a mind. This is his supreme difficulty, and yet it is his very being. (Pascal, 1961, p.56)

This is the "supreme difficulty" that Stirner and Laing appear to differ around. How is the relation between man, or self, and the rest of creation which is not the self, to be viewed? Pascal poses the problem in an open way, recognising both the incomprehensibility and inevitability of the union of body and spirit.

In this chapter I will begin to use two specific philosophical problems to focus the discussion about the self. The problem of knowledge, "the veil of the senses", is used to examine the relation between the self and the world that is not-self, and to address the question of the spatiality of the self. Simply, this problem poses questions about the veracity of sensory experience, based on the possibility of sensory error or illusion, and in particular with regard to the correspondence between sensory experience and the existence of objects beyond and independent of the self, which might be supposed to *cause* sensory experience.

The problem of the continuity of the identity of the self over time, the problem of personal identity, will be used to examine the relation between the self and itself at different times, and to address the question of the temporality of the self. This problem poses questions about the identity of the self with itself at different times by recognising changes in each individual observed over time, and by attempting to reconcile this with the wish to ascribe continuing identity to individuals in spite of evident change. Together these problems raise fundamental questions about the nature of the self by defining the spatial and temporal dimensions of the self, and by encompassing both the relation between the self and the not-self, and the self and itself. Satisfactory solutions to both of these problems are required if any tenable theory of the self is to be formulated. In the following chapters the work of each of the philosophers cited is examined in respect of the way in which either one or both of these problems are set out, and the questions they raise addressed.

Descartes goes deeply and famously into these questions and an examination of the way in which Descartes approaches the issues, and hence poses the relevant problems will throw light on the philosophical background to the dispute between Stirner and Laing.[1] Although Descartes work pre-dates Pascal, in his *Meditations* and the *Discourse on the Method*, Descartes can be seen to be pursuing the enigma set out by Pascal to its ultimate conclusion. The main element in his method is the exercise of sceptical doubt about the existence of the world including his own corporeality. He tries to imagine that there is an omnipotent and malevolent "evil deceiver" operating in his world, a God who is trying to make him believe in a world by providing him with convincing evidence of things that do not really exist. This is not as fanciful as it may sound because, as Descartes says,

> What I have so far accepted as most true I have acquired either from the senses or through the senses. But from time to time I have found that the senses deceive, and it is prudent never to trust completely those who have deceived us even once. (Descartes, 1986, p.12)

His most famous conclusion is the self evidence of his own conscious existence, "*cogito ergo sum*", "I think, therefore I am".

> But there is a deceiver of a supreme power and cunning who is deliberately and constantly deceiving me. In that case I too undoubtedly exist, if he is deceiving me; and let him deceive me as much as he can, he will never bring it about that I am nothing so long as I think that I am something. So after considering very thoroughly, I must finally conclude that this proposition, *I am, I exist*, is necessarily true whenever it is put forward by me or conceived in my mind. (Ibid, p. 17)

In this single step Descartes has done far more than demonstrate the indubitability of his own existence, he has divided the world into two in a way that will defeat the attempts, made by him in the later *Meditations*, and by many of those who followed him, to reunite the parts.[2]

Having reached this point Descartes then goes on to address problems of relation between spiritual and corporeal being, sensory errors and the existence of God. However there is an important sense in which the work leading up to the *cogito* is more significant for the whole of Cartesian ontology, and for the ontology of the self, than anything which Descartes says explicitly about the mind and the body. The method of sceptical doubt with regard to the evidence of the senses depends on a presumption, which if accepted, grounds all of the succeeding analysis, and the whole school of thought associated with this theory of ideas.

Descartes' certainty of his own subjective existence includes the certainty of his own subjective internal experience. That is, while it can be doubtful that what he sees is really, or objectively, present, it cannot be doubted that what he sees is what he sees. So we may say "I see a chair", and this may be true in all cases in which I have the experience of seeing a chair, irrespective of whether a chair is present or not. The truth of my having an experience of seeing a chair is deemed to be independent of the truth of the objective presence of a chair. In this way we understand the way in which my senses may "deceive" me.[3] As Descartes put it when considering dreaming,

> For example, I am now seeing light, hearing a noise, feeling heat. But I am asleep so all this is false. Yet I certainly *seem* to see, to hear, and to be warmed. This cannot be false; what is called "having a sensory perception" is strictly just this, and in this restricted sense of the term *is* simply thinking. (Ibid, p.19)

This is not as daft as it may sound at first, and is the kind of thinking we all engage in as a result of coming to understand the unreliability of our senses. We have all been mistaken about what we see, our senses tell us one thing and then another, about the same apparently objective reality. We rationalise this by saying that we were deceived by our senses, the same senses that later put us right about what is really there. The metaphor of deceit remains powerfully divisive of all of our succeeding thinking. It is from this perspective that Descartes comes to his position, as witnessed by his remarks above, but once arrived at, the separation between subjective internal experience and objective external reality is complete.[4]

Descartes' method allows for a radical separation between subjective experience and objective reality and then trades on the possibility of non-correlation between the two to pose problems about the veracity of sensory experience and the, now problematic, relation between mind and body. If we allow Descartes to proceed to the *cogito* then the rest of what he says is difficult, if not impossible, to refute. If it is the case that my experience of the world can be understood as separated from the objective reality of the world, if we accept the certainty of subjective experience as an issue not necessarily connected to questions of objective truth, then we allow Descartes, and all those who philosophise in this way, to establish the ground for the mind/body problem itself,[5] and, moreover, the ground for all those questions demanding answers about the reality or otherwise of the world we see. By seeking a correspondence between what we see and what we suppose to be there we allow a gap in which questions like "Is there really a world out there?" and ""How do I know the world is like I see it?" can be sensibly posed, to the amazement and confusion of those untutored in philosophy who find it nonsensical to ask such questions.

If the ideal contents of experience are indubitable but say nothing about the world 'beyond' and if the relation between experience and the world is entirely contingent, then we must seek solutions in the way that Descartes does in Meditations Three to Six. This leads to an accession to his belief in a benevolent and perfect God, either this, or we will be left with a profound scepticism about the world. Either way we will waste time and effort trying to solve problems which are essentially of our own making.[6]

Descartes does recognise the deficiency of a system in which objective reality is only contingently related to the contents of subjective experience and, in his own terms, and by the end of the "Sixth Meditation", he does give ground for belief in the objective reality of the world as we experience it. He does not believe that each thinking being exists in a limbo of uncertainty about the existence of things and beings other than himself. Descartes is not a sceptic, and is appalled by the apparent consequences of his doubting, when he says,

> the most pressing task seems to be to escape from the doubts into which I fell a few days ago, and see whether any certainty can be achieved regarding material objects. (Ibid, p.44)

The difficulties primarily concern the relation between mind and body and the certainty of the existence of objective reality, and these problems are only eventually solved by recourse to the certain existence of God.[7] Notwithstanding this aid Descartes' theory still has serious deficiencies especially with the qualitative differences between God, mind and material objectivity. In particular, the relation between the last two is picked out in the correspondence with Princess Elizabeth, which I shall look at below.

To begin with we must return to some of the things Descartes says in the *Discourse on the Method* and in the "Sixth Meditation". First, clearly, in the *Discourse*,

> From this I recognised that I was a substance whose whole essence or nature is to be conscious and whose being requires no place and depends on no material thing. (Descartes, 1954, p. 32)

This deduction follows simply from the original bifurcation of the world leading up to the *cogito*. Given the choice Descartes has no other option than to choose his self-certain subjective being as the locus of his existence. This only can he know certainly and indubitably, all else can be doubted and is therefore rejected as a foundation for his existence.[8] However by coming down on the side of subjective ideality Descartes then has to explain the relation of his existence as consciousness to the, now external, body which he would have as his own. He comes closest to achieving this, though not very close, in the "Sixth Meditation", in this famous passage.

> I am not present in my body merely as a sailor is present in a ship; but that I am very closely joined and, as it were, intermingled with it, so that I and the body form a unit. (Descartes, 1986, p.57)

The significance of this is that it denies what seems to be the most appropriate metaphor for the relation between mind and body that can be supported on Cartesian premises. It would seem that any closer relation than that of sailor to ship would violate the affirmation of essential consciousness so firmly set out above in the quote from the *Discourse*. It is vital to Cartesian ontology that I am a substance the whole essence of which is to be conscious, one that requires no essential relation to any material thing. The self must be given as self subsistent and purely self-referenced. This strongly echoes Stirner's philosophy in which the self creates itself and everything around it, enabling Stirner to glorify in the absolute freedom of his own self, and in himself as "Owner". Descartes never seems to be as fully clear about, or as comfortable with, the connection between mind and body. He would not be comfortable with Stirnerian isolationism and he would have us accept that mind and body are somehow "mixed up".[9] The difficulties come to the surface explicitly in his replies to the pointed enquiries of Princess Elizabeth about the precise relation between mind and body given the essential self consciousness derived from the *cogito*.[10]

Descartes, after admitting that his main aim in the *Discourse* and *Meditations* was to show the distinction between body and soul, says simply, "Lastly, as regards the soul and body together, we have only the notion of their union" (Descartes, 1988, Vol. III, p. 218) and then goes into a lengthy discourse on the notions appropriate to describe the actions of the soul and the body, and warning against trying to apply those appropriate for one to the other, thus mirroring the division he has created between body and spirit. Her Royal Highness is clearly not satisfied with this, and quite rightly so. She reposes the question directly in her letter of 10th June 1643.

> ...<I cannot> understand the idea by means of which we are to judge of the way that the soul, unextended and immaterial moves the body

and,

> I must confess that I could more readily allow that the soul has matter and extension than that an immaterial being has the capacity of moving a body and being affected by it. (Descartes, 1954, p.277-8)

Descartes second reply in his letter of 28th June 1643 is equally unsatisfactory.

> It is the ordinary course of life and conversation, and abstention from meditation and from the study of things that exercise the imagination, that teaches us how to conceive the union of soul and body (Descartes, 1988, Vol. III, p. 227)

and

> Your Highness observes that it is easier to attribute matter and extension to the soul than to attribute to it the capacity to move and be moved by the body without having such matter and extension. I beg her to feel free to attribute this matter and extension to the soul because that is simply to conceive of it as united to the body. (Ibid, p.228)

This sits very uneasily with the idea of the self-subsistent thinking individual that I am certain that I am, and contradicts Descartes' earlier assertion in the *Discourse* that his existence requires no material connection.

The root problem is that Descartes has begun the separation of mind and body through the process of his analysis and by seeking to doubt all that he held initially to be true and self evident. The distinction developed in the First and Second Meditations between the certainty of the contents of my subjective experience and uncertain objective reality eliminates the possibility of an integrated analysis of my experience of the world and leaves the self in subjective isolation. This initial withdrawal from the world irretrievably distorts the following analysis and sets in motion a mind/body duality. This duality then pervades all succeeding methodology. So firm is his commitment to dualistic interpretation, and so potent is the distinction that he has introduced that, in his reply to Princess Elizabeth's second letter, he is moved to suggest a duality of investigative method. If, as he suggests, we are to abstain from meditation and study in order to gain particular kinds of knowledge and understanding we will have no opportunity or ground on which to evaluate the different types of knowledge we acquire and the objects they inform. In the end Descartes' remarks on the relation between mind and body tell us nothing more than that their separation must remain absolute under the premise of the possibility of sceptical doubt, that is, once we have allowed the distinction between subjective experience and objective reality to be made.

It is not my purpose at this stage to go deeply into the attempts of Cartesians, including Descartes, to re-establish the ground for belief in an objective reality in spite of the uncertainty engendered by the exercise of sceptical doubt, nor am I concerned with Descartes' proofs of the existence of God and the effect this has on the mind/body problem and questions about the veracity of sensory experience. To go into these issues now would not only distract from the central theme of my argument but would implicitly accept Cartesian premises and methods, and a pursuit of the investigation of the nature of the self in the style set by this tradition. All I have set out to do above is to indicate that the approach determined by Descartes sets its own problems which then demand resolution. It is my firm contention that Descartes does not solve the mind/body problem nor the problem of the independent existence of objects beyond, or external to, consciousness, and I will argue further that these problems are in fact set by the methodology developed by Descartes and adopted by his successors and may be avoided by the use of an alternative and ultimately more satisfactory methodology.

The most important feature of what Descartes has to say in the *Discourse* and *Meditations* about the self is not the issue of the indubitable existence of the self, however obvious this might appear to be from the continuing importance of the *cogito* in the work of those following Descartes. The certain existence of my own self, given in the *cogito*, is neither in dispute nor very illuminating. Existence itself is not the real issue, more important critically is the complete subjectification of the contents of my experience, the way in which the method of analysis (sceptical doubt) describes the way I perceive, see, and experience, and the possibility that this may be in conflict with the way things really are. The possibility of the self certainty of my subjective experience and the disconnection from a supposed world "beyond" my subjective self is the ground of Stirnerian egoism and the ground which must be won back if Stirner's egoism is to be refuted.

While God rescues Descartes from scepticism the Godless Stirner transmits subjective certainty into the ethical sphere with devastating consequences. Indubitable subjective experience becomes the only basis on which Stirner is prepared to base his behaviour, his only justification for action. The "ownership" of the subjective contents of experience, its indubitability set out in Descartes' work, and the undermining of objective reality through its merely contingent relation to certain subjectivity, becomes the basis for Stirner's rejection of objective morality and his glorification of the Ego and its own. Just as, in Descartes, knowledge proceeds from subjectivity so does value in Stirner, neither is satisfactory.

Personal Identity - The Metaphysical Goldilocks

Of equal importance to the mind/body problem in any theory of the self is the question of personal identity. In this question the "What Am I?" and the "How can I know myself?" are brought together. To begin with, the core of the problem we are concerned with here is the "If" and "How" of the continuity of the same (identical) identity over time. The English Empiricist, John Locke put it in characteristic style when he said,

> Another occasion the mind often takes of comparing is the very being of things, when considering anything as existing at any determined time and place; we compare it with itself existing at another time and thereon form the ideas of *identity* and *diversity*.

And...

> When we see anything to be in any place in any instant of time, we are sure (be it what it will) that it is that very thing, and not another which at that same time exists in another place, how like and indistinguishable soever it may be in all other respects; and in this consists *identity*, when the ideas it is attributed to vary not at all from what they were that moment wherein we consider their former existence and to which we compare the present. (Locke, 1975, p.206)

If the discussion of Descartes' work centres around the relation of the self to the world we experience, then the discussion of personal identity will centre around the relation of the self to time. The process of comparison indicated by Locke makes this much clearer; identity must first mean, identical with itself at the same time, and, beyond this, some circumstance under which the idea of identity indicates the identity of the entity with itself at different times. If only the former of these can be demonstrated then the notion of identity will have no practical meaning, so little can it be formulated. Clearly the task of the philosopher lies in demonstrating the possibility of continued identity of the individual self over time.[11] Once again from Locke,

> But let men, according to their diverse hypotheses, resolve of that as they please. This every intelligent being, sensible of happiness or misery must grant: that there is something that is *himself*, that he is concerned for and would have happy; that this the self has existed in a continued duration more than one instant, and it is possible may exist, as it has done, months and years to come without and certain bounds to be set to its duration; and may be the same self, by the same consciousness continued on for the future. (Ibid, p. 219)

I will now look at one attempt to solve this conundrum.

Hume on Identity

Nowhere is this challenge taken up with more devastating result than in the work of David Hume, the eighteenth century empiricist and sceptic, who elegantly, and relentlessly, pursues Cartesian insights and premises to what he sees as their inevitable logical outcome.[12] By the time he has finished, at the end of the *Treatise of Human Nature*, we are left wondering about the simplest everyday occurrences, and how even these are possible at all. Hume exposes the contingency of principles which we had held to be certain. Causality, knowledge, probability, chance, relation, memory, reason, and the evidence of our senses, are all put under Hume's microscope and found wanting to lesser and greater degrees.[13] Nor does the notion of personal identity escape and in Part IV of Book One of the *Treatise*, Hume, using his version of Cartesian method, undermines our naive understanding of our own identity and then abruptly leaves the scene.[14]

Hume, unlike Descartes, accepts no responsibility to re-establish the ground for commonly held beliefs, and in this respect his work shows more starkly the deficiencies of this kind of theorising about the nature of the self. The fact that Hume's conclusions about the nature of our idea of personal identity appear consistent and unavoidable, highlights the deficiency in the approach he employs, in the same way that Descartes' failure to answer Princess Elizabeth shows up the flaws in his method. Hume, like Descartes, is a mind/body dualist who would like to find some way of describing interaction between the two but who, unlike Descartes, will be prepared to admit that he can find no means to do so. This is clear from the way he sets out the ground for his discussion of personal identity when, in the second section of Part IV of the *Treatise* he discusses "Scepticism with regard to the Senses". A brief examination of this section will show us the way that Hume thinks about the general principle of identity as a prelude to his thoughts on personal identity.

It is important to remember that Hume's scepticism does not deny that we rely on the evidence of our senses, his denial is aimed at our supposedly sure ground for this reliance. Hume admits only that there is no link to be found in experience between cause and effect. This link, it seems, is only constituted psychologically by consciousness which establishes a relation through custom and habit. Hume's scepticism is scepticism with regard to the lessons of experience and not with regard to the actual existence of the world. Hume is concerned to clarify the nature of our belief, and then to demonstrate that this belief has no foundation outside custom and habit.[15]

Hume's empiricism means that he is committed to the thesis that all ideas, notions, concepts etc., are derived from sensory experience, whether directly, as in the case of our impressions of the material objects which surround us in the world, or indirectly, as ideas arrived at by the operation of reason on this raw sensory evidence, ideas like, identity, diversity and continuity. He shares Descartes' subjective certainty of his sensory experience,

> For since all actions and sensations of the mind are known to us by consciousness, they must necessarily appear in every particular what they are, and be what they appear. (Hume, 1959, Vol.I, p. 185)

The world is idealised once again, and...

> it is not our body we perceive, when we regard our limbs and members, but certain impressions, which enter by the senses; so that the ascribing of a real and corporeal existence to these impressions, or to their objects, is an act of the mind as difficult to explain as that which we examine at present. (Ibid, p. 185)

Thus the first and main problem is encountered. Hume is committed to sensory evidence as the source of knowledge about the world including his own self, and yet finds difficulty with grounds for the veracity of this kind of evidence. Even more, he has to admit that simple sensory experience cannot solve the simple identity problem. The senses cannot give us evidence of the continued existence of objects even when these objects are not being perceived by us, but this is a kind of continuity of existence which we very much wish to ascribe to a great many objects in the world, including ourselves. We get over this by a simple act of mind which Hume describes with characteristic understatement and elegance.

> Objects have a certain coherence even as they appear to our senses; but this coherence is much greater and more uniform if we suppose the objects to have a continued existence; and as the mind is once in the train of observing a uniformity among objects, it naturally continues till it renders the uniformity as complete as possible. (Ibid, p.192)

In simple terms this seems like a pretty adequate description of what goes on. The mind finds that its picture of the world works a whole lot better if it assumes, or "supposes" a continued unperceived existence of certain objects which appear to exhibit a sort of coherence in their observed changes. But Hume is greatly troubled with regard to the derivation of this idea of continued existence, or identity, over time. For Hume, as an empiricist, there should be some experience from which our idea of identity, as continuity over time, can be derived. Hume's dilemma is that, a single individual object, even if it is said to be identical with itself, can never give us the idea of identity because this is a relation, and no relation between objects is present in the case of a single simple object. However, were a multiplicity of objects present to us this would not be able to give us an idea of identity either but only the idea of number, or multiplicity, as opposed to the single object which gives us the ideas of singularity and unity. Under this construction it is difficult to see what kind of identity statements could ever make sense, the notion of identity appears to have no possible coherence. Hume is left with the difficult "act of mind" described above. Continuity inferred, despite interrupted perception, allows for the notional separation of the object from itself, and hence its later identification with itself at a different time. Hume can then conclude that "the principle of individuation is nothing but the *unvariableness* and *uninterruptedness* of any object through a supposed variation of time" (Ibid, p.195).

In all of this Hume seems to be saying that the ascription of identity comes out of a mistake, or lack of rigour, in our conception of a succession of similar, but different, objects which pass before consciousness and are loosely identified with one another. A sort of fudge over the contradiction between singularity and number, both of which seem to be required to frame the concept of identity. He expresses his reservations thus,

> This propension to bestow an identity on our resembling perceptions, produces the fiction of a continued existence; since that fiction, as well as the identity, is really false, as is acknowledged by all philosophers, and has no other effect than to remedy the interruption of our perceptions, which is the only circumstance that is contrary to their identity. (Ibid, p.202)

We cannot be happy with a notion of identity which is merely a "fiction" even if it is a convenient fiction, but, in the end, Hume believes that it is easier to ascribe identity to an interrupted succession of similar perceptions than to face up to the contradiction that we have before us, namely a series of distinct and different perceptions and therefore distinct and different objects presented to us, where we had supposed there to be but one object.

> There is a great difference betwixt such opinion as we form after calm and profound reflection, and such as we embrace by a kind of instinct or natural impulse, on account of their suitableness and conformity to the mind. If these opinions become contrary it is not difficult to foresee which of them will have the advantage. (Ibid, p.206) [16]

What has occurred by the end of Hume's discussion of the general theory of identity is that the duality of perception and object is allowed to explain the one (perceptions) as interrupted and discontinuous, while the other (objects) can remain uninterrupted and identical. Hence we are able to make sense of our idea of identity. But since the relation between perception and object is contingent even more problems are introduced. The idea of identity is rendered inaccessible and the notion of our own personal identity placed in serious jeopardy. Hume hints at this when he says,

> we may observe, that what we call a *mind*, is nothing but a heap or collection of different perceptions, united together by certain relations, and supposed, though falsely, to be endowed with a perfect simplicity and identity. (Ibid, p.200)

An idea of identity has only been achieved at the cost of separating the subjectively certain perceptions, or experiences, from objective reality and the ascription of identity between these two is left dependent on the relation between cause and effect, which, in Hume, is much weaker than we might have naively supposed. Hume argues elsewhere, in convincing fashion, that we have no grounds but custom to suppose that cause *determines* effect, he argues that the relation merely denotes an habitually observed past conjunction.[17] Identity is left founded, and foundering, on this denotation. It is on this basis that Hume proceeds to discuss personal identity specifically.

He begins this section by noting that philosophers have imagined that we have a *self*, of which we are always conscious and which subsists through time in a way that is essentially unchanged. This to him seems problematic from within the idealist empiricist framework which is his philosophical base.

> Unluckily all these positive assertions are contrary to that very experience which is pleaded for them; nor have we any idea of *self*, after that manner it is here explained. For, from what impression could this idea be derived? (Ibid, p.238)

and, even more difficult,

> But self or person is not any one impression, but that to which our several impressions and ideas are supposed to have reference. (Ibid, p.238)

Hume also recognises that it is not possible for him to separate his own self from these perceptions, "I never can catch *myself* at any time without a perception, and can never observe anything but the perception" (Ibid, p.239). My "self" resists objectification, by slipping away out of sight when I look or by never being at home when I call, a metaphysical Goldilocks.[18] The only possible conclusion is that self must be made up of, "a bundle or collection of different perceptions which succeed each other with inconceivable rapidity" and that, "The mind is a kind of theatre" (Ibid, p.239).[19] As with the argument about the continued existence of objects in the world, despite their interrupted perception, so with the case of personal identity. Hume is driven to affirm that, in claiming an idea of personal identity we are mistaking our perception of diversity, the changing perceptions over time that make up the self, for an unchanging identity. Despite the fact that we see ourselves as changed over time we wish deduce from this observation that we are identical with ourselves at different times. To Hume this is confusion and contradiction, since what we are describing as identity is evidently a notion derived from the continuous succession of different perceptions, which succession can only truly give us the idea of diversity. Hume is not saying that we are not continuously identical with ourselves, but that we have no possible grounds for saying so, apart from our instinctive presumption. We act as if we, and others, have a continuous identical existence, but in the end this is, in itself, the only reason we can give ourselves for believing it to be so.

The crisis in the theory of identity, when applied to the self, comes when the observing subject becomes object too. No real bifurcation is possible when we try to observe ourselves, hence the way that the self seems to slip out of sight as we turn to view it. In fact the identity we imagine to be there when we are not looking appears to be no more than a fiction we invent to satisfy our requirement for continuity of existence, a fiction that has become necessary as a result of the way we have come to understand the world as divided into subject and object. In this way the contradiction between supposed continuous object and the interrupted succession of subjective perceptions is brought fully into the open.

Hume rejects the thesis that my identical existence is interrupted by sleep, or by forgetfulness and yet is left with no grounds to show how this is not so, according to the theory of ideas and the empiricism he espouses. He is left, finally, with the disappearance of any satisfactory basis for a notion of personal identity and can only say,

> The identity which we ascribe to the mind of man is only a fictitious one, and of a like kind with that which we ascribe to vegetable and animal bodies (Ibid, p.245)

and,

> identity is nothing really belonging to these different perceptions, and uniting them together, but is merely a quality which we attribute to them, because of the union of their ideas in the imagination when we reflect on them (Ibid, p.246)

and finally,

> All the disputes concerning the identity of connected objects are merely verbal, except so far as the relation of parts gives rise to some fiction or imaginary principle of union. (Ibid, p.248)

Hume briefly revisits this problem in his Appendix to the *Treatise* and is frank indeed in admitting his continuing perplexity. He is unable to disentangle his perceptions or experiences from his experience of self and cannot avoid the conclusion that,

> The annihilation which some people suppose to follow upon death, and which entirely destroys the self, is nothing but an extinction of all particular perceptions; (Hume, 1959, Vol.II, p.318)

and he is forced to admit that "all my hopes vanish when I come to explain the principles that unite our successive perceptions in our thought or consciousness" (Ibid, p.319), though he does in characteristic fashion allow for the possibility that, "Others, perhaps, or myself, upon more mature reflections, may discover some hypothesis that will reconcile those contradictions"(Ibid, p.319). A "fiction" is all that Hume has left available to constitute the continuing self and we are left with only fragments of what we took to be a continuous identity. This is silly, as Bennett quotes,

> To say that my successive instantaneous states are not one state but several is one thing, while to say that I in those states am not one but several individuals is to say quite another thing, and a thundering silly one at that. (Bennett, 1971, p.337)

It is silly because it contradicts what appears to be the case. The lack of grounds for belief in the continuity of personal identity which leaves this common sense belief resting on nothing more than a psychological disposition to believe leaves much to be desired. Before going on it will be useful to say something about why this contradiction arises in this kind of analysis.

This kind of contradiction is the product of an attempt by philosophers and particularly empiricists, to objectify the subject which is themselves. Analyses, which can apparently be made to be consistent when applied to objects placed "beyond" the observing subject, go completely awry when applied to the observing subject itself as object. Instead of a process of comparison between the certain contents of my subjective experience, and a supposed objective reality, which causes me to have these sensations, and which, therefore, I can claim knowledge of from the evidence of my senses; there is an attempt to compare the subjective self with itself as an object. Hume, in trying to find himself "at home" with no perceptions, is looking for the objectified self in order to begin the comparison. It is no surprise when he can find no-one there, no surprise that is to anyone except a dualist. Hume can talk quite sensibly about the impressions caused in the observer by objects in the world and deduce characteristics about these objects from the impressions received. Although it has its own problems the relation "if I see/hear/smell etc. something, then something is there, and, if something is there I will see/hear/smell it", is acceptable as a starting point because it seems to fit with the self certainty of subjective experience. However when applied to the self this methodology cannot even find its object, there does not seem to be one when there must be both subject and object for the methodology to be applied. Empirical analysis will not function when the object is made both observing subject, and observed object. The real problem is to be found in the method of approach itself, which employs the subject/object structure in the first place. At the fundamental level of self analysis it is not merely problematic in the way that it is when applied to the world "outside" it simply will not function at all.

Rejection of this approach with regard to the analysis of the self, consequent upon consideration of the problem of personal identity, is the beginning of the questioning of the whole method of approach even as applied to the whole of the observed world. The method appears to create, or to leave, a void at the centre of the observation. Where the self ought to be it cannot be found. The idea of the continuous self cannot be accommodated in Hume's empiricism because Hume, and those like him, are orientated towards questions of essentiality. These questions about what the self *is* will never provide satisfactory answers to questions about the self, more of this later.

This dualist Cartesian approach misconstrues the nature of the world and establishes a division between what I perceive and what might actually be there, thus creating the problem of knowledge. The approach misfires even more when it is applied to the problem of personal identity because, in centring around the problem of the continuity of identity and existence over time, the method of Descartes, Locke, Hume and others like them, objectifies time. The questions they ask about identity divide the self from time in the same way that the questions they ask about the world divide the self from the world. The identity statements they make are closely tied up with questions of essentiality and the continuous and self identical essence of the self. I will show later that this is by no means the most fertile ground in which to develop the theory of the self.

In Locke identity is defined as the idea of a thing being identical with itself at another time, as if time were something apart from the being in question. When he speaks of what *person* stands for his description is,

> a thinking intelligent being, that has reason and reflection, and can consider itself as itself, the same thinking thing, in different times and places, which it does only by that consciousness which is inseparable from thinking. (Locke,1975, p.211)

Time is objectified like place or world, and self is separated from both in a way that poses the dual problems of how they might be once again connected. Hume struggles to connect experiences we have at different times and can find no basis in the end apart from a convenient fiction we call personal identity. He admits that,

> Our chief business, then, must be to prove, that all objects, to which we ascribe identity, without observing their invariableness and uninterruptedness, are such as consist of a succession of related objects. (Hume, 1959, Vol. I, p.242)

But why is it necessary to find some alternative to observation? Only because observation, in this case, is not sufficient to provide ground for the uninterruptedness and invariability that Hume seeks. Hume's ontology, like that of Descartes, objectifies entities in the world as existing at a particular time; this in turn provides an objective view of time as alienated from entities which are then understood as existing "in time". This ignores, or fails to recognise, the temporal dimension of existence itself and it is this objectification of temporality which leads to the formulation of the "problem" of personal identity, a problem which appears to be silly when its solutions, or apparent lack of them, are returned to everyday commonsensical experience.

In the next section I will examine Kant's attempt to solve the problems of relation to the world, and personal identity, with the benefit of the earlier work of Descartes and Hume.

Notes

1. For a description and discussion of Descartes method of doubt see, Wilson, 1978, Chapter One, and Williams, 1978, Chapter Two.
2. Williams, 1978, Chapter Four, "The Real Distinction" and Wilson, 1978, Chapter Two.
3. For an interesting and illuminating discussion of the distinction between perceptions, judgements and dubitability see Kenny, 1993, Chapter Two, and Wilson, 1978, Chapter Three, pp. 101-120.
4. This is Cartesian Dualism, see Wilson, 1978, pp. 177-185 for a strict version of the split which stresses the qualitative difference between intellectual and bodily activity as opposed to simple non-correspondence.
5. Williams recognises something like this when he says of Descartes proof that his essence is thinking. "There is a subtler error that might come into the argument at this point. In saying that one can entertain the idea that one might not have been thinking at another time, or the idea that one might not have been thinking now, one is implicitly taking a view of oneself from what I called in the last chapter the third person perspective - just as much as one explicitly does in invoking others' conception of oneself" (Williams, 1978, p.110). It is exactly this perspective which later radical critics of Cartesian method will deny in subverting the Cartesian project. See Chapter Seven.
6. Richardson, 1986, pp.75-80.
7. Kenny, 1993, Chapter Seven, Williams, 1978, Chapter Five, and Wilson, 1978, pp.136-138.
8. It matters little by this point whether the *cogito* is taken to be a logical inference, a self evident existential truth, or an inevitably performatory truth. All of these are concerned with how the *cogito* is true, none dispute that it is true. These options on the mechanics of the *cogito* have been discussed widely, for a broad sample see, Hintikka, *Cogito, ergo sum: Inference or performance*, Kenny, 1993, Chapter Three, Malcolm, *Descartes proof that his essence is thinking*, and, Wilson, 1978, pp.50-71.
9. See, Williams, 1978, Chapter Ten, and Wilson, 1978, pp. 205-219 and for an alternative approach to this issue, Sayers, 1985, pp.70-72.

10. Princess Elizabeth's letter to Descartes of 16th May 1643, in Descartes, 1954, p. 274-5.
11. See, Bennett, 1971, pp. 333-345, for a discussion of serial and contingent identity statements.
12. Hume, as will become apparent, is a mind/body dualist who wishes to show a connection between these two while retaining a firm footing in empirical method. As such he therefore takes over what becomes apparent as the contradiction between mind and body inherent in Descartes' work and his work is coloured and eventually frustrated by this contradiction which, I will argue, is made acute in all Cartesian founded discussions of personal identity.
13. For a discussion of the extent of Hume's scepticism, see Popkin, *David Hume: His Pyrronhism and His Critique of Pyrronhism* and, Penelhum, 1975, pp.15-26.
14. For a useful and in-depth discussion of Hume's work in this area see, Bricke, 1980. Also, Penelhum, 1975, pp.75-88, and, *Hume on Personal Identity*, and Kemp Smith, 1960, pp.497-516.
15. The view that Hume is not the same kind of subjective idealist as Berkeley and that Hume does not deny existence to the world and to the self is argued by Kemp Smith, 1960, pp.79-102.
16. It is interesting to note that Hume's dualism extends not only through epistemology and personal identity but also to the practise of philosophy which is seen as quite distinct from ordinary everyday thinking about the world in which we are untroubled by questions of epistemology and identity. He says himself, "Most fortunately it happens that since reason is incapable of dispelling these clouds, Nature herself suffices to that purpose, and cures me of this philosophical melancholy and delirium, either by relaxing this bent of mind, or by some avocation, and lively impression of my senses, which obliterate all these chimeras. I dine, I play a game of backgammon, I converse, and am merry with my friends; and when, after three or four hours amusement, I would return to these speculations, they appear so cold, and strained, and ridiculous" (Hume, 1959, Vol. I, p.254). This, in common with much of Hume's empiricism, is pregnant with the insights later taken up by phenomenologists and evokes Heidegger's discussion of *everydayness*, see Chapter Seven.
17. Hume, 1959, Vol.I, Part III, Sections II, III and IV. Also see, Penelhum, 1975 Chapter Two, Bennett, 1971, Chapters XI and XII, and Kemp Smith, 1960, Chapters XVI-XIX, for extensive discussions of this key issue in Hume.
18. In the first part of famous fairy tale the little girl, Goldilocks, finds only the signs of the three bears in the same way that, when he looks for himself, Hume can only find signs of himself. In the second part of the story the bears find signs of Goldilocks and infer a presence from these signs in a parody of Hume's search for the continuing self. In the final dramatic conclusion Goldilocks and the Bears (subject and object, and *vice versa*) finally come together and repel as like poles. Their meeting is actually impossible in the same way that Hume can never find himself at home.
19. This is a curious pre-echo of Heidegger's description of Dasein as the clearing in which beings are manifest in *Being and Time*, H. 133 and H. 170, and I will return to Hume's insight in Chapters Eight and Nine as part of the discussion of Heidegger's (very different) notion of identity.

5
Kant - Let Sleeping Dogma Awake!

Kant's epistemology is a clear and explicit response to Hume's scepticism,[1] an attempt to provide both a foundation for empirical scientific knowledge and to show the limits of such knowledge. As a consequence of this work, given in the *Critique of Pure Reason* and *Prolegomena to Any Future Metaphysics*, in which Kant attempts to explain the relation between the conscious self and the external world, he also provides a theory of the self which, he hopes, will not encounter the shortcomings which so disable theories of the self set out by Descartes and Hume, and which will solve the problems of knowledge and identity. In this chapter I will examine briefly Kant's epistemology and his discussion of the relationship between consciousness and the world, and show how these constitute an advance over the work of his predecessors. This will allow a clear setting out of a Kantian view of the self, which, although it will prove to be less problematic and perplexing than, for example, the notion of personal identity in Hume, will still exhibit significant deficiencies. I will then give an alternative interpretation of Kant's work, particularly in the *Critique of Pure Reason*, which will point the way towards a radically different, but more fertile, understanding of knowledge, experience and selfhood than is possible within the tradition of Descartes, Hume and Kant.

The epistemological problem for Kant is quite simple. Hume is quite unable to provide a foundation for our knowledge about the world beyond the beliefs we have. Hume's empiricism is inadequate to provide the kind of proof which Kant believes is essential to provide justification for the knowledge on which we base our day to day actions. Most significant of all Hume fails to provide proof of the necessary connection between cause and effect. His work clearly demonstrates that inductive reasoning cannot deliver these goods.[2] This is the epistemological crisis which awakens Kant from his dogmatic slumbers and which has to be met in order to provide a foundation for the emerging empirical science of the eighteenth century.

In simple terms Kant wants to show how objective knowledge, that is knowledge about the world, which is independent of our own subjective perception, is possible. This question can be resolved into a question about the presuppositions of experience, or what it is that must be true for us to be able to have experience, as we know it. In this way Kant will bring together both the empiricism of Hume and the nascent rationalism of Descartes and, in so doing, produce a complete epistemology and an explanation of the process of relation between the conscious individual, the world and time. Kant will demonstrate, in the *Critique of Pure Reason*, not only the areas in which knowledge is available to us, but also areas in which the search for knowledge is fruitless, misguided and even dangerous, areas in which belief, or even faith, are all that we can expect.[3]

Kant's enquiry centres on the possibility of *a priori* knowledge, or, what he calls *a priori* synthetic judgements.[4] In other words he is seeking a form of knowledge which is specifically not empirically verifiable but which provides the basis for empiricism itself. This is to be Kant's transcendental deduction and through it Kant will show how empirical experience itself is possible, and will thereby demonstrate how *a priori* knowledge is acquired. In this way Kant's work can be seen as a metaphysics of experience.

Kant's Epistemology - A Rational Psychology

The failure of the Cartesian epistemological project prior to Kant's work is the failure to show how the conformity between our subjective perceptions and objects existing independent of us can be demonstrated. Specifically, the conformity of knowledge to objects remained highly problematic for both Descartes and Hume. Kant makes a subtle but radical departure from the tradition and, instead of investigating the conformity of knowledge to objects, (which exist supposedly behind our perceptions), seeks to develop an epistemology on the presumption of the conformity of objects to knowledge, thereby hoping to recover the objective world from its concealment behind the veil of the senses. This Copernican Revolution is the move away from the focus on objects in the world as the key to problems of knowledge, and towards the conscious self as the source of knowledge. Kant says, in the preface to the second edition of his *Critique of Pure Reason*,

> Hitherto it has been assumed that all our knowledge must conform to objects. But all attempts to extend our knowledge of objects by establishing something in regard to them *a priori*, by means of concepts have on this assumption ended in failure. We must therefore make trial whether we may not have more success in the tasks of metaphysics, if we suppose that objects must conform to our knowledge. (Kant, 1992, B. xvi)

Crucial to the operation of Kant's systems is the distinction between appearance and what Kant terms things-in-themselves. What we see hear feel etc., is only given to us as appearances. We never have anything else, apart from our sensations, as a source of empirical knowledge, and this is both the strength and fatal weakness of the empiricist position exemplified by Hume. We may not proceed to ground knowledge except on the basis of what we see, hear, feel etc., but neither may we proceed beyond this empirical experience to claim knowledge of the super-experiential reality which we believe exists behind appearances. We see what we see but we are unable to pierce the veil and experience the thing-in-itself we suppose to exist behind it. We are unable, through this process; to ground empirical knowledge and we are potentially precipitated into a world in which doubt about the very existence of objects outside us seems unavoidable.

Things-in-themselves, Kant will say, certainly exist but are inaccessible to perception. Appearances constitute what we may call the phenomenal world, while things-in-themselves are the noumenal reality to which we have no sensible access. Parallel to the distinction between appearances and things-in-themselves is the distinction between our capacities of sensibility and understanding. Sensibility, as the term suggests, is our ability to receive sensations or appearances. Understanding, in its pure form, is devoid of empirical content and denotes the capacity for rational thought allowing us to deduce, through logic, truths which are independent of empirical experience. Underlying both these distinctions is a fundamental distinction between content and form. Sensibility and appearance providing the contents for the forms derived from understanding, and, conversely, the forms providing structure to the flux of sensations, the structure that makes them experience.[5]

Kant turns first to the consideration of space and time. In this discussion he concludes that experience can only be possible on the basis of *a priori* (that is, prior to and independent of all empirical experience) intuitions of space and time as the forms of appearance. Space and time are not caused by, or effects of, things-in-themselves but are inherent in consciousness, and experience is not possible except on the presumption of its spatiality and temporality. In the *Prolegomena* he says,

> Pure mathematics, as synthetical cognition *a priori*, is possible only by referring to no other objects than those of the senses. At the basis of their empirical intuition lies a pure intuition (of space and time), which is *a priori* because the latter intuition is nothing but the mere form of sensibility, which precedes the actual appearance of the objects, since in fact it makes them possible. (Kant, 1977, p.28)

Space and time are not qualities of things-in-themselves but the formal conditions for the appearance of substantial qualities. Of space Kant says,

> Space is nothing but the form of all appearances of outer sense. It is the subjective condition of sensibility under which alone outer intuition is possible for us. (Kant, 1992, A. 26 = B. 42)

By outer sense Kant means, "a property of our mind", by which "we represent to ourselves objects as outside us" and these are "all, without exception in space" (Ibid, A. 22 = B. 37). In other words our experience of the world is premised on an *a priori* intuition of space, without which the appearance of the world would not be possible. Of time Kant says,

> Time is not an empirical concept that has been derived from any experience.... Only on the presupposition of time can we represent to ourselves a number of things as existing at one and the same time (simultaneously) or at different times (successively). (Ibid, A. 31 = B. 46)

Just as there can be no motion without space, so there can be no alteration without time. Inner sense is that, "by means of which the mind intuits itself or its inner state" (Ibid, A.23 = B. 37). Once again, as with space, we cannot abstract our experience of the world from the notion of time, "Time is a necessary representation that underlies all intuitions"(Ibid, A. 31 = B. 46). Space and time are the pure forms of outer and inner intuition respectively. All that Kant is really saying is that all of our outer experience must be spatial and all of our inner experience must be temporal and that if it were not it could not be experience at all.[6] This begins to say important things about the relationship of consciousness to the "external" world and the interaction between the two. Most notably Kant is bringing forward a view of consciousness that is more active in terms of its relation to sensibility than the model put forward by Hume. While both admit conscious activity in response to sensations Kant is explicit in affirming the very active role of consciousness in making experience and knowledge possible in the first place through the application of categories, while Hume merely allows that the mind produces ideas the genesis of which must be traced back directly to specific sensible impressions. For Kant, categories are necessary for us even to experience impressions, as he extends the active role of consciousness in framing all sensibility, while for Hume consciousness is more passive in receiving sensations.

Kant's discussions of space and time reflect on the two significantly problematic areas for the Cartesian tradition, the problem of knowledge of objects "outside" the self and the problem of the continuity of personal identity. The former as the problem of the spatiality of the self and the latter as the problem of its temporality. It is no coincidence that Kant must settle on these two notions (space and time) and his treatment of both illustrates a dualism in his thinking that has damaging consequences for the theory of the self which he provides later in the *Critique of Pure Reason*.

After the account of the notions of space and time Kant follows through the initial impulse to elucidate the conditions that make experience possible by setting out the Table of Categories. These are the pure concepts of understanding and are *a priori*.[7] They have no empirical content but are the forms of appearances. They are the pure forms of thought in which all our experiences must appear. As Scruton says, "every comprehensible world (every world which could contain self-consciousness) must also have the appearance dictated by the categories" (Scruton, 1982, p.27). That is, not only is experience made up of appearances but of appearances with particular forms. Categories are not special empirical determinations but general concepts, like substance and causality (precisely those concepts which gave Hume the greatest difficulty). The categories are the forms provided by understanding which when brought together with empirical sensibility produce experiences. The forms "organise" the flux of sensations and the sensations provide contents for, and enliven, the pure forms. Conversely the categories are applicable only to those objects which we can experience, this means that their application to other entities, metaphysical entities, is always mistaken.

Kant accepts, in fact insists, that there is no empirical means for the derivation of these concepts but instead of making this problematic, as does Hume's empiricism, he goes on to assert that the categories must be independent of any particular empirical experience since they are the forms of experience and make experience possible in the first place. This is the bringing together of the rational and the empirical, the capacities of the knower and the objects of knowledge, and is also the beginning of Kant's transcendentalism which I shall discuss more fully below. These structures of experience are logically but not temporally prior to any particular experience, there is no conscious process of bringing together sensations and categories in each individual experience. Kant is providing an analysis of experience in general and not giving a commentary "as it happens". Experience is the central given in Kant's analysis, and the *Critique of Pure Reason* is Kant's way of showing how it is possible or how it is grounded in the kind of beings that we are and in the kind of world in which we find ourselves. As I will demonstrate later this will have profound implications for the notion of selfhood which can be derived from Kant's work.

Kant's transcendental move is a large sidestep from Hume's scepticism, although Kant is still attacking the same problem. He is still attempting to provide a philosophical basis for natural science, which, it seems from Hume's work, has assumed an *a priori* knowledge to which it appears barely entitled. Kant, in common with Hume, wants to show how the assumptions of natural science, like the relation between cause and effect, can be grounded without reliance on the inductive method. Hume is not successful in this but his failure provokes Kant into the search for *a priori* synthetic knowledge and recourse to the categories provided by the understanding. With the setting out of the categories and the recognition of space and time as the forms of outer and inner sense Kant provides an alternative to Hume and deepens the distinction between the forms and contents of experience. This is a distinction not available to the empiricist Hume, but one that enables Kant to make sense of experience in a way that does not simply violate the tenets of empiricism,[8] and allows for transcendental deductions about the structure of experience. Naturally Kant and Hume share much in common, most notably a tradition that provides problems already formulated (and most significant amongst these the problem of the veil of the senses). This means that whatever differences become apparent between Kant and Hume there will remain many similarities born out of their common acceptance of the original Cartesian analysis which first precipitates the problems.

It is now clear that the key difference between Hume and Kant is that Kant is using a method which will allow him to go much further than Hume. By concentrating attention on the forms of experience, by allowing the experiencing self a more active and creative role, and by seeking the conformity of objects to our knowledge rather than the opposite, Kant can move away from Hume's scepticism and show how we can, and must, have *a priori* notions not derived from experience, but which support experience and provide grounds for the certainty of our knowledge of the world, (though not of the world of things-in-themselves but only of a world of appearances). Kant shows how knowledge is only possible through a combination of empirical sensations and rational structures and in this criticises not only Hume's empiricism but also the rationalist metaphysics of Descartes. Kant is trying to show that empiricism and rationalism must combine if we are to have a satisfactory theory of knowledge.

Kant is beginning to show the appropriate extent of our knowledge and, by this limiting of ambition, avoiding some of the deeper pitfalls of the tradition. Kant's method will also enable him to overcome Hume's perplexity with regard to the question of personal identity by generating a transcendental subject, or form of subjectivity, which will be coherent and grounded in a way that the purely empirical self, sought by Hume, can never be. Kant must, however, also show how the transcendental form of the self can be at one with the empirical self. In short he must show how the mind/body problem is to be resolved.

Probably the most serious criticism that can be levelled at Kant at this stage is that he risks the reduction of the world to the subjective experience of an individual consciousness providing no way in which we can deduce a world in common for different subjects. The empirical inaccessibility of things-in-themselves means that this risk looms large in all that Kant has to say. How can I know that there really is something out there? And if there is, how do I know that I am in the same world as everybody else? Kant acknowledges this issue and distinguishes himself from the subjective idealism of those like Berkeley in the section of the *Critique of Pure Reason* headed "The Refutation of Idealism" (B. 275-294).⁹ In this section Kant recognises that,

> The required proof must, therefore, show that we have *experience*, and not merely imagination of outer things; and this, it would seem, cannot be achieved save by proof that even our inner experience, which for Descartes is indubitable, is possible only on the assumption of outer experience. (Kant, 1992, B. 275)

He thereby, appears to grant a primacy to outer sense and to challenge the Cartesian indubitability of inner experience. He then advances the thesis that,

> *The mere, but empirically determined, consciousness of my own existence proves the existence of objects in space outside me.* (Ibid, B. 275)

Beginning with the simple fact that I am conscious of my own existence as determined in time Kant proceeds to the affirmation that all determinations in time presuppose something permanent in perception. Crucially Kant is then able to say,

> But this permanent cannot be an intuition in me. For all grounds of determination of my existence which are to be met with in me are representations; and, as representations themselves require a permanent distinct from them, in relation to which their change, and so my existence in time wherein they change, may be determined. (Ibid, B. xl)

Using the apparently evident truth that any representation must have a reality to which it corresponds, to support the proof of objective reality existing distinctly and separately from my self, and enabling Kant to conclude that the determination of my existence in time is only possible through the existence of actual things which I perceive outside me, and so, "the consciousness of my existence is at the same time an immediate consciousness of the existence of other things outside me" (Ibid, B. 276). Kant hopes that this turns the idealist game against itself and connects inner experience with an external world in a way that cannot be undone, by weaving the methodology of empiricism into the rationalist analysis, thus ascribing to sensation and selfhood their proper and essential places in experience.[10] In this way Kant's refutation of idealism is a critique of the purely rationalist position that leads to Berkeley's subjective idealism.[11] Instead of sticking firmly to the assumed pre-eminence and priority of inner experience, established by Descartes at the beginning of the *Meditations*, Kant makes inner experience dependent on the existence of objects independent of consciousness, and thus the mode of argument which appeared to invite the sceptical conclusion in both Descartes and Hume makes the posing of the question itself impossible.[12] External objects must exist otherwise my own existence would be questionable, which it clearly is not. As Kant says, "inner experience is itself possible only mediately and only through outer experience" (Ibid, B. 277) and

> outer experience is really immediate and ... only by means of it is inner experience - not indeed the consciousness of my own existence - but the determination of it in time - possible. (Ibid, B. 276-277)

Kant's contention against the idealist is clear. The idealist assumption that only inner experience is immediate is held to be false, and it is not allowed to be possible that the cause of representations can lie only within ourselves. If this were allowed then it would contradict my consciousness of the determination of my own existence in time. How much of Kant's argument in "The Refutation of Idealism" rests simply on the implications of using the language of representation is arguable, however, and despite this weakness, the argument does succeed at least in distancing Kant from Berkeley's position, and, more significantly, leaves the door open to a much more radical interpretation of experience and Kant's work in this area which I will discuss later.

Two significant consequences flow from this argument. The first is that we must always bear in mind that when Kant speaks of objective reality he is still discussing appearances and not things-in-themselves, perception of the latter is never a possibility and our knowledge of the objective world external to ourselves is always confined to knowledge of appearances. The second is that this restriction applies equally to the experiencing "I"; in fact we shall see that we can know nothing of this beyond its bare existence. We do not come to know the self in-itself through inner or outer experience. To this extent Kant does not solve Hume's problem with Goldilocks.

Transcendental Idealism - Finding Somewhere to Stand

Before going forward to examine more closely the notion of selfhood in Kant's *Critique of Pure Reason* it will be useful to briefly recognise some of the central points of Kant's methodology and the advance this represents on the earlier work of Descartes and Hume.[13] Kant's transcendentalism is premised on dualism between the self and the not-self and between the phenomenal and the noumenal.[14] It is a method through which Kant hopes to circumvent the problem of how to verify the evidence of the senses by correlating this evidence with external objects which cause the sensory events which make up our experience. His dualism means that he does not seek correspondence between phenomenal and noumenal reality, but instead means to discuss separately phenomenal and noumenal entities. Kant describes transcendental idealism as,

> the doctrine that appearances are to be regarded as being, one and all, representations only, not things-in-themselves, and that time and space are therefore only sensible forms of our intuition, not determinations given as existing by themselves, nor conditions of objects viewed as things-in-themselves. (Kant, 1992, A. 369)

Space and time alone are removed from the list of possible qualities of objects and alone established as fundamental forms of our intuition. Kant continues,

> There can be no question that I am conscious of my representations; these representations and I myself, who have the representations, therefore exist. (Ibid, A. 370)

This is a re-statement of Descartes' premise of the self-certainty of my own existence, *cogito ergo sum*, and it is also a premise central to the empiricist school. However, unlike some Cartesians before him Kant goes on to say,

> objects are nothing but representations, the immediate perception (consciousness) of which is at the same time a sufficient proof of their reality. (Ibid, A. 371)

There is no room for doubtful inference between thing-in-itself and appearance. There is immediate perception, but not perception of things-in-themselves, only of representations. Transcendental realism is rejected in favour of transcendental idealism; disposing of the problem the realist has in attempting to infer the qualities of objects from their appearance. Finally Kant concludes,

> In our system ... these external things, namely matter, are in all their configurations and alterations nothing but mere appearances, that is, representations in us, of the reality of which we are immediately conscious. (Ibid, A. 371-2)

Kant denies that it is possible to show how representation takes place, nor does he attempt to deduce from the representations any qualities that may be attributed to things-in-themselves existing beyond his consciousness. Although this existence is demonstrated transcendentally from our perception of appearances, the representation can tell us nothing of the thing-in-itself, beyond the formality of its existence. This is an evident weak point in Kant's argument since he both requires some connection between things-in-themselves and appearances and yet, equally, requires their qualitative distinction. However this is the best argument that can be constructed from the essentially dualist position inherited from the tradition of Descartes.

Kant takes the argument in another direction and, in so doing, re-defines what we mean by objective knowledge. If all that we have are representations then we seem to have a choice of two alternatives. The first, scepticism, determines that objective knowledge is impossible and that all claims to such knowledge are at best mistaken and at worst malicious. The second, transcendental idealism, is to understand what we have in the way of representation as the foundation of knowledge and objectivity, to abandon the fruitless search for knowledge of things-in-themselves, and to fashion knowledge within the confines of possible experience. This is the course chosen by Kant when he first affirms the existence and immediacy of representations and then later says,

> From perceptions knowledge of objects can be generated, either by mere play of imagination or by way of experience; and in the process there may, no doubt, arise illusory representations to which the objects do not correspond, the deception being attributable sometimes to a delusion of the imagination (in dreams) and sometimes to an error of judgement (in so-called sense deception). To avoid such deceptive illusion we have to proceed according to the rule: *Whatever is connected with a perception according to empirical laws is actual.* (Ibid, A. 376)

Kant is saying that true perceptions will conform with one another, that is, we may deduce from their consistency and conformity that perceptions provide us with a view of the world that is true. Illusion is betrayed not by the non-conformity of the representation with a thing-in-itself "behind" it (to even attempt such a comparison is impossible), but by the fact that the perception of illusory or mistaken representation will not conform to, or fit in with, all our other representations. In this way representations, viewed as constitutive of a whole, form the basis of an objective knowledge against which other representations can be tested. Their conformity to the empirical structure demonstrates their truth, non-conformity indicates illusion. Knowledge is possible, but not in the form of which the sceptic despaired.

Leaving aside questions about the nature of things-in-themselves which, despite all Kant says, we may still feel that it is legitimate to ask, Kant has given a description of the way in which human (empirical) knowledge is apparently acquired and accumulated. Consistency with a received body of knowledge, broad conformity to laws of nature determined through observation, and the repeatability of experiments, are the ways in which we test and affirm what we call knowledge. As we have seen in "The Refutation of Idealism", Kant hopes to overcome scepticism and avoid solipsism by exploiting what he sees as available space between epistemology and ontology and by maintaining a radical separation between the two.[15]

Having established what amounts to a transcendental phenomenology based on an interpretation of apparent facts about human knowledge Kant has circumvented the traditional problem of knowledge. Sympathetically we may say that, by re-posing the questions asked by the sceptics in a wider framework, he has demonstrated how they might be answered and, whereas Hume was unable, Kant is able to provide certain ground for our knowledge of the world, and furthermore, by indicating the areas in which these claims cannot even be made, has outlined the sphere available for knowledge. A more unsympathetic critic can point to the cost for Kant in this manoeuvre. Kant remains a dualist, and at bottom a Cartesian. The dichotomy between what I experience (appearances) and things-in-themselves independent of my consciousness remains and must remain if Kant is to avoid the charge of subjective idealism. Kant's world must not be reduced to the simple contents of my experience, his idealism must remain transcendental. However this necessity creates a realm of the existent unknowable thing-in-itself, indeed a world in which epistemology, as we understand it, is not appropriate at all. Similarly the world which we can know lacks a firm foundation, the mere consistency of our present perceptions with systems and patterns previously observed feels a bit like the blind leading the blind and provides scant defence against a determined sceptic. We can know nothing of Kant's things-in-themselves. It is as if they exist in another dimension. But if this were so then even these gestures in their direction would be impossible, even the naming of such entities would be beyond us. We do "know" some things about Kant's things-in-themselves. We know that they exist: We know that things-in-themselves are unknowable, but this is to know only their bare form. They are, and must remain, empty abstractions, beyond the field of epistemology.

Kant's transcendental idealism can be understood as a way of providing a perspective from which to view the world, an epistemological focus. Kant will continue to succeed only as long as I do no more than gesture to the far side of the duality, despite the fact that the bedrock of things-in-themselves is essential if Kant is to exist in a world in common with others. I have already indicated that dualism is crucial to the whole of Kant's epistemology and that this is not merely an accidental consequence of his work. The notion of the empirically inaccessible thing-in-itself is structurally essential to the Kantian world, and, without it Kant's epistemology may be made to slide into subjective idealism. It is vital for Kant that, although we may all have different representations, things-in-themselves are the same for all of us, whatever they are. I will now examine what Kant has to say specifically about the self in the *Critique of Pure Reason* and see what consequences this has for the Kantian notion of selfhood.

Kant's Rational Self

In the *Critique of Pure Reason* Kant seeks to establish the ground for what he calls a "rational doctrine of the soul".[16] He insists that it is not the case that we have no grounds for our belief in a continuing self, but he is trying to show that the empirical knowledge we suppose we have of such a self is illusory, and that we know the self in quite another way. Kant is recognising and building on Hume's perplexity with regard to continuing personal identity without straying into claims of knowledge which cannot be sustained.

It is clear that despite their differences there is much in common between Hume and Kant with regard to their discussion of the self. Kant takes on much of what Hume has to say about the experiencing self: he does not deny the potency of Hume's empiricism merely its ability to explain all the facets and structures of experience.[17] However Kant's conclusions with regard to the self at the end of this discussion do not admit of the failure expressed by Hume in his Appendix to the *Treatise*. Whereas Hume concludes somewhat pessimistically that he can find no empirical ground for his belief in his own continuing identity, Kant's method allows him to affirm, at least, the existence of the transcendental (noumenal) self, which, though limited, represents an advance on Hume's position. Kant sets out his aim thus,

> I am not here seeking to learn in regard to the soul anything more than can be inferred independently of all experience, from this concept "I", so far as it is present in all thought. (Kant, 1992, A. 342 = B. 400)

Kant wants to chart a course between two undesirable options by giving us a notion of the self which leads neither to materialism nor spiritualism, and which is self sustaining. This is a difficult problem as we shall see, and one which, for all his efforts, Kant is not necessarily successful in solving, but again he is clear as to the task in hand,

> Rational psychology exists not as a *doctrine* furnishing an addition to our knowledge of the self, but only as a *discipline*. It sets impassable limits to speculative reason in this field, and thus keeps us, on the one hand, from throwing ourselves into the arms of soulless materialism, or, on the other, from losing ourselves in a spiritualism which must be quite unfounded so long as we remain in this present life. (Ibid, B. 421)

Kant is making and maintaining a crucial distinction between the phenomenal, or empirical, self and the noumenal self, or self as thing-in-itself, showing how both are necessary to an understanding of selfhood and how they are connected in the individual. This amounts to Kant giving us the forms of the self in the same way that in his deduction of the categories he provides us with the forms of appearances in experience. It is clear already that no empirical ground will be found, or sought, for these forms and that we are here concerned with the noumenal world rather than the phenomenal, the transcendental rather than the empirical self.

The discussion centres on the notion of consciousness itself, the "I" of the Cartesian "I think". This accompaniment to every exercise of thought is not accessible in the same way that the objects of experience are brought into purview through the application of the categories. Deductions about the nature of consciousness cannot operate in the same manner as do judgements concerning the world. Of this "I" Kant says,

> As is easily seen this is the vehicle of all concepts and therefore of all transcendental concepts and so is always included in the conceiving of these latter, and is itself transcendental. But it can have no special designation because it serves only to introduce all our thought as belonging to consciousness. (Ibid, A. 341 = B. 399)

Kant is trying to say some things about that which troubled Hume the most; that is, the experiencing self and its relation to an apparently external world. Hume's empiricism is ultimately unable to ground ideas which are essential to our understanding of ourselves and the world we recognise as not-self. Hume tried to discuss the world, which existed apparently beyond himself, by making it object but found that, through this method, he was unable to adequately account for notions (like cause and effect) which are necessary to make the discussion possible in the first place. Within Hume's strictly empirical method this leads to epistemological scepticism. Hume was similarly disabled when he turned to his own self. While he could not be absolutely sure that the world was exactly as it appeared to be, he was unable even to find a place to stand from which to view his own self, which appeared to disappear when he made any attempt to objectify it. This is because of the problem of observing the observer, or making the self present to itself. Empirically speaking I cannot see myself seeing. The subject which is actually having the experience cannot, by any means, be held at a distance from itself, so the self cannot experience itself in the same way that it experiences that which is not-itself. Therefore empiricist methodology is inadequate when applied to the relation between self and not-self. Kant recognises this, but by abjuring the strict empiricist method for transcendentalism, is able to rise above the difficulties experienced by Hume.

Kant wants to release the argument from the empiricist dilemma but without extending claims to knowledge beyond the legitimate bounds laid out earlier in the *Critique of Pure Reason*. Using the transcendental method he is able to do this by insisting on the distinction between phenomenal and noumenal self and directing attention towards the latter, about which we may have no knowledge, but the existence of which can be certainly and justifiably inferred. This distinction will allow Kant to split epistemology and the knowledge of entities, from ontology and the bare existence of entities, and enable him to circumvent the problem encountered by Hume when he was unable to provide empirical ground for knowledge of the self.

In the next section I will examine the consequences of Kant's transcendentalism for a Kantian theory of the self and attempt to set out what conclusions Kant is able to come to in the *Critique of Pure Reason* with regard to the nature of the experiencing self.

Goldilocks Revisited - Resilient Scepticism

Kant's work on the self represents a clear advance on the work of Descartes and Hume. Descartes, in large part, fails to recognise sufficiently the epistemological problem set by his meditations. He is unable to provide Princess Elizabeth with a convincing answer to her most penetrating questions.[18] Hume recognises the problems associated with sceptical doubt and visibly despairs at his failed attempts to solve the problems of necessary connection and personal identity.[19] Kant also recognises the problems, following the promptings from Hume, and establishes a structure specifically for their solution, central to which is his transcendental idealism. Kant makes the problematic dualism of Descartes, not only explicit, but a pivotal part of the structure of his epistemology and inescapable in any understanding of experience and of the self.

Hume's scepticism does not amount to a denial of the existence of the world or the continuity of personal identity. Hume could simply find no empirical basis to affirm knowledge of these apparently self-evident truths and thereby left the relation between self and the not-self confused and problematic. In this respect Hume and Kant are similar. In both cases evident features of the self are put forward and the lack of empirical footing is made clear. Kant's work is marked as more advanced than that of Hume by his transcendentalism and his use of the Cartesian dichotomy to insist on the bare existence of things-in-themselves, beyond empirical experience, which enables him to transcend empiricism. Kant sees no problem in the location of knowledge in the realm of appearance or representation. He insists on a dual foundation for knowledge, adding rationalism to empiricism. However this manoeuvre is not without problems of its own. In particular the distinction between existence and knowledge and the acknowledgement of a class of existents which cannot be known, asks questions which it cannot answer. At this point there is sharp contrast between Hume and Kant. Hume as a strict empiricist could not have accepted the existence of a class of entities for which no impressions were to be found, empirical knowledge and existence were inseparable for Hume.

In the *Critique of Pure Reason* Kant explores the presumptions of empiricism in a way that empiricists could not. He recognises the essential distinction between form and content in the self, phenomenal and noumenal self and tries to show how these are brought together. The operation of this dichotomy provides Kant with an exit from the problem of Goldilocks which had baffled Hume, by giving Kant access to non-empirical truths about the self. Kant does not avoid the question of claims to empirical knowledge of the self but he is able to limit the extent of such claims without jeopardising our justified belief in continuing personal identity. We may have empirical evidence about the self, the phenomenal self, in the same way that we can have empirical evidence about any phenomenal object, as an appearance. It is as if we may see the signs of the self in the same way that the three bears recognised the signs of Goldilocks. The key to the advance made by Kant is that, although he acknowledges the same limit to empirical knowledge as his empiricist predecessors, he is able, through the use of pure reason, to infer from the possibility of such knowledge in general, further fundamental truths about the self and the not-self. In the end Kant demonstrates how empiricism itself is possible by showing what kind of world and what kind of experiencing being must lie at the root of all experience. So that, for entities to appear they must do so in the forms set out in the Table of Categories. Likewise, if they are to appear they must appear to a self, which is substantial, simple, identical and relational. The result of this is that the Kantian self is active and creative in forming sensibility into experience. This does not, however, make Kant a Berkelian since he stops well short of making the existence of things-in-themselves dependent on the subject. In Kant knowledge is gained in the judgement which is the combining of sensibility and the understanding, so, while the forms of the "world" (categories) are something we all have in common the precise contents of each individual's experience may vary, subjectively, without calling into question the commonality of the "world" or its independent existence.

Despite the advantages of the Kantian approach to questions of the self there remain both uncertainty and shortcomings in the Kantian notion of the self. Although in the *Critique of Pure Reason*, Kant applies the phenomenal/noumenal dichotomy his resolve in this appears to falter when he directly confronts the notion of the self itself.[20] In his work on the self Kant is re-encountering some of the problems I have already exhibited in the work of Descartes and Hume, in particular, the problem of trying to observe the observer in the act of observation. I say that these perceptions, experiences etc., belong to me and then extrapolate from the way in which I apparently experience the not-self, to the unitary and simple nature of the self as necessary to explain these perceptions and give them life. In truth we cannot know (empirically) the simple unitary basis of the self. Only its bare existence in this form can be given through the transcendental deduction. Kant calls this the transcendental unity of apperception. That is, in experience we infer ourselves as the subject of that experience, since experience without a focus is no experience at all. Although it appears to be necessary for experience that there is an experiencing subject, this does no more than point in the direction of the subject. It is at this point that Kant's uncertainty emerges when he says,

> My existence cannot, therefore, be regarded as an inference from the proposition "I think", as Descartes sought to contend.... The "I think" expresses an indeterminate empirical intuition,... But the "I think" precedes the experience which is required to determine the object of perception through the category in respect of time; and the existence here [referred to] is not a category. (Ibid, B. 423n)

He tries to explain further what an indeterminate empirical intuition might be, and how this would fit into the phenomenal/noumenal divide when he goes on to say,

> An indeterminate perception here signifies only something real that is given, given indeed to thought in general, and not so as appearance, nor as thing-in-itself (*noumenon*), but as something which actually exists, and which in the proposition, "I think", is denoted as such. (Ibid, B. 423n)

It seems that the self we know is turning out to be neither phenomenal nor noumenal but something else again, and what this might be Kant begins to say at the end of this note,

> it must be observed, that when I have called the proposition, "I think", an empirical proposition, I do not mean to say thereby, that the "I" in this proposition is an empirical representation. On the contrary it is purely intellectual, because belonging to thought in general.

but then,

> Without some empirical representation to supply the material for thought, the *actus*, "I think", would not, indeed, take place; but the empirical is only the condition of the application, or of the employment, of the pure intellectual faculty. (Ibid, B. 423n)

Evidently the relation between the experiencing self and the empirical world requires still further examination and clarification, but it is clear that the transcendental unity of apperception can never amount to an apperception of unity, that is, direct knowledge of the unitary self.

The difficulty which Kant is encountering here is a difficulty inherent in his methodology. By escaping from the Goldilocks problem via the route of the phenomenal/noumenal dichotomy Kant has given himself the problem of having no apparent way to end the story. He has introduced a fundamental, qualitative, distinction between the players. To resolve the position and end the story Kant must show how the phenomenal and the noumenal can come together, he must show how Goldilocks can meet the three bears. This issue, which can be made to lie, however uneasily, dormant in consideration of relations between self and world, becomes acute in addressing the nature of the self. The self must be singular and without Chinese walls, but within the dualism of Kant's system it is hard to see how this can be achieved. The phenomenal and the noumenal appear to be mutually exclusive and qualitatively different, and yet they must be understood together in the unitary self. The uncertainty expressed by Kant in the note quoted above is Kant's recognition of this dilemma and the resulting conclusion that the self is given neither as appearance nor as thing-in-itself is an attempt to insert a mediating notion between the two parts of the dichotomy.

Kant's model of the self suffers from the same defect as all models provided by dualists. The notion of the self as an object is problematic under the Cartesian premise, because it appears to be contradictory. Object is that which I am not, self is that which I am. The constant attempt by Kant and others to catch themselves at home is frustrated by their dualism. They continually note all the signs of Goldilocks but can never encounter the little girl in the flesh. The dualism which results in the "veil of the senses" and the problem of knowledge of the world that is not-me, can only result in the persistently absent self.

At best in Kant the self becomes an uncomfortable union of phenomenon and thing-in-itself, but this is not even really acceptable to Kant. Kant says that we become confused when we mix up the possible transcendental abstraction from our experience of that which is our own self, with empirical knowledge of the self. This is the confusion of the transcendental self with the empirical self, but it is a conflation which we must be able to make if we are to arrive at the unity of the self. Kant's embrace of dualism and the progressive divorce of experience from the experiencing self move him not closer to, but further from, an understanding of individual consciousness. He embraces dualism and in this way renders the singularity of the self problematic.[21]

In search of a solution to some of these problems I will now turn to a radically different interpretation of Kant's work in the *Critique of Pure Reason* which attempts to build on Kant's work as an advance on that of

Descartes and Hume while developing Kantian insights in a surprising but ultimately illuminating way.

The Best Laid Schemes - Kant and Heidegger

I have shown how, in spite of significant shortcomings which remain in his system, Kant's work represents a clear advance over that of Descartes and Hume. This advance is taken up by both Heidegger and Sartre, and, without pre-empting a fuller exposition and discussion of their work which will be given in Chapters Six, Seven and Eight, it will be useful to indicate here some of the aspects of Kant's work which Heidegger develops, in particular where these refer to notions of selfhood and the relation of the self to the world. It is important to note that there are considerable similarities between the work of Kant, Heidegger and Sartre in this area and explicit continuity between them in the development of notions of selfhood and the relation of self to the world. In this section I will predominantly employ Heidegger's works *The Basic Problems of Phenomenology* and *Kant and the Problem of Metaphysics*[22] to illustrate the similarities and differences between Kant and Heidegger. In the following chapter I will discuss Sartre's existentialism as set out in his *Being and Nothingness*.

Both Kant and Heidegger are attempting to set out the conditions for the possibility of experience, that is, both are trying to explain on what basis experience is possible. Given the failure of empiricism to provide an adequate framework both return, though in different ways to human consciousness as the foundation of human experience. The most significant point developed by Kant and taken up by Heidegger is this shift in focus onto the self as the centre of attention when attempting to solve the problems left in the debris of empiricism. Both Kant and Heidegger use everyday experience to show how metaphysics can be grounded, both begin with the *fact* of experience rather than the presumption of doubt. I will concentrate on four areas of difference between Kant and Heidegger, these are; the notions of thing-in-itself and appearance, Heidegger's discussion of the section of Kant's *Critique of Pure Reason* entitled, "The Schematism of the Pure Concepts of the Understanding" (A.138-147 = B.177-187), the notion of transcendence, and the idea of the active or creative self. It will become clear that these areas are closely connected and the discussion of each will amplify the differences between Kant and Heidegger and add to the development of a notion of the self which goes beyond that set out by Kant, and which avoids many of the pitfalls I have illuminated in Kant's theory of the self.

In Kant's work the distinction between thing-in-itself and appearance is central. Kant uses the dichotomy to liberate epistemology from the empiricists' dilemma by limiting the sphere of possible knowledge to appearance only. This move constitutes the Copernican revolution at the heart of Kant's theory of knowledge in which he seeks the conformity of objects (of experience) with knowledge instead of the other way around. As I have shown the thing-in-itself provides the (unseen) ground for belief in a world distinct from the experience of each subject. This is apparently successful in overcoming the sceptical conclusion but it means that Kant is left with a world divided into two, a division which is not simply accidental but structurally necessary to the Kantian system. The realm of unknowable entities, the things-in-themselves, is completely inaccessible, and equally necessary, to Kant's model of the world, and yet he is unable to satisfactorily show how things-in-themselves are connected to appearances because to do so would be tantamount to a pretending of knowledge of things-in-themselves, a pretence which Kant denies absolutely. Working within the object/subject model of the world this paradox is inevitable for Kant, and as I have shown, becomes acute when Kant discusses the experiencing self and attempts to insert a notion of the self which bridges the divide, and is neither one thing nor the other. While Heidegger follows much of the insight offered by Kant into the nature of experience his interpretation of Kant's terms is subtly but dynamically different. First he says, "The thing-in-itself is not another object but another aspect of the representation with regard to the same object." (Heidegger, 1962, p.37), thereby acknowledging Kant's analysis but seeking to avoid Kant's particular dualism. Then, on the unknowability of the thing-in-itself, he says,

> it is a misunderstanding of the significance of the "thing-in-itself" to believe that it is necessary to prove through a positivist critique that knowledge of it is impossible. (Ibid, p. 38)

This is the beginning of the move in Heidegger's thinking about Kant from the conception of the thing-in-itself as a thing at all and towards a more active and dynamic understanding of entities and our experience of them.[23] It is also the de-stressing of the presence or "thingness" of entities, which dominates the tradition of Descartes, Hume and Kant, and the beginning of an emphasis on activity. Under this kind of interpretation it makes no sense to undertake a positivist critique that knowledge of things-in-themselves is impossible because it is a presupposition of the whole Kantian system itself that "knowledge" is not a notion applicable to this aspect of the representation. Finally Heidegger is explicit when he says,

> the concepts "appearance" and "thing-in-itself" ... can be made intelligible and the objects of further investigation only if they are based explicitly on the problematic of the finitude of man. These concepts however do not refer to two

levels of objects positioned one behind the other in one fixed and completely undifferentiated [field] of knowledge (Ibid, p. 39),

once and for all dispensing with the "veil of the senses" and opening the way to an understanding and interpretation of Kant's system in which things-in-themselves are not separated from appearances but are joined to them as form to content.[24] This begins to reveal the fundamental ontology, knowledge of beings as such, which eluded both the empiricists and Kant because of the radical separation of appearance and thing-in-itself (epistemology and ontology) in the tradition which Heidegger is criticising. In Heidegger's interpretation of Kant appearance and thing-in-itself are distinct but not separate, and their unity is the foundation of ontological knowledge. This is what Heidegger means when he says, "The establishment of metaphysics is the projection of the internal possibility of the *a priori* synthesis" (Ibid, p. 42). This synthesis, between the form and content of knowledge, is the foundation of ontological knowledge and the ground for the understanding of selfhood.

Further differences and similarities occur on consideration of Heidegger's reading of specific parts of Kant's work. Heidegger describes the section in Kant's *Critique of Pure Reason* entitled "The Schematism of the Pure Concepts of the Understanding"[25] as "the central core of the whole voluminous work" (Heidegger, 1990, p.60). In the Schematism Kant says,

> Thus an application of the category to appearances becomes possible by means of the transcendental determination of time, which as the schema of the concepts of understanding, mediates the subsumption of the appearances under the category. (Kant, 1992, A. 139 = B. 178)

Kant acknowledges the gulf that his dualism creates between the *a priori* categories and sensibility and is looking for a way to cement these together in experience. He sees the fundamental part that must be played by a notion of time as the form of inner sense. Experience is not possible except within a time frame, nothing can happen except in time, experience is the result of the bringing together of the categories and sensibility, time must therefore provide the form for this combination. He explains further,

> This formal and pure condition of sensibility to which the employment of the concept of understanding is restricted, we shall entitle the *schema* of the concept. The procedure of understanding in these schemata we shall entitle the *schematism* of pure understanding. (Ibid, A. 140 = B. 179)

Having shown in the "Transcendental Deduction" that experience must be a combining of sensation and categories, in the "Schematism" Kant is trying to say *how* it is that concepts can be enlivened by sensibility, and how it is that sensibility can be presented as experience through the application of the categories. He is trying to describe the actual process. The problem of unifying experience is the problem of bringing together the qualitatively different elements of experience. The unification is sealed when he concludes,

> The categories, therefore without schemata, are merely functions of the understanding for concepts; and represent no object. This [objective] meaning they acquire from sensibility, which realises the understanding in the very process of restricting it (Ibid, A. 147 = B. 187)

thus acknowledging that the categories, or forms in which entities must appear to be accessible to sensibility, are themselves devoid of content and acquire their meaning (as appearances) only when filled up with sensible contents. Similarly sensibility requires the limitation brought through the application of concepts to the flux of perception to make it sensible as experience. Experience is quite simply the coalescence of sensibility and concepts as its contents and form. The agent of this coalescence, in the "Schematism", is the imagination (as opposed to the understanding or sensibility).[26] It is imagination that creates the unity between sensibility and understanding, and this unity is experience. Kant hopes to have explained how these three combine to make experience possible and therefore to avoid the worst consequences of his dualism as well as Hume's scepticism. The "Schematism" contains the mortar which holds the Kantian system together. Kant is not so crude as to characterise experience as a simply sequential and mechanical process, we do not consciously combine sensibility and categories to get experience, this is not really a process at all and Kant's work here is more like an after the fact analysis rather than a description of the process of the genesis of experience. We may therefore perhaps begin to see the "Schematism" as a description of the pre-existing ground upon which discussion of sensibility and understanding can take place, without this ground there can be no experience.

The key to understanding the importance of the "Schematism" is the way in which it shows how experience cannot be separated from time, as Kant says, "The schemata are thus nothing but *a priori* determinations of time in accordance with rules" (Ibid, A. 145 = B. 184), and time is the form of inner sense to which all sensibility and understanding must conform. The apparent abstraction of the notion of time from experience, which is accomplished earlier in the *Critique of Pure Reason*, is therefore a mistake in view of the later essential return to the temporality of experience in the "Schematism". It represents a mistaken objectification of time which results in the equally mistaken attempt to understand the fundamental structures of the self in terms of object and subject. Kant's comments in the "Schematism" come close to the later equation, by Heidegger, of being and time as central to the development of a formal notion of the self,[27] in the same way that Hume came close when he said "the mind is a kind of theatre" (Hume, 1959, Vol. I, p. 239). But this is a further step which neither Hume nor Kant can actually take, although they may be facing in the right direction.

In his *Kant and the Problem of Metaphysics* Heidegger recognises the thrust of Kant's argument in the "Schematism" but is immediately wary of entering the discussion in the same way as it is begun by Kant. He says, "it is precisely the idea that it is a matter of providing a foundation for an edifice already constructed which must be avoided" (Heidegger, 1962, p.4). This edifice is the already apparent fact of our everyday experiences. Kant is beginning with fundamentally Cartesian presumptions about the relationship between world and consciousness and it is exactly these presumptions which Heidegger wishes to call into question. He is clear about what he sees Kant trying to do in the "Schematism" when he says,

> Kant undertakes the revelation of the essential ground of ontological knowledge in the section which adjoins the transcendental deduction and is entitled: *The Schematism of the Pure Concepts of the Understanding*. (Ibid, p. 93)

This may not be quite how Kant would have put it but given Heidegger's comments about Kant's foundationalism it is clear that he is reading Kant as revealing a pre-existing ground rather than inventing a bridging mechanism between sensibility and understanding. The consequences of this shift in emphasis are, however, radical. If unity in experience is taken to be primordial then the distinctions we make between sensibility and understanding, content and form, subject and object, are shown to be derivative of this underlying unity, and not themselves fundamental at all. Heidegger can then say,

> the laying of the foundation as the projection of the intrinsic possibility of metaphysics is necessarily a letting become effective of the supporting power of ground,

and,

> To the extent that metaphysics belongs and factically exists with "human nature", it has already developed in some form. (Ibid, p. 5)

Whereas Kant, working from a subject/object model of the world, needs an argument to unite these elements, Heidegger's acknowledgement of the pre-existing unity within experience turns Kant's work in the "Schematism" into a revelation of the ground for metaphysics and ontological knowledge, and so, "what makes the comporting towards beings (ontic knowledge) possible is the preliminary understanding of the constitution of Being, ontological knowledge" (Heidegger, 1990, p.7). This indicates that the ground which Kant is seeking to establish in the 'Schematism' must itself be presumed by the kind of enquiry Kant is conducting and is therefore deserving of a prominence which is not adequately recognised within Kant's dualism. Heidegger is therefore able to say that "the *Critique of Pure Reason* does not provide a "system" of transcendental philosophy but is 'a treatise on the method'" (Heidegger, 1962, p.21). It is to be read not as a theory of knowledge or experience but as a discussion of the possibility of ontological knowledge or the foundation of metaphysics itself.[28] Once again there is continuity and difference between Kant and Heidegger.

The notion of transcendence is central to Kant's methodology. It enables him to escape from the sceptical conclusions which seemed inevitable to Hume and to open up a route to knowledge which is not empirically demonstrable and which grounds empirical knowledge itself. In the discussion of the self transcendence enables the Kantian argument to progress beyond the simple attempt to glimpse the empirical self as it disappears and allows a reinterpretation of selfhood in ways which lead to a more fertile understanding of the relationship between self and world. If we understand Kant as showing how empirical knowledge is possible through transcendence we may see Heidegger as showing how transcendence itself is possible, recognising the advance made by Kant over the empiricists but taking the investigation further and deeper into the fundamental ontological structures of being. Heidegger makes a strong connection between transcendence and intentionality when he says, "it is precisely intentionality and nothing else in which *transcendence* consists" (Heidegger, 1982, p.63), and moves away from the Kantian position when he asserts that, "misinterpretation lies in *an erroneous subjectivizing* of intentionality" (Ibid, p. 63-64). Heidegger is using the notion of intentionality to develop a highly interactive model of selfhood based on the fundamental characteristic of a conscious being as projecting towards that which is not itself. The being which is intending towards is made into the subject by the Cartesian tradition; Heidegger refuses this interpretation and returns us resolutely to the beginning of the argument by retaining the focus on the activity of intending itself. For Heidegger intentionality is the sign that points to the kind of being which stands out in the world, and it is this standing out (existing) which distinguishes conscious being from being devoid of consciousness.[29] Heidegger refuses the Cartesian notion of subjectivity employed by Kant and in particular its isolation from the world, which leads to dualism because,

> The idea of a subject which has intentional experiences merely inside its own sphere and is not yet outside it but encapsulated within itself is an absurdity

which misconstrues the basic ontological structure of the being which we ourselves are. (Ibid, p. 64) [30]

This is because the self is not at all isolated in the world, in fact transcendence indicates quite the reverse, that is, a unity of self and world instead of a Cartesian/Kantian presumption of separation to the extent that,

> transcending, belongs to the essential nature of the being that exists (on the basis of transcendence) as intentional, that is, exists in the manner of dwelling among the extant. (Ibid, p. 65)

Transcendence is not an activity consciously *engaged in* by the subject but is at the core of its subjectivity, the activity of its being-a-subject. Kant shows how transcendence enables the escape from the empiricist dilemma of scepticism, leading to the notion of the transcendental subject, but bequeathing Kant's system with a constitutive dualism, which will ultimately cripple his notion of selfhood. Heidegger goes further than Kant who has shown how empiricism is possible (through transcendence) and shows how transcendence itself is possible by illuminating the way of being which an experiencing consciousness must have. I will expand on this aspect of Heidegger's work later in Chapters Seven and Eight but the implications of this move are that transcendence and where it leads, (to the transcendental subject) ceases to be the focus of attention as transcending itself comes to the fore and selfhood is revealed as the transcending itself. The presence of the self, or its "thingness", will be shown by Heidegger to be inadequate to fill the notion of the self and, moreover, as derivative of a more primordial notion of selfhood. Heidegger takes on from Kant the question of what kind of being we must be in order to be able to have experience, and, following Kant's demonstration that we must be transcendental as well as phenomenal, Heidegger wants to say that we are intrinsically transcendental, or the transcending itself, thereby encompassing phenomenal and transcendental self in the one notion of transcending selfhood, and avoiding the dualism of Kant's model. Heidegger believes that this unity becomes apparent from a simple reading of the nature of our experience. He says, "I can apprehend something *imaginarily* only if, as apprehender, I *intend* in general" (Ibid, p. 60), that is I must first acknowledge that I am essentially intentional, that is standing out from and projecting into the world that is not-me, and, "We must be able to understand actuality *before* all experiences of actual beings" (Ibid, p. 11). We must already understand what it is to be before we can be receptive to an experience of a particular being.

Heidegger is not only pointing to a pre-experiential understanding of the world but to this kind of understanding of intentional being as essentially descriptive of the structure of consciousness, returning us to the the activity of being as fundamental to understanding the relationship between self and not-self. This means that transcendence is not something incidental but a pre-experiential feature rooted in the nature of the experiencing being. Heidegger's analysis is, in this respect, if anything, more formal than that of Kant. He is not discussing any actual experiences but is only seeking to describe the forms, including the forms of the self, which frame particular experiences. Using his own term "Dasein" to represent the individual conscious being Heidegger says,

> Dasein's comportments have an *intentional character* and on the basis of this intentionality the subject already stands in relation to things that it itself is not. (Ibid, p. 155)

Transcendence is not a move which the subject has to make in order to have experience, rather it is the fact that transcending itself constitutes selfhood that first makes experience possible. This is shown by the fact that the Being that experiences must, as it were, find itself in a world along with other things and Beings which it is-not. This finding is the transcending, and is inescapable. Kant has thus re-discovered transcendence and not invented it and transcendence itself is possible on the ground of, and because of, the nature of the being that experiences. Heidegger's Dasein, by its way of being, creates space in the world, as transcending, and this is the space in which entities become manifest, so that,

> To hold oneself in advance in such a play space, to form it originally, is none other than the transcendence which marks all finite comportment to beings. (Heidegger, 1990, p.48)

The transcendental self in Kant allows a deeper understanding of the possibility of empirical knowledge but Kant cannot go that far because he is ultimately still tied to a Cartesian model of self and world, and to the notion of the self as essentially and fundamentally some kind of thing.

In conclusion I will briefly examine the effect of Heidegger's approach on Kant's theory of the active and creative self. The self in Kant is divided. Despite Kant's best efforts there is ultimately a problematic discontinuity between the phenomenal self and the transcendental self. However, by showing that the notion of selfhood must extend beyond the purely empirical (phenomenal) self of Hume's *Treatise* Kant has moved the argument forward by more than a matter of degrees. The notion of the transcendental self in Kant marks the arrival of the Copernican revolution in the metaphysics of the self. The self becomes giving as well as given, active as well as passive, and the way is opened to a much more dynamic relationship between self and world. The reason for the crippling dualism in Kant's theory of the self is that the roots of Kant's theorising are in the Cartesian model of the self as a kind of object-become-subject. The self is understood as some kind of thing, or fundamentally as presence, as Heidegger puts it,

> However essential Kant's own investigations have become and will always remain for the ontological interpretation of subjectivity, the I, the ego, is for him as it was for Descartes, res cogitans *res, something*, that thinks, namely, something that represents, perceives, judges, agrees, disagrees, but also loves, hates, strives, and the like. (Heidegger, 1982, pp.125-126)

This presumption is reinforced and mirrored in the way in which the world is made object and the self a subject for these objects. The analysis of self and world in terms of simultaneously present but distinct and separate subjects and objects locks us into a subject/object dualism which then defeats all attempts to reunite us with the not-self. The illusion of inner and outer is created and thoroughly promulgated. Heidegger says, "This res cogitans, the something that thinks, is a subject of predicates and as such it is a subject *for* objects." (Ibid, p. 126), the constant search for objectivity creates the subject. Through this model we, and Kant, are led to questions about how this "thing" engages in activity, questions about what kind of "thing" it must be, and what must be its qualities. We are, as Kant is, able to acknowledge the active part played by the self, but are then left struggling trying to explain, and show how, the necessary connections (with the not-self) are to be made. This is what Kant is trying to do in the "Schematism". This is the structural dualism in Kant, and in the Cartesian tradition, to which we are led inexorably when we confine our theorising about the self to its presence, its "being-there", or "thingness". We make objects of the world through our engagement with entities, which are not-self, and, at the same time, we make ourselves the subject, we then forget that it is the activity of engagement to which they owe their objectness, and we our subjectivity. We are left trying to understand these things which we ourselves have created, one of which is our own subject self. This is what Heidegger means by understanding the world as mere presence.

It is at this point that we find perhaps the greatest divergence between Heidegger's work and the Kantian system. Heidegger wants to further develop Kant's notion of the active/creative self but in a way which makes it impossible to go on assuming or accepting the "thingness" of the self, or presence as its fundamental mode. Heidegger recognises presence as only one way of being of the self and as a way of being grounded in more primordial structures of selfhood. The focus is thus moved away from the notion of the self as any kind of thing and towards the activity of being-self itself, so,

> If the ego is determined by the mode of being or acting and hence not a thing, then the beginning for philosophy, which starts with the ego, is not an active thing but an active deed. (Ibid, p.142)

This activity is derived from a dynamic understanding of thinking and the "I think" of the Cartesian *cogito* Heidegger says,

> as Kant expresses it, the ego is "the vehicle of all concepts of the understanding",

but this means that,

> It first of all makes possible the basic *a priori* ontological concepts. For the ego is not something isolated, not a mere point, but always "I think", that is, "I combine". (Ibid, p.129)

The equation of thinking with combining is the outcome of Heidegger's characterisation of being as an activity and a final acknowledgement that the essence of experience is interaction between a creative self and a dynamic world, neither of which has meaning beyond the other and which are therefore inseparable. In Kantian terms selfhood becomes the constant and unavoidable combining of categories and sensibility. The difference between Kant and Heidegger is Heidegger's recognition of this combining itself as the central and fundamental pillar for any understanding of experience and self. This combining is the essence of Heideggerian selfhood and gives the ontological ground for all experience. This ego is, "not one among the categories of beings but the condition of the possibility of categories in general" (Ibid, p. 128-129). The sense of the self as a combining at once overcomes the inherent dualism of the Cartesian model and recognises the fundamental unity of self and world. There can be no structural bifurcation between a self and its world if the self is the combining of self and world.

At this stage it is sufficient to recognise the kind of continuity and discontinuity that Heidegger's work on the self represents as compared to Kant's theories set out in the *Critique of Pure Reason*. I will set out and examine Heidegger's position in more detail in Chapters Seven and Eight.[31] Kant has opened up the field by his development of transcendence and the transcendental self, but is unable to take this active and creative self further because of the constraints of the Cartesian subject/object model and the focus on presence as fundamental to self. Heidegger, as I shall show, uses this opening to subvert and subsume the entire edifice of Cartesian metaphysics and, in so doing, develops a notion of selfhood, which refuses the problems of knowledge and identity.

However to proceed directly to this work would be to fail to provide the Cartesian tradition sufficient opportunity to demonstrate its strength.

Therefore, before going on to set out and discuss fully Heidegger's work in this connection, it will be interesting and useful to examine the work of a modern Cartesian, much influenced by Heidegger, but still remaining within the Cartesian tradition. This will serve to show, if nothing else, that, even under, one of its most radical interpretations, the deficiencies of the Cartesian position are still apparent. I will now turn to the early work of Sartre and in particular his *Essay on Phenomenological Ontology: Being and Nothingness*, in which he sets out, not only a dramatic and dynamic reinterpretation of the *cogito*, but also a theory of the self and being-with-the-Other which owes its origins to both Descartes and Heidegger, and echoes much of the Kantian position.

Notes

1. Kant famously says in the Preface to his *Prolegomena to any future Metaphysics*, "I openly confess that my remembering David Hume was the very thing which many years ago first interrupted my dogmatic slumbers and gave my investigations in the field of speculative philosophy a quite new direction" (Kant, 1977, p.5).
2. Scruton provides a clear and straightforward setting out of the background to Kant's thinking in Chapter Two of his excellent short book *Kant*. Also, Kemp, 1968, Chapters One and Two.
3. Kant says, "Human reason has this peculiar fate that in one species of its knowledge it is burdened by questions which, as prescribed by the very nature of reason itself, it is not able to ignore, but which, as transcending all its powers, it is also not able to answer" (Kant, 1992, A. vii), and, "it soon becomes aware that in this way - the questions never ceasing - its work must always remain incomplete; and it therefore finds itself compelled to resort to principles which overstep all possible empirical employment, and which yet seem so unobjectionable that even ordinary consciousness readily accepts them" (Ibid, A. viii).
4. Strawson doubts the usefulness of the distinction between analytic and synthetic *a priori* propositions and argues that, "Kant really has no clear and general conception of the synthetic *a priori* at all" (Strawson, 1993, p.43). However this, and much of the rest of Strawson's criticism of Kant fails to recognise its significance particularly in the light of Heidegger's interpretation of Kant in his *Kant and the Problem of Metaphysics*, in which it is argued that Kant's dualism, between appearance and thing-in-itself is not fatal in the way that Strawson tries to show.
5. There are many examples of discussion of this crucial distinction in Kant's thought, two good examples are, Strawson, 1993, Part Four, and Paton, 1936, Vol. I, pp. 80-100. Walsh in his essay "Self Knowledge" argues for a distinction between knowable phenomenal objects and the awareness we may have of the noumenal, although it is never clear what this awareness might be and how it

would differ from knowing. See also, Walsh, 1975, pp. 159-167, Cassirer, 1954, Chapter IX, and Williams, 1987, Chapters Seven and Eight. Again the clearest setting out of this distinction, particularly for those untutored in the idiosyncrasy of Kantian terminology is in Scruton, 1982. Chapter Four.

6. Strawson is unhappy with Kant's derivation of space and time as the forms of outer and inner sense and as neither the forms of objects which allow us to become aware of the objects nor forms of our knowing which we bring to objects when we become aware of them. (Strawson, 1993, Part Two). But this is because Strawson is too wedded to the Cartesian tradition to see how Kant might be interpreted other than in this way. For an argument more generous towards Kant see Paton, 1936, Vol. I, pp. 101-171. Also see, Cassirer, 1954, Chapter I, and Walsh, 1975, pp.17-20 for further traditional descriptions of Kant's thinking in this area. For a radically different, though ultimately positive, reading of Kant's derivation of space and time see Heidegger, 1990, pp. 29-34.

7. Ewing quotes Kant as describing Categories as, "concepts of an object in general by means of which the intuition of a object is regarded as determined by one of the logical functions of judgement", and hopes that this will become clearer as the discussion progresses (Ewing, 1938, p.132).

8. Strawson would disagree; see, Strawson, 1993, pp.170-174 and, pp.235-270.

9. This refutation is fully discussed by, Walsh, 1975, pp.189-195, Strawson, 1993, pp. 125-132, and Paton, 1936, Vol. II, pp.377-386. Once again Paton is the more generous to Kant when he says, "Kant's argument is quite general; it asserts only that inner experience in general presupposes outer experience in general" (p. 386). Thus allowing Kant to achieve limited aims, whereas Strawson is less than charitable and has Kant unable to resist, "a very strong temptation to identify whatever he succeeded in establishing as necessary conditions of the possibility of experience of an objective world with what he already conceived to be the fundamental, unquestionable assumptions of physical science" (Strawson, 1993, pp.128-129).

10. This interweaving prefigures Heidegger's later reading of Kant in *Kant and the Problem of Metaphysics* in which the dichotomy between the subjective and the objective is demonstrated as itself derived from a more primordial underlying unity.

11. Berkeley, 1975, *The Principles of Human Knowledge*.

12. Again Heidegger concurs with this manoeuvre in both *Kant and the Problem of Metaphysics*, (p.2) and in *Being and Time* (H. 203).

13. Strawson discusses this in *The Bounds of Sense*, Part Two, Section II, and Matthews provides a useful short commentary on his view in his essay "Strawson on Transcendental Idealism". Paton begins to suggest that Kant is espousing a formal idealism when he says, "the affectation of the self by itself seems to be concerned with determining inner sense as regards its form, which is time" (Paton, 1936, Vol. II, p.389), and this view begins to approach Heidegger's reading in *Kant and the Problem with Metaphysics* although it is still a great way away from Heidegger's position.

14. In fact it is central to Kant's method that the noumenal cannot be discussed as such as far as it is not accessible through sensory experience, and the concept of

the noumenal is used negatively to designate the limits of possible knowledge. See Scruton, 1982, pp. 41-57.
15. This is the difference between things that can be known and things that cannot be known but exist all the same. This is a crucial difference between Kant and, for example Berkeley. Berkeley wants to make the ontological point that things only exist if they are perceived, whereas Kant is making an epistemological point that things are only known if they are perceived. See Matthews, "Strawson on Transcendental Idealism".
16. Kant, 1992, A. 342 = B. 400.
17. Walsh, 1975, pp. 183-189, and Strawson, 1993, pp.169-170.
18. Descartes, Letters, in *Descartes Philosophical Writings*, Trans and Ed. by Anscombe and Geach, pp. 274-286.
19. Hume, 1959, Appendix.
20. Walsh in "Self Knowledge" argues that Kant fails to recognise that, "his own philosophy presupposes in human reason a power of self awareness, and, thanks to this power we do seem to be able to formulate important truths about the knowing subject" (p. 166). Also see, Walsh, 1975, pp.183-189. Though this is to an extent true its necessary importance cannot be fully revealed in advance of the radical re-reading of Kant given by Heidegger. Similarly Strawson holds that it is a weakness of Kant's position that he ignores the fact of a man's persistence through time as a consistent and single basis for experience, Strawson, 1993, pp. 162-169. Once again this is a criticism, as far as it goes, but provides no way forward as opposed to the way in which Heidegger uses this opening in the Introduction to *his Kant and the Problem with Metaphysics* (pp. 1-2).
21. Alternatively a prior embrace of singularity will precipitate Kant into precisely the problems encountered by Berkeley and, as Strawson says, "Thus there arises a certain illusion: the illusion of a purely inner and yet, subject-referring use for 'I'". If we try to abstract this use, to shake off the connotation with ordinary criteria of personal identity, to arrive at a kind of subject-reference which is wholly and adequately based on nothing but inner experience what we really do is simply to deprive our use of "I" of any referential force whatever" (Strawson, 1993, p.166).
22. There are two translations of this important work by Heidegger, by Churchill and by Taft; both have merits and demerits in their clarity of expression of Heidegger's thinking. I have used each translation according to which seems to me to express most clearly Heidegger's thought on the issue in question.
23. Paton is suggestive of this in his discussion of the active Kantian self. (Paton, 1936, Vol. I, p. 570), as is Walsh in the section of *Kant's Criticism of Metaphysics* headed "The Mind as 'making Nature'" (Walsh, 1975, pp. 88-96).
24. Matthews hints at this in "Strawson on Transcendental Idealism" when he distinguishes between the standpoint of experience and the standpoint of action and he appears to agree with Scruton in believing that the most fertile interpretation of the dichotomy between thing-in-itself and appearance is as two different ways of looking at the same entity rather than as a two worlds explanation.
25. See Paton, 1936, Vol. II, pp. 19-76, for a good discussion of this section of Kant's *Critique of Pure Reason*, and Walsh, 1975, pp.65-81.

26. Mulhall describes the schemata as "essentially Janus-faced - at once possessed of the purity of the *a priori* and the materiality of intuition: as the nexus of concepts and intuitions, they form the junction-box through which the Kantian system relates mind and matter, subject and world" (Mulhall, 1996, p.158).
27. Heidegger, 1987, Div. 2, Section III.
28. Thereby deflecting much of the critical thrust of traditional readings of Kant such as that given by Strawson.
29. It will become clear in Chapters Seven and Eight that Heidegger wishes to make a strong distinction between the being of Dasein which is distinguished by its temporal projecting towards a future and which, as such, *exists* or stands out in the world, and simple unreflective being which does not project or stand out. On this distinction will be built the unique temporality of Dasein.
30. Also see Heidegger, 1987, H. 202-208.
31. See also Heidegger, 1987, Section 64 "Care and Selfhood".

6

Sartre - Goldilocks Uncovered?

> ...the only point of departure possible is the Cartesian *cogito*. (Sartre, 1956, p. 251)

> The profound meaning of the *cogito* is essentially to refer outside itself. (Ibid, p. 85)

I have so far tried to show how Descartes, Hume and Kant fail to provide a theory of the self and its relation to the not-self, through the failure of their attempts to solve the problems of knowledge and personal identity. I will now move forward in time and outside the mainstream of the tradition to which these philosophers belong, in order to see if an approach not available to Descartes, Hume and Kant, but still within the tradition, will be more successful in solving the problems which they so precisely delineated and yet could not satisfactorily solve.[1]

In turning to existential philosophy I hope to make even more clear the flaws in the assumptions made by the philosophers I have examined so far, and to find a new way towards a tenable theory of the self, including an account of personal identity and relation to Others like ourselves.[2] Sartre attempts to do exactly this in *Being and Nothingness*.[3] His discussion of the Other and the structures of the self in *Being and Nothingness* are constituted by the attempt to reconcile the self-supporting, self-referencing integrity of the *cogito* with a meaningful reference towards the Other. This really begins in Part II of *Being and Nothingness* when Sartre looks at "Immediate Structures of the For-itself" (Ibid, pp. 73-105). In this part of the work he attempts to uncover the Goldilocks that Hume failed to find, to catch himself at home, and thereby to furnish the ground upon which the description and examination of the conscious self can be made. If successful in this Sartre will escape from the dilemma of the observing observed which frustrated Hume in his search for continuing self identity. To achieve this Sartre characteristically uses a duality, the notions of being-in-itself, and being-for-itself, the former representing simple unreflective being such as might be given to a stone or some other inanimate object without consciousness, and the latter the kind of reflective being of the conscious self, including human being. For Sartre, it seems, we are both, with being-in-itself characterising our material, or as Descartes would say corporeal, self and being-for-itself our conscious or thinking self. Together they form the Sartrean structure of human being.[4]

The Self Divided

The problem of the observing observed need no longer be a problem if we accept reflective activity (consciousness) as having the effect of introducing differentiation into the unitary self. Sartre is able, where Hume and Kant were unable, to positively acknowledge a duality in the structure of the self,[5] and he is therefore no longer frustrated by not being able to find simple identity in his notion of the self. Consciousness, by its very nature, is the separation of the in-itself and the for-itself, and hence the unitary conscious self is an impossibility. As soon as I begin to reflect upon, or become conscious of, my being it is differentiated by this process, and my consciousness, so long as it is conscious, must remain not-identical with my simple being-in-itself.[6] Sartre has both uncovered Goldilocks and rendered her inaccessible to all three bears. Identity belongs only to the simplicity of being-in-itself and once the process of reflection begins, with consciousness as the only witness to itself, the possibility of the simple identity of the self goes out of the window. I can never perceive myself as complete and I can only assume this totality out of the incompleteness in that which I see as myself. I know what I must be, but I can never gather all the parts together and look at them without excluding from my purview the part that looks. This is seen a problem by Hume, but Sartre recognises its sheer inevitability.

Consciousness apparently destroys the simple identity of the self because the observer can never be at one with the observed, if it were to become so then consciousness itself would disappear and lapse into being-in-itself. Sartre seems to have achieved a dynamic model "within the indissoluble unity of one and the same being",[7] by showing how the being is divided against itself in the unavoidable act of self reflection. Consciousness of self cannot be identified with self and,

> In fact the *self* cannot be apprehended as a real existent; the subject cannot *be* self, for coincidence with self, as we have seen, causes the self to disappear. But neither can it *not be* itself since the self is an indication of the subject himself. The *self* therefore represents an ideal distance within the immanence of the subject in relation to himself, a way of *not being his own coincidence*, of escaping identity while positing it as a unity - in short of being in a perpetually unstable equilibrium between identity as absolute cohesion without a trace of diversity and unity as a synthesis of a multiplicity. (Ibid, pp. 76-77)[8]

There is a strong hint of Kant's transcendental deduction in this. The line, "Who's been eating my porridge?" gives us both the diversity, between me and mine, and the Other who must have eaten the porridge, while at the same time unifying my being to that of this miscreant Other through the medium of porridge, which belonged to me but which she ate.[9] In Sartre's tableau we are expected, within our own individual selves, to rush back and forth playing both parts, bear and little girl, continually inferring and re-inferring the presence of the Other from the effects we notice while playing the reverse part. This is a structure applied here to the conscious self which will be used again by Sartre in the explicit discussions of the structure of self-with-Others in Part III of *Being and Nothingness*. In more technical terms we might say that the self, as self-consciousness, is standing out from what it is, in order to acknowledge its being, and yet wishes to acknowledge itself as a unity, of that which stands out, and of that of which it is conscious. Thus there is always a duality present within the self simply because of the nature of consciousness itself. In Sartre's terms,

> The law of being of the *for-itself* as the ontological foundation of consciousness, is to be itself in the form of presence to itself. (Ibid, p. 77)

This is Sartre perhaps at his most paradoxical because it quickly becomes apparent that *nothing* separates these constitutive elements of the self[10]

> if we ask ourselves at this point *what it is* which separates the subject from himself, we are forced to admit that it is *nothing*. (Ibid, p. 77)

This is even more paradoxical, and,

> The being of consciousness qua consciousness is to exist *at a distance from itself* as a presence to itself, and this empty distance which being carries in its being is Nothingness. (Ibid, p. 78)

This use of the idea of nothingness as determinate, and the paradoxical way that Sartre uses the idea, means that an impression is created of a self riven in two, and yet unified, divided only by "nothing".[11] Its division is given in the simple analysis of reflection and its unity in the fact that nothing separates the divisions from each other. Like Goldilocks, the division can be understood or inferred but not produced as evidence. There is also a clear line of descent to Sartre's ideas from the work of Kant.[12]

At this stage we do not need to see how successful a model of consciousness this will turn out to be, it is sufficient for the moment to establish the duality in the structure of the self, which Sartre sets out, and the uses this is put to. From what has gone before it is clear to see that consciousness, as for-itself will never be complete because it will constantly distinguish itself from the in-itself. This attitude of the for-itself is described as a *lack* and is revealed in *desire*. "What the for-itself lacks is the self - or itself as in-itself" (Ibid, p. 89) and,

> But the being towards which human reality surpasses itself is not a transcendent God; it is at the heart of human reality; it is only human reality itself as a totality. (Ibid, p. 89)

The for-itself wants to be both for-itself and in-itself, conscious and self-identical. Inevitably this can only result in suffering since the lack of totality and identity is precisely that which grounds consciousness in the first place. Desire is the manifestation of this lack, "The existence of desire as a human fact is sufficient to prove that human reality is a lack" (Ibid, p. 87). This is because desire is a pointing towards a completeness that is not (yet) existing and hence refers back to the existing as incomplete or lacking. "Desire (says Sartre) is a lack of being" (Ibid, p. 88). Sartre paints a bleak picture of a being the reality of which is a lack, not simply of some quality or another, but an essential incompleteness that it must strive continuously, and unsuccessfully, to overcome, knowing that success can only mean the disappearance of the striving consciousness.

Being as Possibility

Before going on to look specifically at what Sartre says about the existence of Others it is necessary to understand the way that Sartre uses the notion of *possibility*[13] to throw the being of self outside the confines of the *cogito*. Possibility arises through consciousness and the ability of the conscious for-itself to project a state of affairs different to that in which it finds itself, this is the significant feature which distinguishes conscious being-for-itself from being-in-itself. But possibilities are only possibilities and,

> To be sure, the possible state does not exist yet; but it is the possible state of a certain existent which sustains by its being the possibility and the non-being of its future state.

And,

> Just as there can be lack in the world only if it comes to the world through a being which is its own lack, so there can be possibility in the world only if it comes through a being which is for itself in its own possibility. (Ibid, p. 98)

The possibility of possibility is founded on consciousness, but it is not necessarily the only possible way to interpret possibility. In Sartre's construction it is now valid to make the following two deductions. First,

> But if it is true that the possible is - so to speak - an option on being and if it is true that the possible can come into the world only through a being which is its own possibility, this implies for human reality the necessity of being its being in the form of an option on its being. There is possibility when instead of being purely and simply what I am, I exist as the Right to be what I am. But this very right separates me from what I have the right to be. (Ibid, p. 99)

Sartre is beginning to bring the indeterminacy of the future into the compass of being by speaking of options on being, and existing as a right to be some (determinate) being. He then continues in paradoxical form with the second deduction.

> But to be its own possibility - that is, to be defined by it - is precisely to be defined by that part of itself which it is not, is to be defined as an escape-from-itself towards ------. In short, from the moment that I want to account for my immediate being simply in so far as it is what it is not and is not what it is, I am thrown outside it toward a meaning which is out of reach and which can in no way be confused with immanent subjective representation. (Ibid, p.100)

The *not yet* of possibility becomes the *not-me* of my possible being and hence of my being. The possibility of possibility leads to an understanding of being in which my being is defined as something which it is not, that is, its possibility. We are thrown outside the self-certifying circle of the *cogito* into a world which is not-yet, almost wholly contingent, possible, and yet part of the totality that is self and without which there can be no understanding of self. The way is apparently now open to develop a structure of the self, which will admit the Other (the not-me), from the premise of the Cartesian *cogito*.

Sartre and Freedom

In the preceding section I have painted a picture of the model of the self that Sartre uses in *Being and Nothingness*. In this section and in the next I will show how Sartre uses this model as a basis for his notions of freedom and being-with-Others, and thereby as a way of solving the problems of knowledge and identity. The application of the model in the description of the relation of the self to the world is given in Sartre's exploration of human freedom set out in Part IV of *Being and Nothingness*.[14] An understanding of what is meant by freedom in Sartre's work will illuminate the usefulness or otherwise of Sartre's model of the self. Freedom is taken as the measure of our relation to others in the world and the analysis will bring back into consideration problems of externality, which had previously been bracketed by both Sartre and Kant. The effect that Sartre's analysis has on our understanding of freedom will point clearly to the deficiencies in his model of the self and the whole of his suggested ontology.

To begin with Sartre observes that, "an action is on principle *intentional*" (Sartre, 1956, p.433). This simply means that every action is the product of a human intention of some sort, though the actual action or its consequences may not correspond precisely, or even at all, to the intention.[15] Intention is the first bud of the project which is to be realised in action. We project ourselves upon the world intentionally and, based on the model of the self that I have outlined above, Sartre can say that, if intention is required for every action then a situation itself is never a motive, it only becomes so when a being wrenches itself away from its situation and projects an alternative situation. Quite simply, in having an intention I desire a state of affairs, or a situation, which is not my situation now. I project an alternative state of affairs which does not exist at the present. The simple fact that I am cold cannot be a motive for my switching on the heating, unless I make it so by wishing not to be cold. It is only,

> by fleeing a situation towards our possibility of changing it that we organise this situation into complexes of causes and motives. (Ibid, p. 437)

But already "fleeing" is a metaphorical rather than an actual movement. Cause is treated in much the same way as motive. Sartre says that

> We shall therefore use the term *cause* for the objective apprehension of a determined situation as this situation is revealed in the light of a certain end as being able to serve as a means for attaining this end. (Ibid, p. 446)

While motive is "the ensemble of the desires, emotions and passions which urge me to accomplish a certain act" (Ibid, p. 446). A cause, as a circumstance, may exist beyond me, of this I can say nothing since only representation is given to me, but I, by my project, give it its meaning as a cause. Sartre's interpretations of both motive and cause are a product of, or are premised on, my ability to project a possibility which is *not*.[16]

To sum up the argument so far: We exist as individuals in a particular situation, action can only occur as a result of the wish of the individual to alter, or to exchange, this situation in some way. The weight of Sartre's case is that, whatever the facts of the situation may be, they are only given particular meaning by the individual's project, or desire for another situation. I may only say that an obstacle is an obstacle if I wish to proceed beyond it, it then becomes an obstacle *for me*. I determine its meaning in my world. By itself it can neither be cause nor motive for action. These are relational qualities of objects, which can only be inferred in the context of a relation to the self.[17]

It would appear that Sartre, in this brief exposition, has said nothing controversial. He has simply described the premise, and one or two features, of human action, from a certain point of view. True enough, this point of view has led us to an alteration in the notion of cause, from an external factor in action, to one of a set of interiorised features of action, even so, at this stage, the exposition remains consistent within the confines of the model of the self in which Sartre wishes to conduct the analysis. The more radical implications of his ontology only become apparent on closer examination of the point of view he takes, the point of view of the individual subject, and of what his descriptions say about this individual subject. Once we accept Sartre's method of approach and his simple description of action, intention, cause and motive, certain implications for the individual subject consciousness, and freedom, (as the relation of this consciousness to the world), seem to follow. Sartre's statements that "No factual state ... is capable by itself of motivating any act whatsoever" and "No factual state can determine consciousness to apprehend it as a *negatité* or as a lack" (Ibid, p. 435-436) points towards his conclusion that "the indispensable and fundamental condition of all action is the freedom of the acting being" (Ibid, p. 436). The very fact that, for any action, my intention, my free project, is required to give meaning to the whole ensemble of features which make up an action, makes the freedom of the actor a cardinal precept, based precisely on my ability to project a state of affairs, or situation, which does not (yet) exist, and thereby enabling me to aim towards it. Quite quickly Sartre has moved the argument from the simple possibility of human action to the interim conclusion of the fundamental freedom of the conscious subject. Further explanation will be necessary before the validity of this movement is fully apparent, but it will remain basically a simple transition. For Sartre, the root of consciousness is the ability to negate the situation by projection. All that he is doing is to point to the possibility of choice. Essential to Sartre's idea of choice is the nihilating power of the free will, the way in which our proposal (intention) to act is an intentional negation of the existing situation. If I choose to go and make a cup of tea, I nihilate the situation in which I do not have a cup of tea. Though the importance of this description of an ordinary process may elude us, it seems trivial in the extreme, to accept it is to pave the way for Sartre's ontology of freedom. Sartre's emphasis on choice as an everyday individual matter is familiar in the everyday context. It exemplifies what philosophers have called a vulgar conception of human freedom, the idea that, though I did this, I could have done that, a common sense idea of freedom. It is at this point that the trap snaps shut. If choice is an individual matter, if motive and cause are interiorised features of action, if I give meaning to the ensemble of complexes that surround action through my free project, then determinism can have no place, and I can have no excuses. Sartre has not, as it might seem at first glance, posed the problem between freewill and determinism, but decided it conclusively on the side of freewill. My freedom is inevitable because my choice (intention) is unavoidable. I cannot choose not to choose, for this too is a choice. Not acting is to choose to continue as I do now and just as intentional as to choose to change. All that is required by Sartre is that I have the possibility of imagining myself into a set of circumstances different from those in which I find myself at present, not even that I actually conduct such imaginings. By centring his analysis of action within the individual subject Sartre locks the individual into an inescapable freedom, which he can then describe as, "identical with my existence" (Ibid, p. 444) and, "very exactly the stuff of my **being**" (Ibid, p. 439). My free project, what I want, determines my intention, action must be preceded by intention, and the possibility of intention is dependent on the power of the free will to determine its free project as a nihilation of the situation. Through my free project I organise, give meaning to, the complex of cause, motive, and ends, which make up action. Therefore my ability to formulate a free project (my power to nihilate) is essential to action and (again) "the indispensable and fundamental condition of all action is the freedom of the acting **being**" (Ibid, p. 436). There may be a lot wrong with all this, but Sartre, by explaining an ordinary mechanism, one with which we can all identify, in so strangely persuasive a manner, has opened a Pandora's Box of intentionality and action. Sartre has so far arrived at the conclusion that freedom and existence are inseparable. Taking his cue from Descartes and the *cogito* we find that this conscious being that I am cannot help but choose, in this way I am essentially free if conscious.

> One must be conscious in order to choose, and one must choose in order to be conscious. Choice and consciousness are one and the same thing. (Ibid, p. 462)

My freedom is guaranteed not as a quality of my consciousness but as its essential constituent, so that, "We shall never apprehend ourselves except as a choice in the making" (Ibid, p. 479). Translating this back into the context of actual practice, my freedom appears to be the possibility of making a choice. My freedom is represented as my power to negate an actually existing situation in the imagination.

Despite going by a different route to that chosen by Descartes this is the way that Sartre, despite his own efforts to the contrary, can be seen to be effecting a radical separation between self (consciousness) and the world. I am free to negate the facticity of my situation, I cannot help but do so, but how this nihilation applies to the world, to the realisation of my choice, is not at all clear. Following his alarming statements, "success is not important to freedom" and, "the technical and philosophical concept of freedom... means only the autonomy of choice" (Ibid, p. 483), which seem to open a clear breach between the projection of ends and their realisation (I am free to think but not necessarily free to act) Sartre appears to precipitate a divorce between the freedom of the conscious subject and external reality, a divorce which it seems increasingly difficult not to see as a feature of Sartre's model of the self.[18] Given the model of the self that Sartre is using and the Cartesian/Kantian baggage he is carrying this is not really surprising. However, freedom, as the measure of our interaction with others, cannot be denied an external dimension. If this dimension is nullified then any succeeding description of freedom (and of the self) will be inadequate and unrecognisable. Projection does not equal freedom when it is confined within Sartre's model of the self. He attempts to mend the breach by saying that

> It is necessary, however, to note that the choice, being identical with acting, supposes a commencement of realisation in order that choice may be distinguished from the dream and the wish. (Ibid, p. 483)

These distinctions, between choice and wish, success and the commencement of realisation are simply too arbitrary to achieve what Sartre wants, they can amount to no more than sub-division of the contents of consciousness, and, at worst, begin an infinite regress. Even more than that they are surely the distinctions that Sartre has made unavailable to himself. Once the connection between the free choice made by the individual and the free action realised by that individual is broken then no hasty construction of substitute structures can ever succeed in mending the breach. It begins to look more and more as if Sartre's freedom amounts to nothing more than this; "To be free is not to be able to do what one wants but to want what one can" (Sartre.1968, p. 173).

Having provided an interpretation of freedom, as choice, through the notion of a power of consciousness to nihilate, and having tied both this power and the subsequent freedom to consciousness Sartre has, of course, left behind the question of how consciousness is connected to Others existing independent of consciousness, and hence the question of what this kind of freedom means for the acting subject. The problem with Sartre's conclusions about the unavoidability of freedom is that freedom, as the necessity of choosing, is only relevant within the realm of consciousness. Having chosen to conduct the interpretation within the Cartesian metaphysical enclosure the results of the interpretation cannot refer to Others outside the circle of individual consciousness and hence cannot have anything to say about freedom. Choosing is by no means identical with acting, and Sartre's way of talking cannot admit that choosing supposes a commencement of realisation. We can go even further and ask what connection might there be between "commencement" and "realisation"? And what sort of thing is "commencement of realisation"? But Sartre would have no answers to these questions. Sartre has given an ontology of choosing, but not an ontology of action; a description of freedom must include both.

At this juncture we have reached the traditional point of disagreement with Sartre's ontology. Interiorization of all the features of action, including human freedom, and the consequent setting up of a dualism between the individual subject and Others, leave him with what appears to be an unbridgeable gulf. This emerges yet again in his discussion of "Freedom and Facticity"[19] which I will now examine. In this part of his exposition, the final one before going on to apply the structure, Sartre elucidates the idea of limit,

> although brute things ... can from the start limit our freedom of action, it is our freedom itself which must first constitute the framework, the technique, and the ends in relation to which they will manifest themselves as limits. (Sartre, 1956, p. 482)

In other words, our freedom, which we can understand now as nothing more than the formulation of our free project, creates, or gives meaning to, the world. We inform the world with our purpose and in this way freedom limits itself. Even though Sartre in no way wishes to deny existence to the external world, its meaning is given by our free project, and this can, unless he is very careful, begin to add up to much the same thing. If the world were to become the philosopher's creature, then very quickly this mighty responsibility would weigh down the ontological structure to the point of breakdown.[20] Sartre like Kant begins to have difficulty with the world of "brute things" (things-in-themselves). Consciousness and the self become disconnected from the not-self, and hence, ironically, there can be found no limit to the Sartrean freedom of the conscious subject. I may dream all I like.

By coming down so firmly on the side of freewill, and by characterising deterministic existence through the subjective point of view Sartre raises the issue of reconciliation between his two sorts of freedom "the technical philosophical" and "the empirical".[21] His attempt to resolve this difficulty is given in his statement of the paradox of freedom, "there is freedom only in a situation, and there is a situation only through freedom" (Ibid, p. 489). In the same way that freedom gives meaning to the situation, organising it into a complex of cause, motive, ends, limit etc. so my freedom is meaningless in a world without a resisting situation. Freedom from what?

> ...the world by co-efficients of adversity reveals to me the way in which I stand in relation to the ends which I assign myself, so that I can never know if it is giving me information about myself or about it. (Ibid, p. 488-489)

The interdependence between my freedom and my situation replaces opposition and creates a more sophisticated idea of both. The situation is given in my freedom and my freedom is given in the situation. I can have no free project except in a world of resisting "brute things", and, by having such a project I create, give meaning to, these things. This follows quite simply from Sartre's earlier description of action. Moreover because of the inescapable and fundamental nature of my freedom as conscious, I am simply incapable of telling the difference between what is given to me by the situation and what is given by my freedom. Whether or not Sartre succeeds in this argument can now only be judged by examining the relation between the self and Others like it.

A Bit of the Other

Sartre's discussion in Part III of *Being and Nothingness*[22] of the various aspects of being-for-Others constitutes probably the most significant part of the entire work. To gain credence for the paradoxical theorising which precedes this section Sartre must demonstrate that his methods can coherently explain the relation between different Others in the world. A failure at this juncture will lead to a rejection of Sartre's theory of the self. By describing what is there Sartre sets out the path of possibilities available to the human actor in the world. He begins by describing the problem of the existence of Others, sets out a few of the suggested solutions and points out their inadequacies. His methodology is made plain in "The Reef of Solipsism" (Sartre, 1956, pp. 223-232). He then sets out, ambitiously and ingeniously, to demonstrate the certainty of the existence of the Other in "The Look" (Ibid, pp. 252-302).

As is usual with Sartre a clear thread will be discernible throughout his argument, and, despite certain flaws in the case, significant conclusions can be drawn from what Sartre has to say. Sartre divines the problem of the existence of Others from certain self evident aspects of being which seem to require explanation, based on, "the presence of another in my consciousness." (Ibid, p. 221). Primarily, the sense of shame I can feel indicates this presence, shame being, "in its primary structure shame *before somebody*" (Ibid, p. 221), and the problem is thus posed simply, "Nobody can be vulgar all alone!" (Ibid, p. 222). It appears to Sartre that these aspects of everyday existence are *prima facie* evidence of the existence of an Other, like myself, beyond me and separated from me.

Right from the start Sartre attempts to tie this Other into my own being, "shame is shame *of oneself before the Other*; these two structures are inseparable" (Ibid, p. 222). The strict necessity of this method will become apparent later, but here it is sufficient to say that Sartre wishes to create an "Other" the existence of which is as certain as my own, by making the being of the Other an aspect of my own being, by understanding both my own being and the being of the Other in a unified context. This is what Sartre means when he says, "I need the Other in order to realise fully all the structures of my being" (Ibid, p. 222).[23]

In "The Reef of Solipsism" Sartre rejects what he calls the realist argument because it produces confusion since, "the existence of others is certain and knowledge which we have of them is probable" (Ibid, p. 224). It is clear that Sartre does not wish to advance sceptical arguments to deny the existence of Others, but it is equally clear that there is a problem about the knowledge we have of these Others, the same problem that we have already encountered in the discussion of the uncertainty of the Cartesian world beyond the self and in the discussion of Kant's work on the self. The realist will maintain that the existence of Others is indubitable, and then refuse to discuss it further. His realism is constituted by the certainty he holds about the existence of Others, a certainty not wholly supported by knowledge, and therefore vulnerable to the charge of naivety and inconsistency. The assumption of the existence of Others is not supported, but undermined, by the appeal to knowledge, and confusion results. Confusion illustrated and exemplified by realist statements like, "I know it is there but I can't see it". In Sartre's terms, of course, all of this realism adds up to no argument at all. He recognises that uncertain knowledge can provide no basis for the certain existence of Others, this is the "Reef of Solipsism" upon which attempts to square the Cartesian circle founder and which is at the root of the realist confusion.

The way in which Sartre seeks to circumvent the problem is highly original in that he offers no new proof of the existence of Others, and bases his case for the existence of Others not on knowledge, but on aspects of his own being (consciousness), an area in which certainty is available to him, so,

> We can never apprehend the relation of the *Other* to me, and he is never given, but gradually we constitute him as a concrete object. (Ibid, p. 228)

This divorce of the problems of perception and knowledge from the existence of Others is radical indeed, and if it succeeds will immeasurably strengthen Sartre's case, providing it with an impetus that will take it out of the traditional realms of dispute. In common with Kant, Sartre is seeking to develop a theory of being without any possible epistemology.[24] His proof which is not a proof, will be open to attack from those who are not manipulated by the psychology and paradox of Sartre's presentation. When Sartre says,

> my resistance to solipsism ... proves that I have always known that the Other existed, that I have always had a total, though implicit comprehension of his existence (Ibid, p. 251)

it looks like a simple affirmation of psychological facts which Sartre finds in his own consciousness, or even an appeal to everyday common sense. Sartre calls it a pre-ontological comprehension. He must adequately explain what kind of thing it is, if not knowledge, which gives him, or enables him to constitute, the existence of Others: if he cannot, then pre-ontological conception will only stand alongside knowledge, and will not be exempt from the questions which beset explanations and affirmations based on knowledge. This kind of pre-ontological explanation is obviously his intention when he says, "I radically transcend the field of my experience" (Ibid, p. 228), and thus avoids all the problems attendant upon a theory of the knowledge. Sartre, like Kant before him, will attempt to use his own subjectivity to demonstrate, or at least indicate, the existence of an Other. I will argue that all this can achieve is an existential restatement of Kant's position providing only formal truths about the self, and at worst amounts to no more than a description of Sartre's own individual psyche.

We experience the Other-as-object, in the shape of the knowledge we claim we have of the world "out there". Sartre wishes to be able to demonstrate that the Other is more than just a figment in our own subjectively constituted world, and in fact constitutes a world of his own. My knowledge of the Other is no way the same as the Other's knowledge of himself, this seems plain, even when couched by Sartre in more technical terms, "between the Other-as-object and Me-as-subject there is no common measure" (Ibid, p. 243). Sartre wishes his theory to go beyond the simple perception of an Other in the world and show, somehow, that we experience the Other-as-subject, and yet that we do this within our own being. An objective knowledge of our own consciousness as subject is impossible, we have seen this much from Sartre's own discussion of the structures of the self in Part II of *Being and Nothingness* and from the perplexity in Hume's discussion of personal identity. Sartre is now attempting to talk about this problem in terms other than those we would normally employ. Through a description of his own consciousness Sartre hopes that he can literally turn the world inside out, producing an argument for the existence of Others, external to us and independently constituted, and who organise the world as object for themselves, and all this without apparently proceeding beyond certain facts about his own consciousness. It remains to be seen how successful is the structure in which Sartre makes his attempt, both in establishing its own credence and in explaining the relation between different Others in the world.

Look Again

Sartre's necessary and sufficient conditions for a theory of the existence of Others are first and foremost, the divorce between the existence of Others and knowledge of these Others. "A theory of the Other's existence must therefore simply question me in my being" (Sartre, 1956, p. 251). In order to answer the problem of knowledge Sartre must bring forward a theory, which is not simply dependent on knowledge of the Other, any such theory, would simply re-state the problem. Sartre believes that the Other, like the self, is immediately apprehended, and is not *known*.[25]

In the second condition he marries this to the Cartesian *cogito* when he says, "the only point of departure possible is the Cartesian *cogito*"(Ibid, p.251). The *cogito* gives the self *a priori*. I have already set out above the way in which Sartre reinterprets the *cogito* in the sections headed 'Immediate structures of the For-itself'.[26] In his description of the self, it is this interpretation of the *cogito* that must be carried forward into his demonstration of the existence of the Other.

Thirdly Sartre says, "What the *cogito* must reveal to us is not the-Other-as-object" (Ibid, p. 251) thus seeking to overcome the problem of establishing common measure between myself and Others. By elevating my experience of the Other out of the realm of knowledge and into that of immediate apprehension within my own being, I must experience the Other as subject and thereby overcome the problems which beset my knowledge of the Other as object.

Naturally, and finally, having established a structure into which I bring the Other, Sartre's fourth condition must enable him to distinguish between himself and Others in order to avoid a collapse into solipsism. Sartre's fourth condition is that "the Other must appear to the *cogito* as *not being* me" (Ibid, p. 252). The Other is to be constituted as an internal negation, of my own self. Sartre seems to be asking us to begin to accept an inter-connection, or even an interdependence, of different Others. This makes sense, fitting in with his self imposed "restriction" that he demonstrate the existence of the Other from within his own being. In this way the Other would be part of me without being me, an internal negation. The self and the Other would then be understood as united and identified, each needing the other.[27] However this appears to be in direct contradiction with Sartre's second necessary condition, that the only possible starting point is the Cartesian *cogito*. I will argue that Sartre cannot maintain the perspective of the self-subsisting self of the *cogito* which requires no external prior support, while at the same time constituting the self and the Other as one, and depending on each other. In short, I will argue that Sartre's re-interpretation of the *cogito* is unsuccessful in explaining the relation between different Others.

In "The Look"[28] Sartre sets out his theory of the existence of Others. The first thing to notice about "The Look" is that, although it claims simply to be a demonstration of the existence of Others, with relations between these Others discussed later in Part III of *Being and Nothingness*, it is an intensely relational piece of philosophy. Sartre is attempting, from the Cartesian point of view of the individual subject consciousness, to articulate a theory that will demonstrate that other individual conscious subjects exist beyond his own. He is thus making the ground upon which all further discussion of Others will take place and determining the fundamental relation between Others in the world. His object in "The Look" is paradoxical; to remain within the bounds set by the *cogito* and yet to cite the existence of conscious beings, outside his own consciousness, thus answering the problem of knowledge in a way that avoids solipsism. The contradiction between these aims is already apparent, and just how effective Sartre can be in making the *cogito*, as it were, throw the self outside itself remains in doubt. However this is not all that is wrong with "The Look".

In "The Look" Sartre demonstrates the existence of Others through a description of certain self evident psychological facts, which we experience, and through which we gain an immediate apprehension of the Other. These states of mind are pride, shame and, fear. All three operate along the same lines so it is only necessary to give an account of one in operation. Sartre's description of himself looking through a keyhole, suddenly surprised by footsteps coming along the corridor is vivid.[29] His description of the shame he feels strikes a chord. From the simple orientation of himself (as subject) looking at the world (as object), to the transformation of the situation by the look of an Other, and his discomfiture under this look, the movement is inexorable, but may say less than he hopes. Sartre claims to be saying more than simply; "I feel shame, I cannot feel such a thing alone in the world, therefore there must be Others for me to be ashamed before". Such a deduction would be unworthy of Sartre and would miss the point of his entire project. It would, moreover, be ineffective against any sceptical argument of the type that might be advanced by those like Hume. What Sartre wishes to say is that, in shame, I actually and immediately experience the Other within my very being, in a way as if he were me or part of me. This brings the Other into the bounds set by the *cogito*.

Rather less emotionally compelling, and more useful philosophically, is his description of objects he sees in the park in their primary relation to him as subject, and the way in which this description is radically re-orientated when he becomes conscious of the look of the Other. As he says, "suddenly an object has appeared which has stolen the world from me"(Ibid, p. 255). Sartre is most insistent that no space is left for inference between my own self and the Other, my apprehension of the Other is immediate, "the Other is present to me without any intermediary" (Ibid, p.270). As I suggested earlier Sartre is using "The Look" as more than just a simple conventional proof. The only way in which Sartre can be certain of the existence of the Other is to experience the Other as subject, and for this to happen a radical (and alarming) conversion must take place in which object becomes subject and subject becomes object. Sartre argues that this is what takes place in "The Look", and that, far from being a contradiction; it is a satisfactory explanation of everyday conscious experience. Suddenly from the commanding heights of my subjectivity, seeing the world, organising its elements in my own way, I am subjected to the look of an Other and the world, including me, undergoes a re-organisation in such a way that it escapes from my control and I become an object for another subject. Sartre eloquently describes the theft of my world by the Other.

> The Other is first the permanent flight of things towards a goal which I apprehend as an object at a certain distance from me but which escapes me inasmuch as it unfolds about itself its own distances. (Ibid, p. 255)

And "In experiencing the look ... I experience the inapprehensible subjectivity of the Other directly and within my being" (Ibid, p. 270). In the same way that in the *cogito* I apprehend my own consciousness, so in the look of the Other I apprehend the Other. Apart from anything else this means that Sartre is actually experiencing the Other not as object but as subject and is experiencing a radical transformation not only of the world of objects, which is re-orientated towards the Other, but of his own self, which is also re-orientated under the look of the Other, as an object itself.

Despite his careful manoeuvrings in order to avoid the issue of knowledge Sartre's examples are weak on several fronts. First of all we may object that Sartre's examples pre-suppose the existence of Others in their construction. I may be looking through a keyhole, I may hear footsteps, and I may be mistaken. In both cases Sartre would have me feel shame and thus experience the Other in my own being. But on what ground can I be certain of what I hear? The problem of knowledge rears its head again and Sartre's only defence is to point to the fact that the possibility of my shame implies in some way the existence of the Other. That is, I can only be mistaken about something the existence of which is given, but this reduces Sartre's case to the level of inference from my state of mind to the existence of the Other, a position that he specifically wishes to avoid. It remains that, the perception which leads me to feel shame, to experience the look of the Other, may be mistaken every time, and my shame (or pride, or fear) is derivative of a state of affairs (a world of objects and Others) certain knowledge of which remains beyond me. Instead of a position in which my shame serves the purpose of bringing the Other to me, Sartre has described a position in which the existence of the Other is given in order to explain these states of mind.

Following on from this we might say that Sartre has simply described certain features of his own psyche, and explained these findings in terms which serve his argument. No-one needs to argue with Sartre that they do not feel shame, no-one needs to dispute the psychology of "The Look", all that is necessary is to challenge his interpretation of this state of mind. Conventionally shame is a state of mind given in a highly socialised environment, it is usually thought of as secondary to philosophical musings about the existence of the external world and Others in it. Shame, pride and fear are all explicable in terms of the social context in which we all assume we live, and, as I have said, a deduction from these emotions is in no way sufficient to demonstrate an underlying ontological structure in which we exist with the Other.

Finally, before turning to more constructive work with what Sartre has to say in "The Look", we may ask; how does Sartre propose that we distinguish in the world between Others, as independent consciousnesses, and material objects? [30] The perfect robot would function in exactly the same way as an Other in Sartre's world, and Sartre's ontology would not cope with a situation in which I was mistaken in taking for a "look", a reflection in the eye of a tailor's dummy. The simple fact that I react to the dummy in the same way that I would react if it were a real Other is not a ground on which to posit the existence of such Others. There is always the possibility that I am always wrong about what I see, hear etc.

In the end Sartre's attempt to demonstrate the existence of the Other collapses into the mire of difficulties connected with the problem of knowledge of Others.[31] In this case, Sartre attempts to interiorise the Other within the confines of his own subjectivity and fails to cross a void of his own making into the world on the other (Other's?) side. Despite all that he says, everything so far can be interpreted as basically Kantian. I will now attempt to explain the fundamental reason for Sartre's failure and then indicate some of the areas in which his case becomes stronger. The contradiction within Sartre's demonstration of the existence of the Other will become even more apparent and this will throw further light on the problems of knowledge and identity.

I Wouldn't Start from Here

The most striking thing about Sartre's demonstration in "The Look" is his starting point. He is unequivocal in affirming, "the only point of departure possible is the Cartesian *cogito*" (Sartre, 1956, p. 251). This is more than just an analytical device; it is the fundamental starting point of the individualist. When Sartre criticises Hegel for forgetting himself in his description of being and Others,[32] Sartre elevates his own self to absolute pre-eminence and makes his own perspective the constituting force of the Other. Following this, and despite all his efforts, his case is doomed to collapse into solipsism. The starting point of the self-subsistent subject can produce no other result than itself. Stirner looms large. The problem of knowledge of the Other, as traditionally posed, can have no answer, its insolubility is written into its very formulation. A brief examination of some of the things Sartre says about being and Others will illustrate the point.

First of all, the two most promising examples Sartre uses; the shame he feels when footsteps are heard in the corridor, and the re-orientation of objects in the park towards the Other, are both intensely subjective in their construction. Sartre straight away, and without apparent question, takes the individual point of view. Sartre has taken for granted, in constructing his examples, the self subsistence of the individual subject consciousness. He has therefore set himself the problems of knowledge and identity in a way that will resist solution whatever moves he makes.

At the beginning of "The Look" Sartre sets out his task again,

> if the Other is to be a probable object and not a dream of an object, then his object-ness must of necessity, refer not to an original solitude beyond my reach, but to a fundamental connection in which the Other is manifested in some way other than through the knowledge I have of him. (Ibid, p. 253)

And, at once, he can speak of, "This relation, in which the Other must be given to me as subject" (Ibid, p. 253). Problems begin to occur when Sartre describes the radical transformation, which takes place under the look of the Other, and we have what Sartre calls the reflective self, as opposed to the unreflective self peeping through the keyhole.

> This means that all of a sudden I am conscious of myself as escaping myself, not in that I am the foundation of my own nothingness, but in that I have my foundation outside myself. I am for myself only as I am a pure reference to the Other. (Ibid, p. 260)

This unquestionably clashes with Sartre's affirmation of the *cogito* as his starting point. Under the *cogito* the self is self referencing, its existence is not dependent upon anything outside of itself. To accept such an external reference would be to destroy the core of the *cogito* as an escape from reference to anything other than itself, it is its own logical corner and can only return to itself. To continue with Sartre;

> Everything takes place as if I had a dimension of being from which I was separated by a radical nothingness; and this nothingness is the Other's freedom. The Other has to make my being-for-him *be* in so far as he has to be his being. (Ibid, p. 262)

Such a dimension of being as Sartre describes is not available to the Cartesian, and neither is the reciprocity of being which Sartre is affirming when he goes on to say, "Yet by my very shame I claim as mine that freedom of another. I affirm a profound unity of consciousness" (Ibid, p. 262). This unity is entirely inconceivable under the singularity of the Cartesian premise. Sartre attempts to wriggle out of all this "unity of being" and re-establish the singularity of his own consciousness by saying, "my being-as-object or being-for-Others is profoundly different from my being-for-myself"(Ibid, p. 273). This confuses even further what he has already said about bringing the Other within his own being. In order to avoid the division of the self from the world and Others, he begins to set up divisions within his own model of the self in which to accommodate the Other, and his final affirmation that, "being-for-others is not an ontological structure of the For-itself" (Ibid, p. 282), contradicts the project he outlined at the beginning of "The Look". Sartre is playing on the ambiguity of his notion of "nothingness" with which he hopes both to separate the two parts of his being while at the same time allowing that there is nothing to impede their unity.

To summarise, in general terms Sartre insists that his case is based on the *cogito*. The proof or self-evidence of the *cogito* is based upon the impossibility of conceiving myself as an object; in the *cogito* my being is given as pure subject, self-supporting and indubitable. Sartre's conclusions in "The Look" point unreservedly towards my being as dependent upon something outside itself (the Other). If Sartre were to deny this then the Other will remain no more than a function of my subject, and the "outside" has no meaning at all. Sartre's conclusions about the Other indicate a unity of consciousness and unity of being. "The Look" is all about relation between self and Other and its conclusions do not paint a Cartesian picture of the self. The Other cannot be understood except in the unified context of the self and the world, and Sartre's Cartesian premise, which divides the world into subject and object, denies this context to the extent that it cannot lead to a recovery of the integrated ground of selfhood. Either Sartre's argument collapses into solipsism or he must abandon the *cogito*.

Sartre's premise might be Cartesian but his conclusions, in spite of his earlier rejection of this point of view, have a distinctly Heideggerian ring.[33] It looks as if the *cogito*, and the way it determines the setting out of the problems of knowledge and identity, causes the collapse of arguments based on it into solipsism. In Sartre's terms, the reef cannot be avoided given the starting point that pre-supposes its existence. This conclusion obviously has more to say about the *cogito* and the problems of knowledge and identity themselves than it does about attempts like that of Sartre to answer them. It provides ample grounds for questioning the Cartesian structure of the self proposed by Sartre and putting in its place a theory of the self, which, although it rejects the *cogito* as the starting point, may encompass some of Sartre's conclusions about the existence of Others.

Knowing me, Knowing you?

We have seen, in "The Look", how Sartre explicitly and very firmly takes the *cogito* as his starting point, following a specific rejection of alternatives (in particular those of Hegel and Heidegger), which offer a non-Cartesian perspective. However, as soon as the Other is introduced into the scenes described in "The Look", and the radical transformations begin, the argument begins to founder. It founders specifically because of the Cartesian premise, which pre-supposes distinction between me and the Other. This forces Sartre into the unsuccessful attempt to throw his being beyond the confines of the *cogito*. Sartre's attempt to bring the Other within his own being is defeated by the structure of the *cogito*. He cannot both maintain the premise of the *cogito* and gain the "immediate apprehension" of the Other. We could assume, because of what he says about the *cogito*, and his quest to demonstrate the existence of the Other beyond or previous to knowledge, that his contradictory conclusions mean a collapse of his argument into solipsism, and a theory of the self closely akin to that derived from the work of Stirner. However this would not do justice to the advances that Sartre's work represents within the Cartesian tradition.

The alternative is a rejection of the Cartesian premise in the light of Sartre's conclusions, and an acceptance of the principle of the immediate apprehension of the Other. This represents a way forward to a solution to the problem of knowledge based on a refusal to divide the world of subject and object in the first place, and the taking of an integrated approach to the question of the existence of Others. Clearly this could not be the Sartre of *Being and Nothingness*, but if it is an approach that will release the argument from the vicious circularity of the traditionally posed problems of knowledge and identity, then he would surely applaud the attempt.

The strongest part of Sartre's argument for the existence of Others in "The Look" is the notion of the "immediate apprehension of the Other". This notion seems to capture accurately and fully the way we notice Others in the world, describing as it does the way in which Others seem to be spatially distant and yet immediately present to us. It does not matter that the two people we are talking to are six and ten feet away respectively, both are present in exactly the same way. Thus we can say, "it is never eyes which look at us; it is the Other as subject" (Sartre, 1956, p. 277). By the end of "The Look" this penetrating observation has hardened to the conclusion that, "we have established that consciousnesses experience one another without intermediary" (Ibid, p. 301), and Sartre is able to suggest a profound unity of being. Put in plain language this means that my own being is set in inextricable context with that of the Other. The opposite of my self is, as it were, the measure against which I determine my own existence. Just as, under the Cartesian premise, it is inconceivable that I can proceed beyond myself towards the Other, so, under this alternative kind of argument, it is inconceivable that I am alone in the world. I may ask whether it is as I see it, but I may not ask if it is there at all.

A more favourable interpretation of what Sartre says about the Other in Part III of *Being and Nothingness* and freedom in Part IV focuses on this unity of consciousness and the world and the way that Sartre uses the phenomena of everyday conscious experience to describe ontological structures. Sartre uses examples of everyday experience which strike a chord with the reader. His example of looking through a keyhole and the discomfiture we all feel when we suppose that we are discovered, and the way in which he describes our experience of the Other as a counter focus for the material world we perceive as our own, are striking and profound, yet these are simple extrapolations from everyday life. Sartre is using phenomenology in an innovative way, reminiscent of one of his earlier teachers, Heidegger, to re-interpret everyday experience in a way that reveals underlying ontological structures. The importance of this context of *everydayness*[34] is somewhat dulled in *Being and Nothingness* due to the difficulties attendant upon Sartre's insistence on using the *cogito* as his starting point, but it forms a vital component in his conclusions about the Other. Everydayness is the notion, which roots all theorising about consciousness, the self, and all fundamental ontology. The validity of the description of ontological structures must be based in everydayness and confirmed by their re-application to everydayness. The only thing that prevents Sartre from accepting wholeheartedly these kinds of conclusions about the interdependence of being and Others is the *cogito*, and the view of the self that it generates. I will now go on to outline a view of the self, which explicitly rejects the *cogito*, based on Heidegger's approach in *Being and Time* and elsewhere in his work of the same period. This will underpin the work of Laing, and provide a powerful standpoint from which to argue with the egoist Stirner.

Notes

1. While Heidegger's *Being and Time* precedes Sartre's *Being and Nothingness* I have considered Sartre's work ahead of that of Heidegger because although this reverses the chronological order Sartre's work is avowedly Cartesian while Heidegger's work is based on a rejection of this tradition. It will become very clear in Chapters Seven and Eight that Sartre's work owes much to Heidegger's method. Also see Fell, 1992, for comparative discussion.
2. For a discussion of Sartre's relation to this tradition see, McCulloch, 1994, pp. 83-94, and Greene, 1983, pp.32-48.
3. It is important to note at this stage that Sartre was explicitly influenced by the pre-war work of Heidegger. In 1934 he spent a year at the French Institute in Berlin where he gained a thorough knowledge of modern German philosophy and was giving courses in Heidegger's work during his captivity in 1940-41. See Meszaros, 1979, Vol. I, pp. 26-28.
4. For a discussion and criticism of this dichotomy see Warnock, 1966, Chapter Two, Natanson, 1973, pp. 87-92, and McCulloch, 1994, pp. 56-62.
5. See McCulloch, 1994, pp. 97-117 on Sartre's realism.
6. Sartre, 1956, p. 74.
7. Ibid, p. 75.
8. See also Caws, 1979, "Consciousness and Subjectivity", pp. 50-62.
9. See note concerning Goldilocks, Chapter Four, Note 18, and Note 17 below.
10. See, Caws, 1979, p. 82.
11. For a description of the way in which Sartre uses "nothingness" see, McCulloch, 1994, pp. 31-38, and Caws, 1979, pp. 70-71.
12. Kant's influence on Sartre is considerable, for example Sartre's *Existentialism and Humanism* can be read as a modern restatement of Kant's *Groundwork of the Metaphysic of Morals*. It is because of this that much of the criticism made of Kant's work also sticks to Sartre's existentialism. See also Caws, 1979, p. 119-121.
13. Sartre's use of this notion is clearly derived from Heidegger; see especially Heidegger, 1987, Div. II Section I, and Fell, 1979, pp. 59-61 and 99-102. Also, McCulloch, 1994, pp. 31-38, and Caws, 1979, pp. 83-87.
14. For contrasting discussions of Sartrean freedom see, McCulloch, 1994, pp. 38-44 and 66-70, Kirsner, 1976, pp. 11-29, Natanson, 1973, pp. 48-52 and 75-81, Meszaros, 1979, Vol. I, Chapter Five, and Caws, 1979, Chapter VIII.
15. See McCulloch, 1994, pp. 71-81.
16. Natanson sums it up when he says, "Since action is necessarily intentional, no political or economic fact can cause an action in the individual. Motivation is inner" (Natanson, 1973, p. 48).
17. This line of reasoning is close to that taken by Kant in the *Critique of Pure Reason* as part of the Transcendental Deduction, A. 84-130 = B. 130-169.
18. Caws says, "Freedom, as we have seen, is not a *capacity* of the for-itself, but rather a *state*; it arises out of the negation, which at once joins and separates the for-itself to and from the in-itself that surrounds it" (Caws, 1979, p. 114.), and Natanson argues similarly that Sartre does not mean freedom to be an ability and

distinguishes between metaphysical and practical freedom (Natanson, 1973, pp. 48-52).
19. Sartre, 1956, pp. 481-552.
20. McCulloch, attempt to make a case for Sartre's form of direct realism but his position depends on an untenable dualism and as McCulloch admits retains some idealist weaknesses (McCulloch, 1994, Chapter Seven).
21. Sartre, 1956, p.483. Also see, Kirsner, 1976, pp. 11-29 on "Sisyphean Freedom", and Natanson, 1973, pp. 75-81.
22. Warnock provides a clear setting out of Sartre's position in *The Philosophy of Sartre*, Chapter Three. Also, McCulloch, 1994, Chapter Eight, Greene, 1983, Chapter Five, and Caws, 1979, Chapter VII.
23. Caws says, "While we do not create physical objects by our look, however, there is a sense in which we do create one another in this way" (Caws, 1979, p. 97).
24. Sartre follows Kant in this transcendentalism.
25. This is the core of Sartre's existentialism, the belief that consciousness *is* before it is *known*. Existence precedes essence.
26. Sartre, 1956, Part Two, Chapter One.
27. Sartre's use of an internal negation is a clear sign that he is feeding directly on the Hegelian tradition. See especially Hegel's discussion of the master/slave relationship (Hegel, 1977, pp. 111-119).
28. Sartre, 1956, pp. 252-302. Also McCulloch, 1994, pp. 131-135, Natanson, 1973, pp. 34-36, and Greene, 1983, pp. 147-153.
29. Sartre, 1956, p. 259.
30. It should already be clear that, coming from a Cartesian, a straightforward affirmation of the immediate presence of the Other is simply not going to be good enough, even if we could say that Others have the special property of being able to steal the world from me, the knowledge which leads to this conclusion is itself doubtful and vulnerable to sceptical criticism.
31. Caws says, "The Sartrean Ego has the elusiveness of a burst bubble and the outcome of the analysis is an empty I, correlative to a Me reduced to nothingness, together maintaining a spontaneous unity of states and actions." (Caws, 1979, p. 58).
32. Sartre, 1956, Part Three, Chapter One, Section Three.
33. Despite Sartre's explicit criticism of Heidegger in *Being and Nothingness*, Part Three, Chapter One, Section Three. Also see Caws, 1979, p. 98.
34. This is a key term in Heidegger's work and will be discussed fully in Chapter Seven.

7

Heidegger - An Everyday Story of Beings-in-the World

It is clear from the preceding examinations of the work of Descartes, Hume, Kant and Sartre that two central problems remain intractable within the tradition they represent. These are, the problem of knowledge of the world that is not-me, and the problem of the continuity of personal identity. These two problems represent the apparently unexplainable and yet constitutive aspects of selfhood. The first, the problem of knowledge, is the problem of the spatiality of the world, the relation between the self and entities existing, independent of the self. The second, the problem of continuing identity, concerns the temporality of the self, its continuity over time and its relation to itself at other times. These problems are also two sides of the same coin, the one concerned with all that is not me, and the other with what it is that I am. At the core of both problems is the notion of selfhood. The fact that these problems are not satisfactorily resolved within the Cartesian tradition indicates that this tradition does not have, and cannot formulate, a notion of the self adequate to encompass the nature of human existence and experience. This failing is so severe as to call into question the tradition itself. Its fundamental premises, and its methodology, must now not only be subject to rigorous criticism, but also to competition from an alternative, which is based on a rejection of the Cartesian tradition. To be successful this rejection must not only provide the ground for an adequate theory of the self but must also question traditional methodology and show the potential for its replacement by an alternative way of understanding both knowledge and the self.

    The two central problems have been encountered in different forms and in different degrees in the work of each of the philosophers I have so far examined. For Descartes the mind/body problem, the question as to how the corporeal body is affected by the non-corporeal mind, remains without satisfactory answer. It seems that the best that can be done is given in Descartes' rather evasive answers to Princess Elizabeth[1] and in his insistence that I am not in my body as a pilot in a ship.[2] In addition, the way in which he applies sceptical doubt appears to resist his following efforts to restore the world as we see it. In the end Descartes poses more questions than he succeeds in answering. Hume applies Cartesian doubt to the extreme of scepticism and, with regard to his own identity, sees it constantly slip away every time he seeks to identify himself. He can never meet Goldilocks because he is Goldilocks, and he is isolated from the world in similar fashion to Descartes by his never ending, and never successful, search for a means to verify his perceptions. Hume does not deny the existence of the world "outside" himself but can find no empirical grounds for his commonsensical belief in such a world, and resigns himself to accept the existence of the world without any verifiable knowledge of it. Kant, in response to Hume's sceptical resignation, tries to construct a system which will provide a reason for believing, but by this time the bifurcation of the world has become hardened to the extent that Kant must actively posit the existence of things-in-themselves, beyond the reach of human knowledge in order to provide support for his epistemology. This structure has fatal consequences when applied to the notion of the self, an area in which internal division and incoherence are not to be tolerated. Kant's model of the self does not resolve Hume's Goldilocks problem and is not much better, at bottom, than Descartes' not-like-a-pilot-in-a-ship. Using phenomenological methods and an existential approach Sartre attempts re-formulate both of the problems with some success in *Being and Nothingness*. However his ontology is flawed, most apparently in the way it affects his idea of freedom. There is a strong sense in which he too holds too firmly to the distinction between consciousness and materiality, and this subverts his analysis of human action. In respect of the self, in terms of its own identity, Sartre's conclusions are much more fruitful. In fact by his brilliant use of phenomenology in "The Look"[3] Sartre paints a picture of a self existing only in conjunction with Others, a self in which the Other is immediately present to me despite any physical distance which may separate us. I experience the Other within my own being; my isolation cannot be maintained in the look of the Other. Paradoxically, Sartre's understanding of the immediacy of the Other is his strongest contribution to the development of an alternative to the Cartesian notion of the self, and it grows out of his contextual understanding and interpretation of entities and consciousness bound together in the matrix of phenomenological presentation. All of this is in spite of his rejection of Heidegger's idea of *Mitsein* (Being-with).[4] Curiously, Sartre is determined to stay with the starting point of the Cartesian *cogito*, albeit a re-interpreted *cogito*, and this appears as the significant barrier in his thought to a real phenomenological/existential breakthrough in the deadlock surrounding the problems of knowledge and personal identity. Sartre's virtual unity of consciousnesses at the end of "The Look" contradicts his Cartesian premise despite his attempts to have the *cogito* throw the self outside itself.

All of the philosophers I have so far examined have, in one way or another, taken as their starting point the Cartesian premise that my own existence as a thinking being is the only thing of which I can be certain. All of them would accept Descartes' First Meditation, which affirms the dubitability of sensory evidence and the idea that the contents of my consciousness may be entirely unconnected with any reality/materiality/being "outside" or "beyond" my own self, or at least that any proposed connection is required to be, or can possibly be, demonstrated. It is not coincidental that Stirner would probably also agree with the contents of Descartes' First Meditation, since, if the separatedness of the self from the world cannot be resolved in the succeeding Meditations, Cartesian doubt prepares the ontological ground for Stirner's egoism. It is this premise that begins the tradition, which separates *being* from the world and thereby begins to misunderstand being itself. This premise is the source of the problems of knowledge and identity. In this chapter, and in the succeeding chapter, I will set out an alternative to the Cartesian tradition (as represented by Descartes, Hume, Kant and Sartre) focussing on the two central problems, of knowledge and identity, and, as a consequence, develop a theory of the self which will comprehensively and consistently explain human being and experience.

In this chapter I will concentrate on the problem of knowledge of the external world, the epistemological problem. Primarily, I will use the work of Heidegger, in the first division of *Being and Time*[5] and in Part One of his *Basic Problems of Phenomenology*, to show how spatiality can be understood in a way that does not lead to the problem of knowledge. In the following chapter, using the second Division of *Being and Time*, and Part Two of *Basic Problems of Phenomenology* I will discuss the problem of temporality, the problem of personal identity.

Phenomenal Insight

In his books *Being and Time* and *The Basic Problems of Phenomenology*[6] Heidegger recognises what he calls "the central philosophical problem",[7] this is,

> How do we proceed from inside the intentional experiences in the subject outward to things as objects?

and...

> How do experiences and that to which they direct themselves as intentional, the subjective in sensations, representations, relate to the objective? (Heidegger, 1982, p. 62)

This is the problem which has taxed all of the philosophers I have studied so far and to which Heidegger returns, but in a radically different way to that used by his predecessors.

Heidegger uses phenomenology both to interpret everyday experience and to retain its dynamic context. He uses the expression *everydayness*[8] on many occasions, but leaves definition of this term until close to the end of *Being and Time* where he says, "'Everydayness' manifestly stands for that way of existing in which Dasein maintains itself 'every day'" (Heidegger, 1987, H.370-371), which is not very illuminating. He then goes on to say, "what we have primarily in mind in the expression everydayness is a definite *how* of existence by which Dasein is dominated through and through 'for life'", and,

> "Everydayness" means the "how" in accordance with which Dasein "lives unto the day", whether in all its ways of behaving or only in certain ones which have been prescribed by Being-with-one-another. To this "how" there belongs further the comfortableness of the accustomed. (Ibid, H. 370-371)

And finally,

> Everydayness is a way *to be* - to which, of course, that which is publicly manifest belongs. But it is more or less familiar to any "individual" Dasein as way of existing which it may have as its own. (Ibid, H. 371)

Clearly this is a key term in Heidegger's work and little more than a flavour of its meaning can be given by sheer definition. Its full significance will only become apparent as the exposition of Heidegger's work unfolds.

Heidegger shares the starting point of everydayness with the phenomenological tradition[9] but this does not mean that Heidegger is necessarily a phenomenologist. He is at odds with the phenomenologists premise that phenomena cannot provide access to noumenal reality and affirms, rather than denies, the possibility of phenomenological ontology.[10] Heidegger uses the methods of the phenomenologist to support his own interpretations of experience and being. In the same way he uses existential ideas and approaches without becoming an existentialist. His work, in *Being and Time* and *The Basic Problems of Phenomenology*, represents a radical departure from the prevailing philosophical tradition and is constituted as a subversion of this tradition.[11] Consequently it requires us to take up an entirely different position to those taken by all of the philosophers I have so far examined.

Heidegger takes involvement to be central to any interpretation of experience and being, and, in this respect, his starting point has some similarity to that taken by Hume. In the same way that Hume, in looking for (sensory) impressions as the source of all of his ideas, is seeking to empirically ground understanding of the world and experience, so Heidegger, by beginning with the everyday and the given circumstance of involvement, can be seen to inherit some of the strengths of the empiricist position.[12] Phenomenology becomes the key to understanding experience, containing all that is required for a description of the everyday, and the basis for a deeper interpretation of experience.

Sartre, as a Cartesian, forms an important bridge between the tradition and Heidegger's alternative, his *Essay on Phenomenological Ontology: Being and Nothingness*, is an attempt at a Cartesian phenomenological ontology. I have shown in Chapter Six how Sartre, despite his avowedly Cartesian premise, arrives at a most un-Cartesian idea of the self which, even after his attempts to re-interpret Descartes *cogito*, it cannot consistently generate.

Heidegger's own use of phenomenology is derived from his close association with Edmund Husserl, his early mentor, who raised the method to prominence at the beginning of the twentieth century. Heidegger was Husserl's pupil and his debt to Husserl he readily acknowledged.[13] Heidegger uses phenomenological methods and insights to aid him in his own elucidation of fundamental ontology and in the process of this work necessarily leaves Husserl, and phenomenology, behind. Heidegger says that, "*the expression 'phenomenology' is the name for the method of scientific philosophy in general*" (Heidegger, 1982, p. 3). If we take phenomenology to be "taking things as they are", and, "the study of things as they appear",[14] we see how this can be a starting point for Heidegger. Heidegger sees phenomena as a window on the wider question of being. Phenomena, though imperfectly, are our only avenue of approach to the world; they are therefore the only point at which to begin the inquiry. Heidegger does not simply take things as given but seeks to interpret phenomena through what is termed *hermeneutic phenomenology*.[15] In the case of Heidegger's phenomenology this means that we can say nothing about the phenomena apart from the context, which includes the conscious self, and *vice versa*. It is not possible to discuss either in isolation; we can gain no perspective on the world from which to isolate phenomena because we are a part of that from which we attempt to stand apart. Meaning and significance can only be determined within the hermeneutic circle of our involvement with the world.

Heidegger brings the interpretive method of Husserl's phenomenology to the starting point of average everydayness and is able to construct a methodological standpoint for himself in the lived world as immediately experienced. Heidegger will brook no separation between things-in-themselves and phenomena. Phenomena must be the showing of the things-as-they-are. Heidegger is not simply accepting sensory experience as the truth of reality, but is taking from phenomenology the insight that, truth must be contained in our phenomenal experience, and that the distinction between phenomenal experience and "noumenal" reality is a distinction that only we can create. As a starting point this serves two purposes. First, by starting from the point of view of average everydayness, Heidegger cannot make the mistake of establishing, or trying to establish, the conscious self simply as an observer in the world. Dasein is not the subject. It is a fact of experience that we experience ourselves as immersed in a world.[16] We may ask, is the world exactly as we see it? But we may not doubt the existence of the world. To do so contradicts the foundation of everyday experience. Secondly, from the starting point of average everydayness Heidegger's world cannot become a simple function of the subject consciousness. Our experience of the world demonstrates that our subjectivity is derived from involvement. The reduction of the self, its objectification as a subject, and the separation between self and the world are the principal sources of the difficulty experienced by Cartesian theorists of the self. An understanding of the significance of the constitution of Dasein as possibility is vital to understanding Heidegger's ontology, which is made up not of a system of things with qualities and essence, but existents with a multiplicity of ways of being their Beings[17] (what they are). Heidegger describes possibility like this,

> Possibility expresses the relationship of the object with all its determinations, that is of the entire reality, to the understanding, to mere thinking. (Ibid, p. 46)

Heidegger rejects the search for essence both in the act, and in the subject, and in so doing refuses to objectify either. All entities, including the self, are to be interpreted *in situ* with a constant refusal to crystallise any fundamental objective individual essence. We must examine the phenomena, which make up our experience, to see what they reveal about the world. In this way we develop ontology, an idea of how things may be over and above the simple description of what we see, and an understanding of how it is that they exist. Heidegger wants to go beyond description into the disclosure of fundamental being, this is the move from phenomenology to ontology and the point at which the breach with Husserl is located.[18] Phenomenology, for Heidegger, is a method, its object is to let things show themselves as they are, and how they are possible (ontology). This means that only as phenomenology is ontology really possible. Furthermore, the deeper meaning of phenomenology is interpretation, hence the equation which comes to characterises Heidegger's method;

Phenomenology = ontology = hermeneutics.

Hermeneutics enables Heidegger to give primacy to the taking from and returning to everydayness. Everydayness is the referential context for Being and its interpretation. It is Heidegger's firm belief that no success will be gained by attempting to move outside the appropriate referential context, and, only by clinging to the value of everydayness, is an interpretation of Being possible. As he says,

> We say that the Dasein does not first need to turn backward to itself as though, keeping itself behind its own back, it were at first standing in front of things and staring rigidly at them. Instead, it never finds itself otherwise than in the things themselves, and in fact in those things that daily surround it. (Ibid, p. 159)

The other significant feature of traditional phenomenological method, which Heidegger imports into his own theories, is *Mineness*.[19] The interpretation of Being begins with the interpretation of the Being of the individual, because, through its own self consciousness, individual Dasein can be aware of Being itself and is able to question itself in its own Being.[20] In true Heideggerian style, we should say that it cannot be unaware of itself because this is the average everydayness of self consciousness. Mineness is inherited from the phenomenological roots of Heidegger's thinking. It is *my* interpretation of the phenomena that Heidegger studies. The disclosure of the world is a revelation of what *I* see, hear, feel, etc. Hence the phenomena appear as "mine", within the context of my sensory fields, so that,

> The Dasein exists in the manner of being-in-the-world and as such *it is for the sake of its own self*. It is not the case that this being just simply is; instead so far as it is, it is occupied with its own capacity to be. (Ibid, p. 170)

Experience cannot be understood at all except as phenomenally specific to an individual consciousness. There is no more possibility of doubting that I exist as an individual than there is in doubting that there is a world at all. We might question the exact nature of the thing, or even its "thingness", but not its existence.

Heidegger's ontology means that he does not really belong to the "Phenomenological School". He is interested in what makes phenomenology possible. Traditional phenomenology, as the careful description of the contents of our experience, betrays itself by refusing to question its own possibility. The possibility of phenomenological investigation itself must imply engagement with, or involvement in, a world of entities. This, for Heidegger, is the beginning of the revelation of ontological knowledge. The precise status of these entities may be a suitable subject for investigation but only premised on the fact of our actual and inescapable involvement as part of the world which they constitute.[21] Phenomenology is therefore only possible on the basis of involvement in the world and provides the route by which we may leave everydayness and study the possibility of this involvement. Fundamental phenomenological ontology is impossible with Cartesian phenomenology, because it refuses the possibility of investigating the possibility which forms its origin. Heidegger's phenomenology attempts to allow the phenomena to disclose what is there, without preconception, and, in so doing, makes the phenomenological "ontological". We are enabled to see things as they appear in the necessary context of our involvement with entities in the world, and therefore to understand the nature of this involvement and our being-in-it. This means that Heidegger's ontology will not look like traditional ontology with its clear definition and determinations, it will never have the satisfying completeness of the, "this-is-what-it-is" way of thinking, Heidegger's way is more akin to a "this-is-what-it-can-be" answer.[22] It is true that Heidegger's "things" do not look like the things-in-themselves of the Kantian world, even if we could see them, but this only serves to illustrate that Heidegger both takes over and rejects that tradition. For Heidegger there can be no self contained, self referential and independent things-in-themselves, because this kind of evasion of the referential context of the world is an impossible self deception. The answer to the question, is Heidegger a phenomenologist? Is the answer to the question, is there, can there be, phenomenological ontology?

Heidegger can practise phenomenological ontology because the only sense of phenomenology is that it leads to ontology, not to the kind of ontology that those who came before Heidegger hoped for, but to a more or less accurate notion of the world as it is, in all its unevenness, complexity and unfinishedness. Before going on to Heidegger's implementation of phenomenological method in this way I will now briefly consider the remaining preliminaries to Heidegger's analysis of everyday being.

Preliminaries to Heidegger's Preliminary Analysis of Dasein

The point of origin of Heidegger's work in *Being and Time* and *The Basic Problems of Phenomenology* is the rejection of the Cartesian position in the most fundamental sense.[23] Heidegger will not address the question "What is it?" with regard to Being, because this is the beginning of the exit from everydayness which leads to Cartesian epistemology. At the beginning of *Being and Time* he makes his aim plain, if not clear, "Our aim in the following treatise is to work out the question of the meaning of *Being* and to do so concretely" (Heidegger, 1987, H. 1). Rather than trying to find out what it (Being) *is* Heidegger wishes to know what it *means*, or what makes it possible.[24] Heidegger is looking to clarify that which underlies the multifarious ways of being of entities in the world, including consciousness. As a preliminary to this enterprise he makes two important points in respect of the way that the question stands under the prevailing tradition. First, the question of the meaning of Being has been obscured by the search for essence in the Cartesian tradition. The constant search for essence has misdirected efforts away from the meaning of Being and concealed the question almost altogether. The question of the meaning of Being and the understanding of what makes Being possible are devalued in the tradition which regards the work of clarification and differentiation of the contents of Being as paramount. Heidegger's second point is more positive and reminds us of the vague everyday understanding of Being which we already have. Being is familiar to everyone but only indeterminately. This is at least a beginning, and a beginning without which further progress is impossible. The simple fact of *Being* and our awareness of this Being is sufficient in itself to fuel our own enquiry into what it is to be. It is with the vague indeterminate understanding of everyday Being that Heidegger begins. In particular, the everyday understanding of the being of individual consciousness, the Being which can question itself in its own being. He denotes this perspective by his term *Dasein*. This term will bear further clarification but, for the moment, all that needs to be said is that this is not the Cartesian subject denoted by the *cogito*.

Heidegger's work is subject to considerable terminological difficulties. The philosophical tradition, which he rejects, has moulded not only explicit theory, but also language and thinking itself. Heidegger discusses experience and everyday Being in a way that is difficult to accommodate with the systems of thought that he inherits from the tradition. His work in *Being and Time* and elsewhere subverts the subject/object dichotomy, which has come down from Descartes and thereby sets problems not only for those who wish to understand his work but also, inevitably, those who wish to criticise. In particular, because of the dynamic nature of Heidegger's analysis of experience, terms usually used as nouns, in the tradition I have so far studied, will be used as verbs by Heidegger. Most notably, Being will be used in the sense of Be-ing rather than as an object (or subject) for enquiry. This change of sense will become apparent as the detail of Heidegger's analysis is set out. The terminological problem indicates, obliquely, the radical nature of Heidegger's work, in that, from the beginning it is an attempt to reject and refute a tradition, which had not only dominated philosophical theory but language and systems of thought, which extend far beyond such theory, and which penetrate far into common understanding.[25]

Although Heidegger, as I have already indicated, will use some philosophical methods familiar to the tradition, including phenomenology, he will do so in a way unacceptable in the tradition. Heidegger may be understood to focus on the interaction between Being and the world rather than on the world, or on Being, separately. This is so except for the fact that Heidegger refuses to acknowledge such a space in the terms given by the tradition, and even to explain the difference between a Heideggerian and traditional post-Cartesian phenomenology in such terms is to fail to appreciate the extent to which Heidegger's work subverts the Cartesian tradition. They speak different languages.[26]

Heidegger's methods make his work unapproachable along some of the usual critical avenues and it is important to understand how, and whether, he is successful in gaining this immunity from criticism. I will try to show how Heidegger's work can be approached critically, that is, to show what criticism can be made without simply invoking the tenets of the Cartesian tradition which he rejects.[27] Whatever the conclusion it is obvious that Heidegger is trying something different, posing and answering different questions, and it is only rarely possible to make parallels between the arguments that are put forward by Heidegger and those used by Descartes, Hume, Kant and even Sartre. It is pointless to expect Heidegger's conclusions to be valid in Cartesian terms and consequently the value of Heidegger's position, and the validity of his theory, will more often than not be given indirectly in terms of its relative success in areas where the Cartesians fail, for example the problems of knowledge and personal identity, and the extent to which it can be seen to explain the genesis of the Cartesian position. In particular the notion of the self, and the relation between the self and the not-self, provides a testing focus for both Cartesian and Heideggerian approaches. In this context I will seek to demonstrate how the Cartesian notion of the self is derived from authentic Heideggerian selfhood.

In the next section I will set out Heidegger's preliminary analysis of Dasein (given in Division One of *Being and Time*) which will serve as an alternative to Cartesian epistemology and answer some of the difficulties encountered by this tradition, both by refusing to generate the problem of knowledge and by providing an alternative interpretation of experience, and which will, in turn, reflect an alternative model of the self.

Absence Makes the World Appear

Heidegger's term *Dasein* will, from now, become increasingly prominent in the setting out of his argument. So far I have only tried to indicate what it is not, particularly with regard to similarities between Dasein and the Cartesian subject. It may seem appropriate, or even necessary, before going any further, to more closely define this term, however this would be a mistake. First it would be an attempt to objectify Dasein in a way counter to the force of Heidegger's argument. We do not seek that which *is* Dasein, but to understand what makes it possible. Secondly, an attempt to define Dasein at this point would be an attempt to circumvent the entire project of Heidegger's work in *Being and Time* and elsewhere. The object of the exercise is to set out a

Heideggerian theory of the self as a counter to the models provided by the Cartesian tradition, and the idea of individual Dasein is certainly central to this theory. If we were simply able to define Dasein then there would be no problem. The question, "What is the meaning of Dasein?" is the question to be answered in this chapter and the next. In short, we cannot attempt the conclusion without first making the case. Finally, the attempt to define Dasein misunderstands the way in which the meaning of Heidegger's terms becomes apparent. Heidegger's work is revelatory, a process of continuous clarification, we must allow the notion of Dasein to become clear as we progress in the establishment of Heidegger's phenomenological ontology. Just as we come to know the meaning of entities in the world through our involvement with them so we come to understand the meaning of Heidegger's terms through the use of them in setting out his argument. For the moment we must be satisfied with the "definition" provided by Heidegger at the beginning of *Being and Time*.

> This entity which each of us is himself and which includes inquiring as one of the possibilities of its Being, we shall denote by the term "*Dasein*". (Heidegger, 1987, H.7)

And, "the kind of Being which belongs to Dasein is of a sort which any of us may call his own" (Ibid, H. 42f). Not a lot to be going on with.[28]

Instead of starting with the individual thinking subject Heidegger begins with our own vague understanding of Being. Central to this understanding is the idea that the Being of Dasein is being-in-the-world. Dasein understands itself as in a world, though this understanding is by no means clear.

> Dasein's understanding of Being pertains with equal primordiality both to an understanding of something like a "world", and to the understanding of the Being of those entities which become accessible within the world. (Ibid, H. 13)

Even our vague understanding of our own being tells us that we are in a world.[29] The how and the why of this circumstance will bear further clarification, but our being in the world is beyond dispute.

It is important to understand that Heidegger does not simply assert the fact of being-in-the-world; it is arrived at from the preliminary assessment of Dasein. The question we can ask about the meaning of our own being cannot make sense outside of the concept of a world which we are in. The only evidence that Heidegger has to go on at the beginning of his inquiry is the indication that we have some sort of indeterminate understanding of Being given in the presuppositions we have, and which Heidegger outlined. Although all that this "evidence" gives us is the fact that we are able to question ourselves in our own being, that is, we are self conscious, this is enough for Heidegger. His case almost comes down to the idea that, if we can ask questions about "Being" and "the world" then this presumes that we have some sort of relation to the world, and that this is not separateness, otherwise the questions would not be meaningless but impossible. The attempt by Descartes and others of the tradition, to set asunder those which are already joined together, and then to ask "How can these two separated be joined up?" fails to recognise its error and therefore neglects the potentially more fertile ground of questions like "What does it mean to be?". Heidegger wishes to concentrate on the actual existing relationships he finds in the world, in preference to establishing a secondary structure of subject and object and then attempting to solve the problems created by this structure. It will be his contention, throughout, that he is asking questions and exposing structures of Being that are "primordial", more fundamental than those addressed by the philosophers I have already discussed.

In beginning to look at the way that Heidegger describes the relation between Being and the world the method he employs emerges. A brief examination of the way in which Heidegger interprets work, will demonstrate this. In the world we encounter entities. These entities are one of two types. Present-at-hand, merely there but of no immediate use or relevance to us; or, ready-to-hand, that is existing in an active relation to us and relevant directly to the accomplishment of goals and the carrying out of projects which we see as our own. These entities, ready-to-hand, are seen as *equipment*[30] for us. They are understood in terms of tasks in our practical context. The relevance of this distinction is revealed when we consider the ways in which this relation we have to equipment is manifest.

Heidegger highlights three modes of the being of equipment; these are, *obtrusive, conspicuous*, and *obstinate*. All three are actually ways of not being useful to us as equipment; all three represent ways in which items ready-to-hand fail, in some way, to assist us in our projects. Equipment is obtrusive by its absence. The tool we wish to use for the job in hand makes its presence felt when we cannot find it. Its Being-for-us is revealed by its absence; its Being-as-functioning is made clear and evident by the gap it leaves in the world of our project. Similarly, equipment is conspicuous when, although present, it malfunctions. The axe with the broken handle, the bent screwdriver, the car that will not start, all of these are conspicuous. Their failure to perform highlights their function, and this constitutes their Being-for-us. Obstinate is the item that is in the way. It is an object of our concern not because it is useful directly to us but because the progress of our project demands its removal. It is in the way and will have to be moved. In this way it is imposed on our situation and its Being is illuminated.

What we have here is a kind of notion of "existential Being-residual", an existing rather than essential being, in which Heidegger reveals the being of items through their absence, through their not fulfilling their function, or through their opposition. In this way he avoids the immediate objectification of entities, characteristic of the Cartesian tradition, and allows their meaning to emerge in the light of their relation to Dasein and within the context of this relation. There is no separation of world from the self; Being is simply brought to light, revealed in the context of our projects. Items are disclosed as equipment by the work through which we impose ourselves on the world through our practical concern. Heidegger looks for ways of revealing what is already there, through imaginative ways of looking at simple things that we do, his method combines empiricism, phenomenology, transcendentalism and existentialism, taking from each its strength in the everyday. The implications and power of this methodology will become progressively more evident as we follow Heidegger in his development of the structures of Being-in-the-world.

Alternative Exit

In the sections of *Being and Time* headed "Being-in-the-world in general as the basic state of Dasein" (H. 52-62) and "The Worldhood of the World" (H. 63-113), Heidegger uses the method I have outlined to describe the world and the relation of Being to the world. Being-in-the-world is not like being-in in the strict spatial sense, to understand the relation between being and the world in simple spatial terms would be to misunderstand in the same way that the Cartesians have misunderstood, and to allow the language of the tradition to recapture the analysis. This alternative understanding is important if we are to retain the sense of unity of Being and the world for, as Heidegger says, "Being-in-the-world cannot be broken up into contents which may be pieced together" (Heidegger, 1987, H. 53).

> It is not the case that man "is" and then has, by way of an extra, a relationship-of-Being towards the "world" - a world with which he provides himself occasionally. (Ibid, H. 57)

It is already clear that Heidegger's concepts "Dasein" and "the world" are not equivalent to the individual subject and the world as object, were they to be understood in this way this would precipitate an immediate problem of knowledge.[31] Knowing, says Heidegger, "is a mode of Dasein founded upon Being-in-the-world" (Ibid, H. 62) and so,

> the perceiving of what is known is not a process of returning with one's booty to the "cabinet" of consciousness after one has gone out and grasped it; even in perceiving, retaining, and preserving the Dasein which knows *remains outside* and it does so *as Dasein*. (Ibid, H. 62)

The possible conception of knowledge as such already implies being-in-the-world. As I have already illustrated, "Taking up a relationship towards the world is possible only *because* Dasein, as Being-in-the-world, is as it is" (Ibid, H. 57). Heidegger sees no inside and outside to the world, this kind of relationship of Being to the world is erroneous, a false construct from which we, and philosophy, must be freed by returning to the fundamental question of the meaning of Being. The world is dynamic and constantly in flux, with Dasein taking on modes of Being according to its disposition. As a further consequence of this perspective we can see what Heidegger means when he says, "Because Being-in-the-world belongs essentially to Dasein its Being towards the world is essentially concern" (Ibid, H. 57). *Concern* is the term Heidegger uses to describe the way in which entities in the world become equipment. Concern is the orientation Dasein must have towards the world as a function of its being-in-the-world. Our own projects, Dasein's possibilities, light up the world through our concern with the entities in the world, which we require to complete our satisfaction. No emotive content is given to the term concern, it is an expression used to denote the practical concern we have for the world as a result of our being in it.[32] Our engagement in the world, and our concern, is inescapable.

In demonstrating how Heidegger describes the world in "The Worldhood of the World" (Ibid, H. 63-113), we must return to the notion of equipment to see how this approach, through practical concern, will give us the world, and to see what kind of a world this will be. Equipment is the ensemble of bits and pieces that makes up our world. "We shall call those entities which we encounter in concern - *equipment*" (Ibid, H. 68). Our concern defines what is to be equipment. Therefore, the room - "that which we encounter closest to us" - is not simply the room in spatial and geometric terms, it is illuminated by our concern and becomes "equipment for residing".[33] Language is not a system of signs and meanings but a way in which we communicate. Our actions, our orientations towards these entities, our projects, plans and possibilities, in short our involvement in the world, characterise the entities we encounter in the world. Heidegger's conception of the world is a kind of functionality, so that, to understand things in the world we must deal with them, put them to use, "do" with them, use them as equipment. Above all we must avoid the interpretation of ourselves as separated from the world. This enables Heidegger to make the important distinction, already referred to, between entities present-at-hand, and those ready-to-hand. The distinction is founded not in the entities themselves, nor in Dasein alone, but in the relation of the entities to Dasein.

As we have seen the non-functioning of equipment illuminates the being of entities, their use is disclosed. In the same way the same failures to function illuminate the task in hand. The work, or assignment, is disclosed through the failure of equipment. So, when we find something missing we understand what the ready-to-hand article is, by understanding what it was ready-to-hand for, and not the other way around. Heidegger is then able to go on to say,

> That with which our everyday dealings proximally dwell is not the tools themselves. On the contrary that with which we concern ourselves primarily is the work.

"The work bears with it that referential totality within which equipment is encountered" (Ibid, H. 69). Taken in isolation the failure of the required tool discloses both the Being of the ready-to-hand and the task being undertaken. However in a wider context the entire structural totality of the world can be inferred from the simple example. Heidegger expresses the extrapolation like this.

> The context of equipment is lit up, not as something never seen before, but as a totality constantly sighted beforehand in circumspection. With this totality, however, the world announces itself.

And

> The environment announces itself afresh. What is thus lit up is not itself just one thing ready-to-hand among others;... it is in the "there" before anyone has observed or ascertained it. (Ibid, H. 75)

The individual entities, which we illuminate as equipment through the work that constitutes our projects, can only be understood as part of a much wider referential context. It is not as if we are all operating in isolation with different and disassociated pieces of equipment. The equipment we encounter is the product of the endeavour of someone else, the project of another Dasein. It was made, fashioned by someone, from something, as part of the purpose of the Dasein for which it was disclosed as equipment. It already takes part in the world as the experience of an Other. All the entities we eventually disclose were there already, part of the totality "constantly sighted before in circumspection".[34] Clearly the entire process of the disclosure of the world depends on the notion of revelation through absence, failure or resistance, and the functional structure of the Being of entities in it. Conversely this must allow for the world to remain hidden under certain circumstances. As Heidegger puts it, "If it is to be possible for the ready-to-hand not to emerge from its inconspicuousness, the world *must not announce itself*" (Ibid, H. 75). Heidegger does not say this out of any belief that the world might not announce itself, but to illustrate that the world, or to be precise its "worldhood", is given in the context of the human existence within it. The "worldhood of the world" is the product of the operation of Dasein in its involvement in the world, its actions and its projections. The world is then revealed as a very human place and the unity of Dasein and the world is further reinforced.

But if the world can, in a way, be lit up, it must assuredly be disclosed. And it has already been disclosed beforehand whenever what is ready-to-hand within-the-world is accessible for circumspective concern.

> The world is therefore something "wherein" Dasein as an entity already *was*, and if in any manner it explicitly comes away from anything, it can never do more than come back to the world. (Ibid, H. 76)

"Things-in-themselves", the mind/body problem, and questions about how do we know when we know, all these become irrelevant if we understand the world in the terms which Heidegger uses. A structural totality that is progressively disclosed by the operation of our projecting, or standing out in the world. Entities may be worldly as well as natural, and nature may be understood as the sum of entities viewed as present-at-hand, while the world is that which has worldhood through its association with Dasein.

Critics may say that Heidegger has achieved the unity between the world and Dasein simply by making the world the kind of place that can only be understood in terms of such a relation with Dasein. In other words Heidegger's world is simply a derivation of the individual subject's use of it with no overall "reality" or continuity, beyond the individual Dasein. A sort of Berkelian world, which disappears when we glance away.[35] This is not so. Heidegger reveals how the world is revealed to us, and explains how our ordinary actions in the world illustrate how we understand the world in which we live. The way we "do" in the world presupposes our presence in it and it is this "doing" which is the Dasein. The conclusions Heidegger draws are based on an explanation of practice, and that which makes this practice possible. Furthermore Heidegger is not describing the world, and things in it, in the kind of terms usually employed. Heidegger's world is not the natural world of science or the TV documentary. He is describing ways of being, not "things-in-themselves". Ways of being, and the possibilities, or options, that are available to individual Dasein, reveal more about Dasein and about Being in general. By looking at the way that Dasein understands itself as being involved in the world, (a world in which it already is) and by trying to see how this involvement is possible, that is, by looking at the way that entities become equipment through the operation of practical concern, and by seeing what this implies, Heidegger is able to explain the world and to show how it gets its worldhood. He has, in his own terms, begun to exhibit the kind of Being which equipment possesses - a kind of Being which cannot be divorced from Dasein, a kind of Being which, because of Dasein's involvement in the world, exists as a unity with Dasein. Heidegger shows us the process of being-equipment and of being-in-the-world; he gives us a metaphysics of the world and ultimately a foundation for metaphysics.

Before going on to look at the detailed layout of the structure of Being, given by Heidegger under the heading "Care as the Being of Dasein" (Ibid, H. 180-230) it is necessary to examine the way that Heidegger places individual Dasein in the world of Others like itself, and to begin to see the possibilities for *authentic* and *inauthentic* Dasein opened up by this relation. Not surprisingly Heidegger begins by saying,

> the positive interpretation of Dasein which we have so far given already forbids us to start with the formal givenness of the "I", if the purpose is to answer the question of the "who" in a way which is phenomenally adequate. (Ibid, H. 116)

Heidegger's idea of man is very different from those who talk in terms of body and spirit, "man's *'substance'* is not spirit as a synthesis of soul and body; it is rather *existence*" (Ibid, H. 117), and from the discussion of equipment, it is clear that when the world announces itself,

> "Things" are encountered from out of the world in which they are ready-to-hand for Others - a world which is always mine too in advance. (Ibid, H. 118)

This must follow from the deduction of the worldhood of the world from the simple example of individual Dasein and the equipment required for it to effect its projects. But, finally and conclusively, Heidegger says,

> By "Others" we do not mean everyone else but me - those over whom the "I" stands out. They are rather those from whom, for the most part, one does *not* distinguish oneself - those among one is too. (Ibid, H. 118)

Heidegger wishes to avoid the position in which the "I" is taken as the starting point, because this sets the problem of how to get from the isolated individual subject to the "Other". His contention is simply that this supposed isolation is itself an error, and its assumption groundless, according to how we actually find the world.

> Being-with is an existential characteristic of Dasein even when factically no Other is present-at-hand or perceived. Even Dasein's Being-alone is Being-with in the world. The Other can *be missing* only *in* and *for* a Being-with. (Ibid, H. 120)

And "Being missing and 'Being-away' are modes of Dasein-with" (Ibid, H. 121). Just as the absence of entities makes them obtrusive, so absence is a form of the Other's being-present. The world of others is given in the same way as the world of things, it is what Heidegger calls a phenomenological assertion. That it is so is revealed through the interpretation of the phenomena we experience, which shows us the world of the equipment of Others.[36]

The questions, which Heidegger has to answer in this context, are: How to distinguish entities that are already merely present-at-hand from those which are other Dasein? And, How are we to distinguish our own Dasein from that of others? To the first of these questions Heidegger answers,

> But those entities towards which Dasein as Being-with comports itself do not have the kind of Being which belongs to equipment ready-to-hand; they are themselves Dasein. These entities are not objects of concern, but rather of *solicitude*. (Ibid, H. 121)

This seems to deflect the question by saying that we already do have a distinct relation to other Dasein. The fact that Dasein has, as one of its possibilities, a mode of Being towards others with the same kind of Being (Dasein), and that this mode of Being is different to that which Dasein has towards other entities, those which may be equipment, points to the difference in the world between, entities which may be equipment, and other Dasein, though once again we must be careful not to objectify Dasein or the entities which make up the world. Both exist as possible ways of being, not as things-in-themselves or isolated essence. This may become clearer on consideration of Heidegger's answer to the second question, which says,

> The phenomenological assertion that, "Dasein is essentially Being-with" has an existential-ontological meaning. It does not seek to establish ontically that factically I am not present-at-hand alone, and that Others of my kind occur. (Ibid, H. 120)

Heidegger is trying to say that the questions I have posed above do not need to be answered because the fundamental way of Being of Dasein is Being-with-Others, and Others with the same kind of Being as Dasein. Heidegger admits that this can create problems for Dasein, and that Dasein-as-Being-with, by using the same equipment as other Dasein, can lead to the apparent dissolution of individual Dasein.

We care about how we stand in relation to the Other in this relation of Being-with; we notice a difference between ourselves and Others like us, because there is a difference. Heidegger calls this *distantiality*.[37] The alternative to standing out in the world of Others appears to be to disappear into it, to take over, passively, the world as we find it. In effect the world we encounter is already made up of entities present-at-hand, and, ready-to-hand, these entities have already been given meaning as equipment through the operation of the Dasein of Others.[38] We do not have to make our world, we find it and lose ourselves in it, but this is to lose the distance between ourselves and Others, however Heidegger argues that this loss is not fundamental to our way of being and,

> The *ontologically* relevant result of our analysis of Being-with is the insight that the "subject character" of one's own Dasein and that of Others is to be defined existentially - that is, in terms of certain ways in which we may be. In that with which we concern ourselves environmentally the Others are encountered as what they are; they *are* what they do. (Ibid, H. 126)

This now begins to make possible distinct notions of *authentic* and *inauthentic* Dasein. When we encounter the world we have a choice; to stand out in the relation of Being-with, to impose our own possibilities on the world, and to give our own meanings to the entities we find as equipment, or, to accept what we find and to attempt to dissolve distantiality and submerge our own Dasein into that of "the they".[39] In taking on the way of Being of "the they" Dasein is disburdened, disburdened of the need to create its own meanings, to stand out in the world, to be spontaneous. Everyone becomes no-one, "the they". Heidegger's notions of authenticity and inauthenticity are grounded on this opportunity of Dasein, as he says of Dasein, in the mode of Being of "the they", "In these modes one's way of Being is that of inauthenticity and failure to stand by one's Self"(Ibid, H. 128).

> The Self of everyday Dasein is the *they-self*, which we distinguish from the *authentic Self* - that is, from the Self which has been taken hold of in its own way. (Ibid, H. 129)

Authenticity is the standing out of individual Dasein from the Dasein of others by the disclosure of the world through the application of the projects of the individual Dasein in a world it finds already in place. Authenticity and inauthenticity are ways, or forms, of Being.[40] As we will see this is only part of what it is to be authentic. How authentic Dasein is possible and how it is further constituted will only become apparent when the analysis of Dasein proceeds beyond the everyday. It is not the world we actually disclose or give meaning to, not the result of this process, which distinguishes individual Dasein but the operation of the process itself. We may adopt the meanings we find already in the world, but to be authentic we must do so actively and positively, as opposed to the passive acceptance of the ways of being of "the they". We may all arrive at the same end point in our illumination of the world, but we must all have made our own way there. As we shall see as the

Heideggerian case unfolds, Heidegger is not concerned with which meanings we adopt or refuse, his notion of authenticity is solely concerned with the way in which we orientate ourselves to the world we find, it is about how we do and not what we do.[41] I will now examine how this preliminary setting out of Heidegger's system impacts on the problem of knowledge and the spatiality of the self.

The Epistemological Project

The problem of knowledge as encountered in the work of Descartes, Hume and Kant is a product of the search for a foundation for human knowledge. This search is well described by Richardson in his book *Existential Epistemology* as the "Epistemological Project".[42] It is the problem of the relation between self and world, a problem of the possibility of spatial relation.

To begin with our everyday experience becomes unsatisfactory when we notice that it cannot always be relied upon to guide us through the world. Things are not always what they seem, perceptual error is common in everyday experience and the contents of experience are recognised as highly conditional, variable according to circumstances and an uncertain foundation on which to project actions and their outcomes. However this is how we are *"proximally and for the most part"*, as Heidegger would say,[43] and it is with this everyday experience that we must begin and with this pragmatic approach to the problem that we must proceed. In everyday experience we are involved with the world in a fundamentally practical way, we operate in the world using the entities we find there. In this unreflective way of being we encounter and use objects in the world according to the purposes we have. We behave as if we exist in a world of entities with which we can interact according to our choice. We do not theorise about the actual existence of these entities, nor the ground for the possibility of our relation with them. To do so would appear irrelevant to the project in hand, even perverse. We know entities according to what we use them to do, and the ways in which they impact on our own existence. This is the beginning of Hume's investigation, the search for a justification for these commonsense assumptions and beliefs, the problem of how to-be-in-the world.

At this point it is important to recognise a vital difference between a Kantian (which is essentially Cartesian) and a Heideggerian way of understanding everyday experience. For Kant concepts and their mastery are essential to the understanding of experience, concepts enable us to form the world into something meaningful. For Heidegger ends, and the relation of entities to ends is the foundation of everyday experience, we come into a world that is already operating, orientated and illuminated by us. In fact Heidegger says,

> The ego is not one among the categories of beings but the condition of the possibility of categories in general (Heidegger, 1982, p.128-129)

and

> I am already conscious of this ego as "I experience" the ontological ground of the possibility of all experiencing. (Ibid, p. 129)

Under the Heideggerian analysis entities are given in one of two ways. They are either ready-to-hand, or present-at-hand. Entities present-at-hand become ready-to-hand at any time which we become involved with them. Similarly, the ready-to-hand may lapse into present-at-hand as we move on. This distinction can be made in order to differentiate between an understanding of entities from the subjective point of view, ready-to-hand, and an understanding apart from their involvement with any particular subject, present-at-hand, though this is not the way in which Heidegger intends the distinction. The way in which this distinction is interpreted has profound consequences for the development of ontology and the way in which the self is understood.

The work of Hume and Kant indicates a dissatisfaction with everydayness and the beginning of a search for unconditional knowledge, not dependent on the whims (projects) of individuals but somehow unconditional. This is characterised in the Cartesian tradition as objective knowledge and the approach itself is called the theoretical attitude. If we understand everyday being and experience in the way of an arena in which we exist, then the theoretical attitude is the search for an exit from this arena, from the domination of the subjective point of view and conditionality, to a (transcendental) position in which entities can be seen for what they really are. This is the realm of Kant's thing-in-itself and we are propelled towards it as a result of our dissatisfaction with the everyday. This particular exit from everydayness, towards the *essential* understanding of entities primarily as present-at-hand, is the one chosen by the Cartesians, and is the root of their difficulties with the understanding of experience. It is the very attempt to escape from everydayness that frustrates Cartesians in their attempt to provide a more satisfactory understanding of experience. Kant recognises this frustration and its inevitability and therefore does not seek knowledge of things-in-themselves, redefining objectivity within the sphere of phenomenal experience.

The question "What is it?" is central to the Cartesian epistemological project and it is constituted as a question by the attempt to separate entities from their context in everydayness. This is driven by a belief that it is not only possible, but necessary, that entities can be understood independently of all other entities, and involvements with those entities, including self-conscious entities who use them, in short, the belief that entities must be rendered self supporting and self subsistent. This belief powers the drive towards unconditional knowledge and under it the Cartesian self, based on the *cogito*, becomes the ultimate isolated entity - a self supporting, self- subsistent and self conscious being. In Heidegger's terms the epistemological project attempts to render all entities present-at-hand, that is in disassociation from all involvements, and this extends not only to hammers and other such tools, but also to perceiving and projecting entities like self-conscious human beings. We have seen how Hume attempts to find his identity apart from his sensations, how Descartes isolates his consciousness behind the *cogito* and finally how Kant affirms the existence of the thing-in-itself so devoid of subjective content that it cannot even be known by the subject. We have also seen the difficulties encountered by all of these philosophers, difficulties which become so evidently intractable when attention is turned to the question of the self. In the Cartesian tradition the self is made object because of, and by the fact of, being made subject. In effect the epistemological project is betrayed by the exit from everydayness chosen by the Cartesian theoretical attitude. Entities are understood in everydayness, this is, and should remain, the foundation of our understanding and knowledge of entities. By divorcing entities from this context the project ends, at a stroke, any possibility of understanding, by removing the foundation of understanding. The epistemological project is an enquiry, which begins because of dissatisfaction with everyday experience and effectively ends as soon as experience is removed from its everyday context. It is self defeating. Entities which were known uncertainly in everyday experience, once removed from the encounters and involvements that led to their discovery, become inaccessible.[44] There is no transparent access to the being of these entities as they really are once this route is taken. They become *merely* present-at-hand. While the theoretical attitude of the Cartesians places such a high premium on tearing entities from involvement it fails to recognise that this involvement is central to any possible understanding of the entities and the being with which they are involved. As Richardson puts it, "It is our competent striving towards the ends that may be 'realised' with hammers, for example, that lays out what it is for something to be a hammer" (Richardson, 1986, p.29). How else are we to know what a hammer is? Furthermore,

> Only because we are "attuned" in some particular manner, can the entities we encounter matter to us in the definite ways they do - because it is only as mattering to us that we encounter these entities in our everyday way, such

attunement is a further "condition of the possibility" for our everyday experience. (Ibid, p. 33)

It should be self-evident that the theoretical attitude and the whole of the epistemological project is centred on the removal of this condition and hence destroys the possibility of the experience it seeks to refine. It can therefore have nothing to say about this experience, and, as we have already seen, produce no knowledge not because this knowledge is not accessible but because this is precisely the kind of thing which knowledge is *not*.

The mistake is repeated in respect of the self, and this is at the root of the Cartesian problems with notions of the self. The self, in Heidegger, will turn out to be not the sort of thing they thought it was going to be. It will, essentially, be no sort of thing at all. Kant was correct in saying that we can have no knowledge of things-in-themselves, if only because we must be able to become involved with entities before we can begin to know them. Knowing them is knowing what it is to be involved with them. But we cannot know without the possibility of involvement, hence the thing-in-itself remains not open to us. Knowing is always, and must be, conditional. The Cartesian epistemological project fails,

> because for it theory comes first, before fulfilling the requirement to open our eyes and take the phenomena as they offer themselves as against all firmly rooted theory and even despite it, that is, the requirement to align theory according to the phenomena rather than the opposite, to do violence to the phenomena by a pre-conceived theory. (Heidegger,1982, p. 62)

Cartesian theory of the self makes assumptions about the nature of the self, in particular that it is the subject. This pre-conceived theory does not accord with the phenomenal experience of selfhood so graphically described by Hume, Kant and Sartre, in their different ways.

Heidegger's interpretation of experience is not simply an alternative to the Cartesian epistemological project it also provides an explanation of how, and why, this project arises in the first place and why, and how, this particular theoretical attitude is favoured. We have seen how the theoretical attitude seeks to understand entities as *merely* present-at-hand, despite the fact that in our everyday experience the meaning of these entities is given in their being ready-to-hand. The theoretical attitude renders entities as objects to establish unconditional knowledge in order to serve the purpose of more easily pursuing and gaining the everyday ends we seek.[45] The theoretical attitude provides us with a means to disconnect entities from the context and to apply them to different uses; our mistake begins when we begin to take this disconnected understanding as fundamental and as somehow giving us access to the being of the entity. We need the assumption of unconditionality in order to be able to operate within the everyday context, diminished understanding for a diminished context, but we must never make the mistake of taking this for far more than it really is. The aim of the theoretical attitude is to establish a framework in which a more generalised control of the environment can be achieved, it is an attempt to render entities adaptable to all, or at least many, purposes and suitable for engagement in Dasein's projects. Under the Cartesian theoretical attitude entities are to be understood only as present-at-hand, that is devoid of context.

Yet the knowledge thus acquired in the epistemological project is intended for use in precisely this context. For this use to be possible the notion of purpose in general must already be apparent - it must already exist in everyday particular to give rise to this generalisation or thematization. That is, the epistemological project itself assumes the notion of purpose in order for any particular purpose to be manifest in the everyday, and for this to be possible the notion of purpose must be inherent in the everyday in advance of the framing of the epistemological project. Primacy is thus returned to the everyday. Moreover the theoretical attitude must eventually come to rest on the kind of purpose and *concernful understanding* from which it attempts to sever the objects of its enterprise, that is if it is ever to become purposeful. At every turn, and despite all its efforts, the Cartesian epistemological project finds itself entwined in everyday conditionality. It is its beginning and its end, and without this the project is meaningless. Despite its own best efforts theory is always founded on being-in-the-world, and consequently, when Cartesian epistemology, as theory of knowledge, misinterprets its situatedness and attempts to deny it, it is impelled towards scepticism. Once the connection between entities and Dasein has been broken, like Humpty Dumpty, no amount of philosophers can stick them together again. Cartesian epistemology fails to explain, and to recover, the world because of its reliance on narrowly present-at-hand interpretations which try to ignore situatedness and lead eventually to scepticism or solipsism. It is a method that must deny it own purpose. It is responsible both for the questions posed by the epistemologist and the unavailability of answers. As Richardson says,

> it is precisely the features of our everydayness responsible for the theoretical attitude's dissatisfaction with it, that also prevent that attitude from grasping this everydayness in its present-at-hand terms. (Richardson, 1986, p. 97)

The theorist cannot escape concernful understanding; the mistake is to think that this escape is possible. The kind of knowledge that the epistemological project provides is not the transparent apprehension of reality it purports to be. Instead it is a distorted and diminished version confined to the narrows of the present-at-hand and suitable only for a narrow range of possible involvements with the world. Like a series of snapshots with little or no apparent connection between each item and lacking the dynamic element which characterises experience, it is knowledge of, and for, the everyday and is no better, and often worse, than the commonsensical beliefs it sets out to improve upon. The consequences of this "attitude" for Cartesian notions of the self are a diminished selfhood, and a preoccupation with either the object-ness of the bodily self, or the spirituality of the subject.[46]

Heidegger's alternative response to the dissatisfaction with the everyday begins with the everyday and is grounded in the everyday. Concernful understanding or involvement is kept at the centre of the interpretation of experience in order that distortions and misunderstandings do not creep in. In place of the epistemological project Heidegger interprets experience as the history and possibility of involvements, as an alternative exit from everydayness.

Heidegger's work on Kant is particularly revealing of his radical departure from the Cartesian tradition. In his *Kant and the Problem of Metaphysics* he questions the very basis of the Cartesian epistemological project.[47] Whereas Kant in the *Critique of Pure Reason* is attempting to provide a foundation for metaphysics Heidegger says that,

> it is precisely this representation which we must keep out of the idea of a ground laying, namely that it is the matter of the byproduct from the foundation of an already-constructed building. Ground-laying is rather the projecting of the building plan itself so that it agrees with the direction concerning on what and how the building will be grounded. (Heidegger, 1990, p.2)

And...

> Laying the ground as the projection of the inner possibility of metaphysics is thus necessarily a matter of letting the supporting power of the already-laid ground become operative. (Ibid, p. 2)

It is as if Kant fails to see the implications of his own work, implications which Heidegger makes explicit, and, in so doing, dissolves the problems encountered by Kant. Experience is a process and is not just about entities and consciousness. Experience happens, it is not something that *is*. The self becomes the happening of experience. Kant's bifurcated self and Hume's sheer perplexity about his own identity[48] arise because both are looking for a "self" that can be identified as object (or subject). With his transcendentalism Kant comes closer than Hume, but only because the self is the transcending itself. Heidegger recognises that for transcendence to be possible there must be a Being the essence of which is transcending. While Kant and Hume look closely for that which is the movement in the escalator, Heidegger watches the world go by and understands what it is to move.

Preliminary Conclusions with Regard to Heidegger's Preliminary Analysis of Dasein

At this point it is possible to draw some preliminary conclusions with regard to Heidegger's work in *Being and Time* and *The Basic Problems of Phenomenology*, conclusions with respect to the Being of everyday Dasein. These conclusions must necessarily be sketchy since they precede examination of the analysis of authentic Dasein given in the second Division of *Being and Time*, and the discussion of temporality in Part Two of *The Basic Problems of Phenomenology*. Even so it is already evident that the route of enquiry taken by Heidegger is less problematic and more fruitful than that chosen by the Cartesian tradition.

By the end of the first Division of *Being and Time* and Part One of *The Basic Problems of Phenomenology* Heidegger has not answered the problem of knowledge, his work has not contributed to the Cartesian epistemological project; on the contrary it has questioned the project at the most fundamental level. In particular Heidegger has re-focused phenomenology, directing attention to the possibility of Dasein. He has undermined the Cartesian position and brought the epistemological project into question. In the context of Kant's work Heidegger has provided an alternative demonstration of what it is that makes experience, and the understanding of experience, possible. There is no question as to how the evidence of my senses can be verified; this is not how phenomenology works. There is no "veil of the senses" and the problems formulated by the Cartesians are both insoluble and yet presuppose their own solutions. That is they fail both to prove Being-in-the world and are premised on Being-in-the-world. As Heidegger says,

> Dasein exists in the manner of *being-in-the-world*, and this *basic determination of its existence* is the *pre-supposition for being able to apprehend anything at all*. (Heidegger, 1982, p.164)

Heidegger's analysis of everyday Dasein is simply the use of phenomenal experience to illuminate Being, not an attempt to see what it is that the phenomena conceal. Heidegger chooses to see what others have refused to see.

In relation to early Cartesians (Descartes and Hume) Heidegger's concentration on the meaning of Being, as opposed to its essence, de-fuses the problem of knowledge. Entities are what they become, and what they become cannot be disassociated from the consciousness with which they are involved. In respect of Kant's *Critique of Pure Reason* Heidegger argues that experience is not given through the application of categories but as a result of the necessary involvement of Dasein in a world in which it already finds itself. Without such involvement no experience is possible. Heidegger shows how categories are possible in the first place. The signs of this involvement, phenomena, provide the starting point, and the only viable starting point, for the understanding of the world. Knowledge comes through the interpretation of phenomena and knowing is a way of being of Dasein. Phenomena are the window on the world. Heidegger shows that phenomenology can only be ontology, and that ontology can only come from phenomenology. However the kind of ontology, which results from Heidegger's analysis, is not like the ontology sought by the Cartesians. We do not discover what things really are, or their essential nature. Heidegger makes no attempt to isolate unconditional knowledge of entities in the world; the present-at-hand is not elevated to this pinnacle. On the contrary we are forced to consider entities in relation to other entities including Dasein and to focus not on entities at all but on their coming together. Contextuality is the key to understanding, and not the attempt to de-contextualise. In the everyday, entities are multi-functional, multi-relational, everything and no-thing.

The analysis in Division One of *Being and Time* is concerned with everyday Dasein and as such adds to our understanding of Heidegger's use of both these terms. So far we have been unable to say any more of Dasein than to deny that it is the Cartesian subject and that it *is* what *we are*. Following the analysis of everyday Dasein we must go further. Dasein is like a space in which things let themselves be seen. If the phenomenal world is like a wood crowded with trees then Dasein is the clearing in the forest, the space in which phenomena are made manifest. Dasein itself is how it chooses to be and its way of Being determines which involvements it will have and which entities will emerge from the present-at-hand and come to be ready-to-hand, but it is the choosing itself which makes Dasein what it is. Dasein is not the transcendental ego of the Kantian world, it is the transcendence itself. In Heidegger's terms, as existing, Dasein is standing out in the world. In a way that is to say nothing at all of Dasein, it is a formal analysis.

Entities are illuminated by Dasein and thereby show themselves in the clearing which is Dasein. Hume seems to have had an inkling of such a notion when he said in the *Treatise*,

> The mind is a kind of theatre, where several perceptions successively make their appearance; pass, repass, glide away and mingle in an infinite variety of postures and situations. (Hume, 1959, Vol.I, p. 239-240)

However Hume then goes on to suggest that we must not be misled by this analogy.

> The comparison of the theatre must not mislead us. They are the successive perceptions only, that constitute the mind; nor have we the most distant notion of

the place where these scenes are represented, or of the materials of which it is composed. (Ibid, p. 240)

It is as if Hume can see the answer and yet is unable to recognise it. At this point there is very little separating the positions of Hume and Heidegger. Hume's theatre is Heidegger's clearing. The difference is in the conclusions they draw from their observations. Heidegger recognises involvement as the key to understanding the mind, as Dasein. Hume recoils and continues the fruitless search for the essence of selfhood.[49] Hume is seeking to constitute the self as the contents of being while Heidegger is content to rest with its form. Experience is possible because of the involvement of Dasein in the world, or, even more accurately, because of the approachability of Dasein. For there to be experience Dasein must be the kind of Being which is open to disclosure, capable of being approached. Without this approachability the world could not announce itself, could not be disclosed to Dasein. Everyday experience leads therefore to the first concrete conclusion about Dasein, that is, the Being of Dasein is being-in-the-world and,

> The idea of a subject which has intentional experiences merely inside its own sphere and is not yet outside it but encapsulated within itself is an absurdity which misconstrues the basic ontological structure of the being which we ourselves are. (Heidegger, 1982, p. 64)

"For the Dasein there is no outside, for which reason it is also absurd to talk about an inside" (Ibid, p. 66). This is the form of everyday being.

The preliminary analysis of Dasein ends with the conclusion that the Being of Dasein is *Care*, a term denoting Dasein's necessary involvement in the world of entities. Care is the way of being which all Dasein must share. Care is the metaphysical basis of experience. If Dasein exists then it exists in the form of Care, and, "the totality of Being-in-the-world as a structural whole has revealed itself as care" (Heidegger, 1987, H.231). Again this seems to express very little about Dasein, but it is the move from the idea of Being which is separated, or at least separable, from the world to the idea of Being which is inextricably connected to, and involved in, the world, constituted in fact as this involvement. From the *cogito*, to Care as the meaning of the Being of Dasein, is a world of progress that provides the ground for the development of a notion of the self outside the Cartesian tradition. Premised on Dasein, as Being-in-the world, a Heideggerian theory of the self will encounter none of the problems of knowledge encountered by the Cartesians. The problem of knowledge evaporates once the perspective of the self "outside" the world disappears. As being-in-the world Dasein cannot take this perspective, it is already in the world as Being-alongside.

But this is only the preliminary analysis of Dasein and at the end of Division One of *Being and Time* Heidegger is quick to insist that this is not the end of the story. The Cartesian epistemological project is confounded in the first Division of *Being and Time*, but Heidegger has not yet put forward a complete alternative, only the grounds for doing so. This has been only the analysis of Dasein in everydayness. The issue of the space of the self is settled, for the moment, by Heidegger's notion of being-in-the-world. However it is already clear that experience is about more than just space. Experiences are successive, the world and Dasein appear as framed in time and it is this succession which both confounds Hume in his discussion of personal identity and to which Heidegger turns in Division Two of *Being and Time* and Part Two of *The Basic Problems of Phenomenology*. In order to flesh out "Dasein", the analysis must be deepened. We must now go forward and see how Heidegger interprets Dasein in temporality and authenticity and how this avoids the pitfalls of subjectivism with regard to the self and relativism with regard to the world.

Notes

1. Descartes Letters to Princess Elizabeth, in Descartes, 1988, Vol. III, p. 218 and pp. 227-228.
2. Descartes, "Sixth Meditation" (Descartes, 1986, p.56).
3. Sartre, 1956, pp. 252-302.
4. Ibid, pp. 233-252. Also, Fell, 1979, Part One, pp. 29-93.
5. All page references to *Being and Time* use the pagination of the later German editions, as shown in the outer margins of the text and are prefaced "H".
6. Also see other works of this period including, Heidegger's *History of the Concept of Time, Kant and the Problem of Metaphysics, Hegel's Concept of Experience, The Essence of Reasons, What is Metaphysics?,* and *Hegel's Phenomenology of Spirit*.
7. Heidegger, 1982, p. 62.
8. See p. 122 and pp. 133-134 for clarification of Heidegger's use of this key term. Also, Schatzki, "Early Heidegger on Being, the Clearing and Realism" (Dreyfus, 1992, Ed.) for some definition of this term. See Richardson, 1986, Chapter One, for a discussion of everydayness as our basic condition, and Zimmerman, 1986, p. 38, on the primacy of everyday life.
9. For a discussion of Heidegger and the Phenomenological School see, Spiegelberg, 1960, pp. 271-353, and Waterhouse, 1981, Part One. For opposing discussions of Heidegger's place in the philosophical tradition see, Rorty, "Overcoming the Tradition: Heidegger and Dewey", and, Okrent, "The Truth of Being and the History of Philosophy" (Dreyfus, 1992, Ed.).
10. See Dreyfus and Haugeland, "Husserl and Heidegger: Philosophy's Last Stand", (Murray, 1978, Ed.) and, Habermas, 1987, Lecture Six: "The undermining of Western Rationalism: Heidegger".

11. Marx, W, 1971, pp. 85-121.
12. Heidegger's attempt to propose an ontology without presumption echoes Hume's attempt to offer an epistemology without presumption. By attempting to bring into doubt all that cannot be empirically demonstrated Hume finds that common sense beliefs cannot be supported without presumption. Heidegger, unlike Hume, is not sceptical either with regard to the actual existence of the world or the basis for our claim to knowledge of such a world. For Heidegger scepticism is either unnecessary or impossible.
13. Waterhouse, 1981, pp.35-48, "Husserl and Phenomenology" and "Heidegger's Early Development", and Heidegger, 1982, p. 21 and elsewhere.
14. The *Concise Oxford Dictionary* says, "phenomenon - Thing that appears or is perceived, esp. thing that the cause of which is in question; that of which a sense or the mind directly takes note, immediate object of perception". Also see Macquarrie, 1968, p.10, where he describes phenomenology as the "showing of that which shows itself".
15. See Waterhouse's discussion of hermeneutics in both Husserl's and Heidegger's work, in the section headed "Husserl's Development of Phenomenology" in Waterhouse, 1981 pp. 20-34.
16. See Macquarrie, 1968, Everyday being in the world, pp.14-28.
17. It is one of the particular problems of discussing work such as that of Heidegger that there arises a potential confusion around the use of the verb "to be". I have endeavoured to forestall at least some of this confusion by using "Being" to denote the notion of ontological being, and "being" for the everyday use of the verb, however in view of the nature of the whole of Heidegger's enterprise, that is the question of Being, this confusion may not always be wholly avoidable. Also see the translator's first footnote on H. 1 of *Being and Time*.
18. See Harries, "Fundamental Ontology and the Search for Man's Place" for a discussion of Heidegger's going beyond the merely descriptive, and, for a discussion of the relation between Husserl's work and Heidegger, see, Waterhouse, 1981, pp.35-48, and Dreyfus and Haugeland, "Husserl and Heidegger: Philosophy's Last Stand".
19. Waterhouse, 1981, p. 68.
20. Heidegger, 1987, H. 7.
21. Habermas, 1987, pp. 147-149, and Haugeland, "Dasein's Disclosedness".
22. Mulhall, 1996, pp. 5-12 on the role of philosophical enquiry assumed by the Cartesian tradition.
23. For a good exposition of this rejection as a starting point see, Richardson, 1986, especially pp. 80-125, and Mulhall, 1996, especially, Introduction, and Chapter One.
24. For a brief discussion of this aim see Gelven, 1970, pp. 180-189.
25. See the Introduction to Zimmerman, 1986, for a discussion of how far from the tradition Heidegger is attempting to move. Also, Marx, W, 197, 1 Part II.
26. See the interjection by Pos in the Appendix to Heidegger's *Kant and the Problem of Metaphysics* (1990, trans. Taft), p.180.
27. Rorty, "Overcoming the Tradition: Heidegger and Dewey", which begins to raise the kinds of questions we might expect Heidegger to have to answer and suggests

that Heidegger appears to leave no standards intact though which we might judge his own work.
28. However it is already beginning to emerge that Dasein will turn out to be no sort of "thing". See Poggeler, "Being as Appropriation", and Habermas, 1987, p. 142.
29. For a discussion of pragmatism in Heidegger, see Okrent, 1988, Fell, "The Familiar and the strange: On the Limits of Praxis in the Early Heidegger", and Rorty, "Heidegger, Contingency and Pragmatism".
30. Heidegger, 1987, H. 73-76. Also see Dreyfus and Haugeland, "Husserl and Heidegger: Philosophy's Last Stand", for a discussion of equipment and functionality also Richardson, 1986, Chapter Two and Brandom, "Heidegger's Categories in *Being and Time*".
31. Zimmerman says, "The world is the interrelated set of relationships which give form and content to my experience" (Zimmerman, 1986, p.27).
32. Whether Heidegger is successful in achieving this value neutrality for his terms is ultimately doubtful since this is not an isolated instance and is soon joined by such terms as *solicitude*, *care* and eventually *authentic*, all of which Heidegger claims have no ethical content. This is called into serious question by my conclusion with regard to Heidegger's theory of the self in Chapter Nine where the normative nature of Heidegger's position becomes apparent.
33. Heidegger, 1987, H.68.
34. Ibid, H. 75.
35. Waterhouse, 1981, pp.151-161 and Habermas, 1987, pp. 149-150.
36. This is taken up in some detail by Sartre in his discussion of my relation to my fellowman in *Being and Nothingness* (Sartre, 1956, pp. 509-531).
37. Heidegger, 1987, H. 107.
38. See "My Fellowman" and the discussion of technique in Sartre, 1956, pp. 509-514.
39. Heidegger's use of this notion (translated from the German *das Man*), does not represent an actual congregation of other Dasein, it is a way of being open to each Dasein. Others are defined, existentially, in terms of what they do, in the same way that entities are denoted as equipment in view of their function, or use value. In speaking of "the they" we are not dealing here with any common essence shared by all Dasein. The mode of being of "the they" has the character of eliminating distantiality and submerging our Dasein in a world of meanings as we find it. It is made manifest in a kind of preoccupation with the here and now, to the extent that individuality is dissolved into *publicness*. See, Heidegger, 1987, H.126-130 and H. 138.
40. This distinction can usefully be seen to parallel Sartre's Good and Bad Faith in Sartre, 1956, Part One, Chapter Two, and the notion of the alienated self developed by Hegel and Marx, see especially Marx on Estranged Labour in the "Economic and Philosophical Manuscripts" in Marx, K, 1981, pp.322-334.
41. This leads to a kind of moral formalism similar to that found in Kant's ethics, see Kant, 1956, and even the potential "vacuity" of the notion of authenticity, see Waterhouse, 1981, pp.179-192, and, his "A Critique of Authenticity".
42. Richardson, 1986, Chapters One and Two, and, Dreyfus and Haugeland, "Husserl and Heidegger: Philosophy's Last Stand".
43. Heidegger, 1987, H. 16.

44. Hence the apparent contradiction between what we might call common sense epistemology which refuses to question the existence of the physical world because its non-existence is inconceivable, and epistemology based on sceptical doubt which can, for example in the case of Hume, apparently undermine the same belief which drives our refusal to question.
45. The essence of everyday knowledge is the control we seek over our environment, hence we do not question the metaphysics of tools, like hammers, when we come to use them to knock in a nail as part of our project to put up a picture. Universal applicability is the key to the success of this kind of knowledge.
46. In an echo of this Marx says, "In tearing away the object of his production from man estranged labour therefore tears away from him his *species-life*, his true species activity and transforms his advantage over animals into the disadvantage that his inorganic body, nature, is taken from him" in "Estranged Labour", (Marx, K, 1981, p.329). Where species-life is read as authentic Dasein and estrangement, or alienation, is inauthentic being. Either way the individual is rendered incomplete and distanced from true being.
47. See also final section of Chapter Five, pp. 77-87.
48. Hume, 1959, Vol. II, Appendix, pp. 317-320.
49. In similar fashion to the way in which Kant recoils from his potential conclusions about the role of the imagination in experience. See, Heidegger, 1990, Part Three, pp. 87-138.

8

Heidegger - Goldilocks Divined

In the preceding chapter I have shown how the Cartesian Epistemological project saddles itself with a theoretical attitude, which frustrates its very aims. The removal from the context of being-in-the-world immediately removes all possibility of understanding of the entities in question. In application to the self this means that the self can only be understood and studied in the context of being-in-the-world, beyond this context it has no possible basis or meaning. Furthermore, we have seen that, where the Cartesian tradition sacrifices the everyday in the search for essence, Heidegger returns to the everyday as the source of all meaning and attempts an interpretation that will both surpass the everyday and retain its dynamic insights. In Division One of *Being and Time* he seeks to interpret the being of everyday Dasein in order to understand what makes it possible. He arrives at the end of Division One at the notion of Care. Care defines Dasein's position in the world. To use Heidegger's less Cartesian terminology, Dasein is already alongside the world. The perspective of the isolated objective observer is specifically denied, and our understanding of spatiality is radically altered.[1]

Although important features of Heidegger's system are in place by the end of Division One he is quick to point to the inadequacy of the analysis so far. Being-in-the-world and the notion of Care as the meaning of Dasein do no more than unseat the Cartesian tradition. As an explanation of the Being of entities, and the self, the analysis is incomplete, and as an explanation of how experience works it is inadequate. Being-in-the-world alone will not provide a full explanation of experience and what it is to *be*; it contains no notion of the succession of experiences, happening apparently in time.[2] Neither, therefore, can it alone provide the ground for an adequate theory of the self. To achieve this it is necessary to use another philosophical problem. The problem of personal identity, which frustrated Hume, provides not only a focus for exploring temporality, but also brings the entire analysis to bear specifically on the self in a way that opens the possibility of setting out a Heideggerian alternative to the Cartesian model of selfhood. To begin with it will be necessary to see in what ways the analysis in Division One is inadequate and incomplete in order to prepare the ground for the interpretation of authentic Dasein against the horizon of time. Just as in the discussion of knowledge, in the previous chapter, it will be possible to show not only how everyday understandings and structures are surpassed, but also how they arise out of more primordial authentic structures.

I will then be able to set out a Heideggerian model of the self and solve the Goldilocks problem, at least in epistemological and ontological terms. Finally an assessment of the conclusions of Heidegger's work in *Being and Time* will lead to possible avenues of criticism of his work from a somewhat surprising quarter.

A Glimpse of the Grail - The Interpretation of Inauthentic Dasein

It is illustrative to return now to some of Heidegger's explanations of the being of entities in the world. Having seen how he uses some important techniques to unseat Cartesian epistemology I will now examine these techniques in terms of how well they replace the mechanisms of the tradition which they seek to supplant. In other words, how do Heidegger's explanations of how we come to know things in the world stand up to criticism?

The main thrust of Heidegger's argument is the argument from absence, misfunction, or obstruction, that is, he describes how we come to know entities through their not being there, through their failing to function, or being-in-the-way. The terms he employs, conspicuous, obtrusive and obstinate are negative, they are all ways of describing things that do not work as they should and which frustrate rather than facilitate our projects. At first sight this seems to be idiosyncratic and unnecessarily oblique, particularly when it appears that we come to know entities through their not being present and not being useful, the opposite of what we might have expected. We have seen that Heidegger's use of these notions is not simply quirky but is quite deliberate, and is intended to avoid the objectification of the world and the removal from spatial context. Heidegger's own theoretical attitude is to derive understanding and knowledge from use, in relation to the projects of individual Dasein. It is designed to relate everyday experience to a deeper understanding of that experience in preference to the construction of super-experiential structures like Kant's categories and Hume's ideas. Heidegger's method is ingenious but it still fails to grasp the full extent of the being of entities in the world. This is evident if we revisit the kind of examples that Heidegger uses.

The screwdriver which is broken (conspicuous) gives us an understanding of the screwdriver at the moment we attempt to use it: furthermore it gives us the screwdriver as part of the referential context of equipment in general and of the work. This simple use model, while maintaining the entity in its spatial, equipmental and work context, does not say anything about the entity either before, or after, the moment of our involvement. It cannot account for the history of the entity nor encompass its future. It makes no attempt to do so since it is focused on the present use in the everyday. Nor can it account for the history of the work, it is timeless. Timelessness betrays everydayness. The missing part of the jigsaw was not always missing and the obstacle to our progress may operate in a quite different manner at another time. Just as entities exist, and have meaning in the spatial and project referential context of other entities and Dasein, so they have meaning in the temporal context. This temporal dimension has been explicitly absent from the analysis in Division One of *Being and Time*, from the analysis of everyday (inauthentic) Dasein. But entities are related not only to the entities with which they co-exist in time but also to themselves, and to these other entities at other times. History and future are the temporal context of entities, and therefore of Dasein. The analysis of entities and of Dasein given in Division One is momentary understanding only of the "now".[3] This is clear if we consider the way in which entities can be manifest. To understand entities as absent, misfunctioning or obstructive we must have a prior understanding of their effective function. Our attention is not usually drawn to this prior understanding and meaning and the entities do not usually stand out, precisely because their function is seamless with our project. However our attempt at use must be premised on this prior understanding, we must have an idea of what we can do with the equipment we encounter before it can become equipment for use. In short we must learn. Similarly we would not attempt to use entities without some end in view and this end is futural, projected away from the present. In this way Dasein exists in advance of itself and its involvements can only be understood as directed towards a future and grounded in a past. We must have an idea of what we are going to do with the equipment, before it can become equipment. The possibility of our becoming involved with an entity must be founded on an understanding of the history both of the project and the equipment under consideration, and the future towards which we are aiming, without these even the examples of these simple tools have no foundation. They indicate the grounding of Being in Care, but say nothing about that which makes Care itself possible. This is the further interpretation that Heidegger intends in Division Two of *Being and Time* and Part Two of *The Basic Problems of Phenomenology*.[4] Heidegger's work at this point connects directly and explicitly with the Kantian heritage and the close focus on the relationship between Dasein and temporality echoes Kant in the "Schematism" section of the *Critique of Pure Reason*, when he says.

> Thus an application of the category to appearances becomes possible by means of the transcendental determination of time, which as the schema of the concepts of understanding mediates the subsumption of the appearance under the category. (Kant, 1992, A. 139 = B. 178)

Kant recognises the need for a temporal framework if experience is to be possible and, in so doing, in the 'Schematism', attempts to describe structures in which this might be achieved. His only mistake, according to Heidegger, is to think that this is at all necessary. Crucially, for Heidegger, no mediation is required between appearance and category, and it is Kant's inevitable error to think that this mediation is required. Whereas Kant sees the need to lay a foundation for metaphysics, Heidegger only seeks to reveal what is already there, and to interpret its meaning.[5]

By the end of Division One Heidegger has successfully unseated the perspective of the isolated Cartesian subject and opened up the possibility of an alternative non-spectatorial starting point for the understanding of the self, the world, and experience. However were we simply to proceed on the basis of Dasein as being-in-the-world this would be to risk the re-instatement of the subject consciousness in a new spatial model of the world. The phenomenological interpretation of human action has shown how Care grounds the being of Dasein, but Heidegger recognises that, for the interpretation to be complete, action, and the possibility of action itself, must be interpreted. Care must be grounded.[6] Without this grounding Dasein will re-assume the mantle of subjectivity. Human action is temporal and it is this temporality that makes involvement and Care possible. Heidegger will show in Division Two of *Being and Time*, and Part Two of *The Basic Problems of Phenomenology*, that Dasein is the source of this temporality and hence demonstrate how any interpretation of the world of entities and Dasein, which ignores temporality, will be dysfunctional and inauthentic.

The inadequacy and incompleteness of the analysis of everyday Dasein given in Division One of *Being and Time* means that only an inadequate and incomplete model of the self can be derived from this part of Heidegger's work. Although the interpretation of everyday inauthentic Dasein does provide dissolution of the problem of knowledge, and illuminates the way in which the self encounters entities, it does not show how this is possible. It is no more than the description of a process. Heidegger sets about the task of the interpretation of authentic Dasein by recognising that action is temporal, made up not only of a present, in which we encounter entities as equipment, but also a past, in which we learn what to expect from equipment, and a future, into which our expectation is projected.

The substantive interpretation in Division Two begins with the Heidegger's interpretations of death, as indicative of Dasein's futurity, and conscience, which brings back Dasein from the forgetfulness of inauthenticity to its basis in its own past. It is to these interpretations that I will now turn as the beginning of the setting out of the Heideggerian notion of selfhood.

"Freedom towards Death"

Dasein is able to project itself forward in time, to imagine a state of affairs that is not-yet, to frame itself in terms of its future possibilities. This is so up until the end of Dasein's Being, until death, and yet in death Dasein is precisely not that which it has been. On death Dasein loses its being-there. Death, as the ultimate possibility of Dasein, is the possibility of the impossibility of Dasein. To gain a more complete understanding of Dasein an interpretation of all that is outstanding in Dasein must be brought forward. Everyday Dasein lacks wholeness and as lacking can never be fully interpreted or understood. In Heidegger's words,

> One thing has become unmistakable: *our existential analysis of Dasein up till now cannot lay claim to primordiality.* It's fore-having never having included more than the *inauthentic* Being of Dasein, and of Dasein as *less* than a *whole*. If the Interpretation of Dasein's Being is to become primordial, as a foundation for working out the basic question of ontology, then it must first have brought to light existentially the Being of Dasein in its possibilities of *authenticity* and *totality*. (Heidegger, 1987, H. 233)

Heidegger uses the interpretation of death as a cipher for the interpretation of the entire futurity of Dasein. His interpretation of death will not objectify this phenomenon in any way, but bring this phenomenon back into the Being of Dasein.[7] This means understanding death as "dying".[8] The problem is the wholeness of Dasein, which must include all that Dasein is not-yet. This will even include possibilities, which Dasein may never be but which are still a part of Dasein, as Being which exists as projecting and futural.

It is easy to see why Heidegger rejects the experience of the dying of others as an entry into the analysis. Not only is this an experience we cannot have,[9] it is also the specific focus on death as an event in the "life" of Dasein, and provides no ground for an understanding of Dasein as futural. Not only can no-one take away the other's dying, but my own dying is not central. Just as Dasein is not simply objective existence, so death cannot simply be the end of this existence.

There appears to be no starting point for the interpretation, death is phenomenally elusive.

> When Dasein reaches its wholeness in death it simultaneously loses the Being of its "there". By its transition to no-longer-Dasein it gets lifted right out of the possibility of experiencing this transition and of understanding it as something experienced. (Ibid, H. 237)

I cannot experience death, neither that of an other nor my own, but without some interpretation of death I can have no understanding of Dasein as a whole, nor of its temporal structure, or even a clear notion of time itself. Heidegger's interpretation concentrates on death as a possibility of Dasein. The death of Dasein is not like the final payment of a debt, nor is it to be understood in the same way as the ripening fruit. Death is not the timely closing of an account and is not the fulfilment of life. Death may be untimely, tragic, pointless, unjustified and accidental. As Heidegger says,

> Death is a way to be which Dasein takes over as soon as it is. "As soon as man comes to life, he is at once old enough to die". (Ibid, H. 245)

"Dasein is dying as long as it exists" (Ibid, H. 251), and, "Any Dasein always exists in just such a manner that its 'not-yet' *belongs* to it" (Ibid, H. 243). Heidegger is bringing death back within the compass of the Being of Dasein. Death is encompassed within the dynamic interpretation of Dasein. Death is a possibility of Dasein, the possibility of the impossibility of Dasein. It is the fate which Dasein cannot avoid or evade, and which no other Dasein can take over. It encompasses all that is still outstanding in Dasein, it stands as the ultimate futural possibility of Dasein. Heidegger expresses this vividly,

> Thus death reveals itself as that *possibility which is ones ownmost, which is non-relational and which is not to be outstripped.* (Ibid, H. 250)

In this way death underlies the whole of my Being. It is not merely a final phenomenon, not just the last act of Dasein, but is part of what makes Dasein possible in the first place, Dasein is futural and death denotes futurity.

On returning to the everyday interpretation of Dasein, which lacks the possibility of understanding Dasein as a whole, it is clear that this lack is grounded in a misunderstanding (inauthentic interpretation) of death. For everyday Dasein death is both objectified, as a certain event in an uncertain future, and alienated or disowned, as something that we only experience as happening to others. In everydayness, "'Dying' is levelled off to an occurrence which reaches Dasein, to be sure, but belongs to nobody in particular" (Ibid, H. 253). Dasein is imbued with a fear of death and seeks interpretations that annul these fears, interpretations provided by the way of Being of "the they". Everyday Dasein understands death as certain. We understand that everyone must die but choose to evade this certainty in the case of our own being, so that "Along with the certainty of death goes the *indefiniteness* of its 'when'" (Ibid, H. 258). By putting it off till later "the they" betrays the certainty of death. The inauthentic interpretations of "the they" de-individuate Dasein by trying to rob Dasein of the non-relational possibility of its own death,

> As falling, everyday Being-towards-death is a constant *fleeing in the face of death*. Being-*towards*-the-end has the mode of evasion in the face of it - giving new explanations for it, understanding it inauthentically, and concealing it. (Ibid, H. 254)

Death is turned into something which everyday inauthentic Dasein must fear, and then,

> *The "they" does not permit us the courage for anxiety in the face of death*

and,

> The "they" concerns itself with transferring this anxiety into fear in the face of an oncoming event

and even further,

> In addition, the anxiety which has been made ambiguous as fear, is passed off as a weakness with which no self-assured Dasein may have any acquaintance. (Ibid, H. 254)

So that anything other than fear of death is made illegitimate, and Dasein that does not fear death lacks self assurance.

> What is "fitting" according to the unuttered decree of "the they" is indifferent tranquillity as to the "fact" that one dies. The activation of such a "superior" indifference *alienates* Dasein from its ownmost non-relational potentiality-for-Being. (Ibid, H. 254)

Heidegger is not simply urging us to be brave enough to stand up to the fact of our own death. He has no interest in this kind of heroism.[10] Heidegger's aim is to show how Dasein can be understood as a whole stretching across its temporal being and in the context not only of other entities, including other Dasein, but also in the temporal context, which he aims to show underlies and makes possible the Being of Dasein itself. The distortions and "ontological perversions"[11] of the interpretations of "the they" fail to represent the Being of Dasein adequately, and fail to provide sufficient ground for Dasein to identify itself.

The distinction between fear and anxiety is crucial and Heidegger uses these terms quite specifically to distinguish between two ways of understanding death and the future.[12] The distinction is central to the structure of Dasein, as inauthentic and potentially authentic. Fear must have an object, that is, there must be something of which I am afraid. I fear that which endangers or threatens my existence, the object provides a focus for my state of mind and makes it fear. We have seen that the notion of "object" itself is derived from the meaning of the Being of Dasein, which is care, my necessary involvement with the world that makes objectness possible. This indicates that fear does not operate at a fundamental level but is a state of mind concerned with these secondary structures of Being. As such, it is unlikely to reveal anything about the fundamental Being of Dasein. Fear is possible only on the ground of Care and says nothing about that which makes Care possible. Furthermore, fear is a state of mind wholly concerned with the present; it is immediate and concentrates attention on the present danger. Fear can be seen as the ultimate preoccupation of Dasein with the present, a simple self preservation exercise entirely out of context with Dasein's projecting. By objectifying death "the they" provides the focus for fear, that is makes fear possible, and simultaneously alienates Dasein from its destiny, in death, locking Dasein into a world of objectification and presence. As death is objectified so is Dasein made into the object/subject and thereby loses its character.

In fleeing towards inauthentic interpretations of death Dasein not only disables itself from understanding itself as a whole but also, since death denotes the futurity of Dasein, fails to take on its own temporality and alienates itself from its own future. Dasein that cannot encompass its own death cannot identify with any of its not-yet, it cannot identify with the Dasein that encounters this not-yet, it does not have a future and has a problem with the continuity of its own identity through time. It is a characteristic of inauthentic Dasein that it exists in a series of "now" moments each disconnected from the other, and succeeding the last seemingly without connection in the same way that Hume describes the constant flux of impressions and ideas which he finds when he looks to discover the source of his own personal identity.[13] In fear, inauthentic Dasein forgets its past, awaits the future and makes present its everyday concerns.

In simple terms anxiety is objectless fear, nameless dread. Anxiety is fear of nothing, apparently ungrounded and unresolvable. In fact, as Richardson explains, Dasein experiences anxiety in the face of what it is, authentically,[14] and anxiety is used by Heidegger as the state of mind, which reveals Dasein's potentiality for Being a whole and for authentic Being. The nameless dread of anxiety reveals twin nullities at the heart of the Being of Dasein. Dasein as existing has not chosen its origins, it is "thrown" into its present from a past that it did not determine, and to which it can never return. Similarly Dasein as futural, that is as existing with possibilities, projects for itself particular ends chosen from amongst these possibilities, just as the available possibilities themselves are in part determined by the past of Dasein, so the choices Dasein makes for the future are entirely contingent, that is, there is no ultimate ground for choosing one possibility above another. The future of Dasein rests on the choices made by Dasein. So although,

> Pursuing our ends, attempting to realise some broad for-the-sake-of-which, we are choosing or determining what we are and will be; this projection, indeed, provides us with our identity. (Richardson, 1986, p. 131)

The identity is undermined because

> our pursuit of just these ends, our choice to be so, rests inevitably on a basis not laid by this prospective pursuit. Our struggle towards ends determines who we are, but is due to who we have been. And this stands always before any current determination of a self, showing that this self we define ourselves as, can never be simply identical to that self responsible for the defining. (Ibid, p. 131)

The truth of our Being is that it is never wholly under our control, never wholly grounded in certainty. In anxiety Dasein is momentarily released from its concerns in the everyday and understands the contingency of the existence that it had previously thought constituted its identity. In anxiety Dasein is unseated and thrown onto its own null basis, Dasein understands itself as without foundation apart from its own choices. In Heidegger's words,

> Only because Nothing is revealed in the very basis of our *Da-sein* is it possible for the utter strangeness of what-is to dawn on us. ("What is Metaphysics?" in, Heidegger, 1968, p. 378)

It is no wonder that we experience anxiety in the face of this inescapable predicament. It is equally unsurprising that everyday inauthentic Dasein refuses to face this contingency of Being and flees from anxiety, and not simply out of desperation. Everyday Dasein is not afraid of anxiety, but anxiety, as unseating, makes Dasein unable to function in the everyday. Everyday Dasein exists as preoccupied in the world of "now" moments and involvements with entities in the world. If Dasein is to be able to live in the present, as it must, it must be able to forget the full extent of its temporal stretch and engage inauthentically with the world. Dasein cannot spend its entire existence in the total perspective vortex of anxiety; authenticity is a possibility of Dasein not its permanent state of being.

Everyday experience abounds with alternative and inauthentic interpretations of death and these interpretations, (morbid expectation, attempts at realisation, euphemistic evasions etc.), the idle talk of "the they", serve to blot out the authentic interpretation and provide a refuge from anxiety. Dasein is anxious in face of its own potentiality-for-Being-a-whole. Faced with the alternatives of anxiety before the twin nullities of Being and fleeing into the comfort of "the they" everyday Dasein flees. In fleeing Dasein is attempting to compress its own temporal stretch from the richness of thrown and projecting Being to the narrow safety of the merely present, fallen, Dasein, eternally incomplete.

The explanation of death given by "the they" is not adequate, and is contradictory in terms both of the death facing each individual Dasein and of the sense of continuing identity felt by each individual Dasein. "The they" de-individualises death in order that Dasein can avoid anxiety. In order to release Dasein from everyday confinement, and realise its potential-for-being-a-whole Heidegger develops the notion of anticipation.

Anticipation is not awaiting, nor is it expecting, even less is it the active attempt to realise death or the future. All of these attitudes betray an inauthentic interpretation of death, which objectify death as an event instead of as a possibility of Dasein. All of these alienate Dasein from its end, and from its future. Authentically Dasein's Being-towards-death must be Being-towards-a-possibility, but not in the sense that death is made ready-to-hand. We must *"put up with* it *as a possibility"*.[15] Anticipation is to be taken as that way of taking over the fact of death without making an object of death, so,

> *The closest closeness which one may have in Being towards death as a possibility is as far as possible from anything actual.* (Heidegger, 1987, H. 262)

Only in this way can death be held as a permanent possibility without being actualised or "made possible", and,

> Anticipation turns out to be the possibility of understanding ones *ownmost* and uttermost potentiality-for-Being - that is to say the possibility of *authentic existence.* (Ibid, H. 263)

If, as Heidegger says, dying is grounded in care then,

> In anticipating the indefinite certainty of death, Dasein opens itself to a constant *threat* arising out of its own "there". In this very threat Being-towards-the-end must maintain itself. So little can it tone this down that it must rather cultivate the indefiniteness of the certainty. (Ibid, H. 265)

Anticipation is taking over this ultimate and unalienable threat to the Being of Dasein, a threat which is grounded in the way of Dasein's Being, that is in Care. Dasein must be involved with entities in the world as long as it exists and as existing it must have the possibility of no longer existing, of dying. Anticipation is the understanding of both the finitude and futurity of Dasein. In anticipation Dasein understands its death as the limit to its projecting, and as one of its possibilities, the possibility of the impossibility of its Being. This is a unique possibility which brings to its attention its potentiality-for-Being-a-whole, and for authentic Being, by denoting the authentic future of Dasein.[16]

Anticipation is a liberation from the constricting distortions of the 'they self', and releases Dasein for anxiety and choice, so restoring the temporal stretch, and replacing Dasein within its authentic temporal context. In anticipation Dasein can understand the nature of its projecting, not only in terms of the individual projects with which it concerns itself in the everyday, but in terms of its own existing. The entire existence of Dasein is the ultimate project, the ultimate and overarching for-the-sake-of-which. As anticipating Dasein can understand itself as such

> When by anticipation one becomes free *for* one's own death one is liberated from one's lostness in those possibilities which may accidentally thrust themselves upon one; and one is liberated in such a way that for the first time one can authentically understand and choose among the factical possibilities lying ahead of that possibility which is not to be outstripped. (Ibid, H. 264)

Heidegger calls this "freedom towards death".[17]

In the analysis of death Heidegger shows how it is possible to understand the Being of Dasein as a whole despite the fact that, as projecting, Dasein is always something that it is not yet. The analysis of death brings this phenomenon within the sphere of the Being of Dasein; it does not however show how this possibility can be realised. If the analysis of death and the temporality of Dasein is to be credible Heidegger must go further and show how, from the basis of the meaning of everyday Dasein, Dasein can come to understand its potentiality-for-being and authentic existence. Heidegger must show how Dasein can become ready for anxiety.

Guilty Conscience

Inauthentic Dasein lost in "the they" must find itself. The analysis of death shows the possibility of Dasein's potentiality-for-being-a-whole and for being authentic. The attestation of this potentiality is achieved through the voice of conscience. We have already recognised that Dasein flees in the face of the authentic interpretation of its own death, and is comforted by the inauthentic interpretations offered by "the they". Authentic selfhood exists as a modification of the they self; most of the time Dasein is in flight from anxiety and disowns its potentiality-for-being-a-whole.[18] Anxiety is first revealed as the feeling of uncanniness, or, not-at-home in the everyday, and this feeling is articulated in the call of conscience. Heidegger uses the notion of conscience in a very specific way quite apart from any moral or religious uses.[19]

The call of conscience, existentially understood, makes known for the first time what we have hitherto merely contended: that uncanniness pursues Dasein and is a threat to the lostness in which it has forgotten itself. (Heidegger, 1987, H. 277)

Or more vividly, "Man alone of all beings, when addressed by the voice of Being, experiences the marvel of all marvels: that what-is *is-*" ("What is Metaphysics?" in, Heidegger, 1968, p. 386). Everyday Dasein is lost and forgetful of itself and, using the argument from absence, Heidegger contends that losing and forgetting are only possible on the basis of possible finding and remembering. So Dasein, lost in *publicness*, implies the possibility of Dasein returning to itself as authentic. The call of conscience comes to everyday Dasein as if from beyond itself, and phenomenally this is the everyday way in which we experience conscience. Heidegger then interprets the phenomenon of conscience in the context of the structure of Dasein;

> *Conscience manifests itself as the call of care:*
> the caller is Dasein, which, in its thrownness (in its Being-already-in), is anxious about its potentiality-for-Being. The one to whom the appeal is made is the very same Dasein, summoned to its ownmost potentiality-for-Being (ahead of itself...). Dasein is falling into the "they" (in Being-already-alongside the world of its concern), and it is summoned out of this falling by the appeal. The call of conscience - that is, conscience itself - has its ontological possibility in the fact that Dasein, in the very basis of it's Being, is Care. (Heidegger, 1987, H. 277-8)

Inauthentic Dasein lacks wholeness. It cannot grasp the temporal stretch of its Being because it is alienated from its future and preoccupied with present concerns. As such it disowns both future and past for it cannot grasp time itself, having no basis for understanding the connection between the successive "now" moments. Present concerns arrive and pass to be replaced by new concerns. As fallen, preoccupied with the present, inauthentic Dasein can have no sense of responsibility because it cannot understand itself as temporal, that is, it cannot find the ground on which to identify itself as continuous with itself at other times. Its Being is temporally disjointed. Time appears as something beyond Dasein, an objective reality outside Dasein, to which Dasein is subject. However this alienation from time is at odds with the involvement of Dasein in the world. Dasein, as Care, is involved with entities in the world, Dasein acts in the world and this involvement is inescapable because it makes possible the everyday Being of Dasein. As long as Dasein *is*, it is involved. Care, though sufficient to ground everydayness (being-in-the-world), cannot ground the continuing existence of Dasein (identity through time), and consequently cannot make Dasein responsible, despite its undoubted involvements.[20] In this way Heidegger interprets the call of conscience as the call of Dasein to itself lost in the way of Being of "the they", a way of Being in which anxious Dasein seeks refuge and comfort and seeks to disown the involvements which ground its very Being "In the face of its thrownness Dasein flees to the relief which comes with the supposed freedom of the they-self" (Ibid, H. 276). Dasein is alienated from its conscience, conscience is understood inauthentically as something which is from beyond Dasein, an objective and separated existence, something present-at-hand, a call which Dasein can choose to ignore. Dasein even appears to be exercising its freedom in choosing to ignore the call of conscience, when in fact inauthentic Dasein is free only to remain incomplete.[21]

In order to understand the way of Being to which Dasein is called forth by the call of conscience we must seek that which grounds care. When Heidegger says, "*Conscience manifests itself as the call of care*",[22] he is making the point that Dasein is responsible because of care, and the call of conscience reveals this responsibility and calls Dasein back to its authentic being. "The they", through its inauthentic interpretation of phenomena like death and conscience, enables Dasein to be distracted and to forget its temporality by evading anxiety.

The style of argument here is familiarly Heideggerian. Conscience is admitted as an everyday phenomenon, and it is the strength of Heidegger's case that he begins with the everyday. Conscience is interpreted by inauthentic everyday Dasein as a voice from beyond Dasein, from God or some higher authority, a voice calling Dasein to do something other than what it is doing, a voice seeking to make Dasein responsible. Heidegger takes this phenomenon of the call of conscience to indicate a characteristic feature of Dasein, refusing to objectify the phenomenon in order to avoid recreating the object/subject in Dasein. This feature he calls, Dasein's Being-guilty,[23] in the sense that if Dasein were not guilty, or responsible, the call of conscience would not be possible. In a kind of "no smoke without fire" sort of way, if I hear a call of conscience then there must be something for me to have a conscience about. My responsibility for my own actions, whatever they may be, my Being-guilty, makes possible the call of conscience. Just as reality is inferred from appearance, in response to the problem of knowledge, so responsibility and temporal continuity with the past are inferred from the call of conscience. Furthermore because my actions are only possible because of the nature of the Being of Dasein as care, conscience is only possible on the ground of care and as such becomes a phenomenon of Dasein itself. In Heidegger's words,

> only because Dasein is guilty in the basis of its Being, and closes itself off from itself as something thrown and falling, is conscience possible. (Ibid, H. 286)

This assertion is not left unsupported, as Heidegger has already demonstrated the possibility of Dasein being-a-whole in the analysis of death, and conscience is simply cited as the phenomenon that attests this possibility. Conscience is a phenomenon on which Heidegger places great weight. It is central to Heidegger's argument that we understand the call of conscience as coming from Dasein itself and calling itself back to its potentiality-for-being-a-whole and authenticity, a call which inauthentic Dasein blots out in order to avoid facing the fact that it is its own null basis. It cannot choose the past that belongs to it and for which it is responsible. The phenomenon of conscience further reveals the ontological structure of authentic Dasein as temporal. It is hard to ignore the heroic overtones of Heidegger's words in the interpretations of both conscience and death and I will return later to this aspect of the analysis of these phenomena in the conclusion to this book.

Having interpreted conscience as the call of Dasein to itself as lost in "the they", Heidegger sets out how Dasein may understand the appeal authentically and so become ready for anxiety. Inauthentic Dasein interprets conscience as a call from beyond itself, thus disowning its own responsibility, failing to take over its own past, and remaining alienated from its own temporality. Authentic Dasein allows conscience to disclose its own potentiality-for-being-a-whole and the effect of Dasein's hearing the call is dramatic:

> When Dasein understandingly lets itself be called forth to this possibility, this includes *becoming free* for the call - its readiness for the potentiality of getting appealed to. In understanding the call Dasein is *in thrall to its ownmost possibility of existence*. It has chosen itself. (Ibid, H. 287)

Clearly it is possible for Dasein to refuse to listen to the call of conscience, or to wilfully misinterpret the call, in order still to disown its past, at the undoubted cost of the compression of its temporal stretch and ground for its identity over time. Inauthentic Dasein cannot but have problems with its own continuity since it cannot connect with its own past. All that remains is to deduce the authentic orientation towards conscience, which enables Dasein to hear the call and to interpret it authentically. This is wanting-to-have-a-conscience. In the same way that Dasein must be approachable in order to authentically understand its being-in-the-world, so, in order to understand itself as temporal, Dasein must want to have a conscience. Just as anticipation is the authentic mode of being-towards-death and the response, which admits Dasein's possibility for being-a-whole, so wanting-to-have-a-conscience is the way, in which Dasein has to be, authentically, towards the call of conscience and, "Wanting-to-have-a-conscience becomes a readiness for anxiety".[24] This wanting-to-have-a-conscience, or readiness for anxiety, is the fundamental characteristic of authentic Dasein. In the same way that approachability denotes Dasein's authentic spatiality, so wanting-to-have-a-conscience denotes Dasein's authentic temporality. Wanting-to-have-a-conscience *is* being ready for anxiety, refusing the inauthentic interpretations of "the they" and taking back the phenomena of death and conscience which the "they self" objectifies and alienates from inauthentic Dasein. In taking over anxiety Dasein can understand itself as being-a-whole. By taking over its authentic future in death and its authentic past, or having-been, by understanding the appeal of conscience, and its being-guilty, Dasein understands and takes over its authentic temporality.[25]

Anxiety in the face of the twin nullities of Dasein's Being opens the possibility for Dasein of taking over these nullities, the contingency of future choices and the already-chosenness of the past. The future is authentically taken over in anticipation and the past in resoluteness. In anticipatory resoluteness Dasein is adequately understood as temporal and restored to its authentic Being from lostness in "the they". Heidegger says, "'Resoluteness' signifies letting oneself be summoned out of the lostness in 'the they'".[26] With authentic future and authentic past restored Dasein is able to understand itself as a whole. Dasein is able to interpret itself in the world, and not simply as being-in-itself but in the context of its involvements:

> When the call of conscience summons us to our potentiality-for-Being it does not hold before us some empty ideal of existence, but *calls us forth into the Situation.* (Ibid, H. 300)

Authentic past and authentic future restore not only the temporal identity of Dasein, as having-been and projecting, but also restore authentic present by framing the present in which Dasein is situated. Dasein as fallen, as preoccupied with present concerns can, by being ready for anxiety, by wanting to have a conscience, understand the context of its present preoccupation and so, along with anticipation of the future and resoluteness in the face of being-guilty, authentic Dasein holds the present in the "moment of vision",[27] in which present concerns are understood in the context of future projections and past thrownness.

Having arrived at an ontological basis for the being-a-whole of Dasein, and having shown how Dasein can understand itself temporally, we must now go on to further investigate and interpret the Being of authentic Dasein. It is already clear that the self that is emerging from Heidegger's work is nothing like the self of Descartes or Hume or Kant, nor even that of Sartre. As Heidegger says, "we must establish what possible ontological questions are to be directed towards the 'Self' if indeed it is neither substance nor subject"(Ibid, H. 303).

Dasein, Care and Temporality

Having attested the possibility of Dasein's potentiality for being-a-whole it is now appropriate to look more closely at the relation between Dasein and temporality and to see how it is that temporality makes possible care.[28] In the section headed "Temporality as the ontological meaning of care"(Heidegger, 1987, H.324-331) Heidegger provides something of a "definition" of temporality.

> This phenomenon has the unity of a future which makes present in the process of having been; we designate it as *"temporality"*. Only in so far as Dasein has the definite character of temporality is the authentic potentiality-for-Being-a-whole of anticipatory resoluteness, as we have described it, made possible for Dasein itself. *Temporality reveals itself as the meaning of authentic care.* (Ibid, H. 326)[29]

Heidegger chooses his words carefully, temporality is not set up as an alienated phenomenon apart from Dasein, it cannot be "defined" as such since this would mean treating time as present-at-hand or objectified.[30] Neither can an explanation of temporality be made which does not also include an explanation of Dasein as what it *is*. It is clear that the relation between Dasein and temporality is at least intimate. "The unity of a future which makes present in the process of having been", is as good a description as we might make of Dasein from the preceding analysis of death and conscience, and the authentic futurity and being-guilty of Dasein. It is no coincidence that Heidegger's description of temporality uses the same threefold structure (past, present and future) and the identity of Dasein with temporality and *vice versa* will become more prominent as the argument develops.

We have already seen how anticipation releases the authentic future of Dasein:

> Anticipation makes Dasein *authentically* futural, and in such a way that the anticipation itself is possible only in so far as Dasein, *as being*, is always coming towards itself - that is to say, in so far as it is futural in its Being in general. (Ibid, H. 325)

This denotes the authentic futurity of Dasein.

> Anticipation of one's uttermost and ownmost possibility is coming back understandingly to ones ownmost "been". Only in so far as it is futural can Dasein *be* authentically as having been. The character of "having been" arises in a certain way from the future. (Ibid, H. 326)

Thus authentic futurity is linked with authentic having been or the past. And finally,

> Only as the *Present* in the sense of making present, can resoluteness be what it is: namely, letting itself be encountered undisguisedly by that which it seizes upon in taking action. (Ibid, H. 326)

That is, we can only be resolute in the present, as situated. Heidegger's simple point is that past, present and future cannot be undone and are inextricably linked to one another, providing the unity for the phenomenon that we call temporality. Conversely temporality conceptually unites the three ecstases of past present and future, which form the temporal context in which Dasein exists. Hence,

> Temporality makes possible the unity of existence, facticity, and falling, and in this way constitutes primordially the totality of the structure of care. (Ibid, H. 328)

It is easy at this stage to take Heidegger to mean more than he actually says. To appreciate the full import of what he actually says we must strive to gain the quite simple insight that Heidegger's work offers with regard to time and the nature of the existence of Dasein. Just because Heidegger is trying to say something about the fundamental structures of Being it should not be surprising to find that what he actually says is simple. It is therefore a mistake to make these simple insights carry more weight than they are meant to bear. Heidegger is not trying to describe the world as it is, but the conditions under which the world, and Dasein, is possible. At this fundamental level it is more likely that insights will be simple, rather than complex, and if we are to capture the simple clarity of Heidegger's thought it is vital to avoid theoretical over elaboration.

An analysis of care, or involvement, quickly reveals that the structure of this involvement is temporal. All of our involvements with the world have a "when-now-then" attached to them, a before, a doing, and an after. Whenever we do anything we act on the basis of things we did before, we learn from our experience and look for its repetition, but all of our doing is also projection, we do things with a certain future (expectation) in mind, we imagine a state of affairs that is not-yet and aim towards it. All of this doing takes place in a present (now), and fundamental to all of it is the unified temporal structure, without which our involvement in the world becomes meaningless. We do things in the present towards a particular future and we aim our present action towards the future on the basis of what we have learned about doing in the past. In Heidegger's rather more florid terms,

> Letting something be involved is constituted rather in the unity of a retention which awaits, and is constituted in such a manner, indeed, that the making present which arises from this, makes possible the characteristic absorption of concern in its equipmental world. (Ibid, H. 353-4)

And similarly,

> Letting something be involved must, as such, be grounded in the ecstatical unity of the making-present which awaits and retains, whatever we have made accessible in dealing with the contexts of equipment. (Ibid, H. 355)

Even the Being of everyday inauthentic Dasein has a temporal structure, though in this way of Being Dasein strives, through inauthentic interpretations, to forget this temporality.

> Inauthentic *understanding* projects itself upon that with which one can concern oneself, or upon what is feasible, urgent, or indispensable in our everyday business

and

> Factically, Dasein is constantly ahead of itself, but inconstantly anticipatory with regard to its existentiell possibility. (Ibid, H. 337)

Authentic Dasein, through anticipatory resoluteness, remembers this structure. Inauthentic Dasein is spontaneously forgetful because it lacks understanding of itself and its meaning as care, and hence of authentic temporality. At bottom we see that

> *Temporality gets experienced in a phenomenally primordial way in Dasein's authentic Being-a-whole, in the phenomenon of anticipatory resoluteness.* (Ibid, H. 304)

To set out the argument sequentially: The Being of Dasein is Care (involvement, engagement, doing). The meaning of Care is temporality, since temporality provides for the possibility of Dasein's involvement because this involvement is necessarily characterised in the form of when, now, then; awaiting, retaining (learning), projecting. Involvement therefore takes place against the backdrop of temporality. But if the meaning of Dasein's Being is Care, temporality becomes the horizon against which the Being of Dasein is disclosed. Dasein's involvement makes temporality possible because without it there can be no temporality. The structure of temporality (past, present, future), which discloses authentic involvement, can have no meaning without this involvement. Entities become significant through their involvements, through being equipment for Dasein. Dasein discloses the being of entities, and the work, instrumentally, through its chosen possibilities. The historical significance of entities depends on the passage of the world(s) in which they were significant as equipment for Dasein. Worlds pass as the choices made by Dasein change; new choices bring new involvements, new equipment in a new work (context). Dasein is thus the source of historicality because only Dasein discloses the world. In a real sense, no Dasein means no world and no history. Without Dasein the world cannot appear and there can be no history of the world, therefore Dasein is the source of temporality.[31]

The relationship between Dasein and temporality is circular. Temporality is revealed through Dasein as involvement/care. Dasein and temporality provide the ground for one another and are thereby identified. The analysis of the one simply provides an analysis of the other from a different perspective. Dasein is revealed against the horizon of temporality, and Dasein, as involvement/care is the source of temporality, that is, it provides for its possibility. Without Dasein's temporal structure time has no foundation, its terms fall as empty. Authentic Dasein is the stretching along of temporality. If Dasein is the transcending, the Dasein is the temporal.

Heidegger goes to considerable lengths to show how the phenomena that make up, and are encountered by, Dasein, as set out in Division One of *Being and Time*, are temporally structured.[32] In particular he shows how the three elements that make up the care structure (understanding, mood, and falling) characterise the three temporal ecstases, future, past and present. Understanding, or projection, is the most important and is characterised as futural. Mood or state-of-mind is understood in terms of the past, or having-been of Dasein. Falling is Dasein's Being-present. Though these three all have meaning in the context of one temporal ecstasis all are connected to every other ecstasis. Their unity, and the unity of Being, is retained within the temporal structure. Phenomena like anxiety and fear and curiosity are also analysed in this way and are shown to be temporally structured. I will not go into the detail of Heidegger's exposition of these notions, however it is useful and instructive to briefly outline the way in which he explains the everyday idea of time or "clock time" which we all use in our everyday dealing with the world.

Public time, or clock time, is the representation of activity in a common way that can be shared.[33] Our ability to represent activity, and hence ourselves, as the possibility of that activity in terms of clock time, is derived from the fundamentally temporal structure of our own Being. Clock time is the inauthentic way in which we share authentic temporality. The temporal structure of Being makes care possible and provides for the possibility of clock time. Clock time is a kind of equipment, which we encounter in the world and use instrumentally. Its meaning is already given to us through its use by other Dasein. What Heidegger is saying is that the ordinary everyday conception of time is made possible because of, and through, the temporality of Being-in-the-world itself, and that clock time, or public time, is not an overarching objective phenomenon to which Dasein is subject but is derived from the fact of Dasein's being-in-the-world and the temporality of this involvement.[34]

The distinction we are finally able to make between authentic temporality and inauthentic time is all the more important because of the identification of Dasein with temporality. Inauthentic Dasein will see itself adrift in public time and forget its fundamental temporal structure. Inauthentic Dasein will fail to see that authentic temporality is the basis of the clock time to which it sees itself as subject. Inauthentic Dasein is alienated from temporality and thereby alienated from itself. Authentic Dasein remembers itself as the source of temporality, through its Being as Care, and understands the derivation of clock time from authentic temporality. In this way authentic Dasein is at one with itself and can understand itself as thrown, and projecting, Being-in-the-world. Authentic Dasein can thus have a sense of its past as its own and of its future as open and available and ownable. Heidegger's intention is quite clear when he says,

> Dasein does not fill up a track or stretch "of life" - one which is somehow present-at-hand - with the phases of its momentary actualities. It stretches *itself* along in such a way that its own Being is constituted in advance as a stretching-along. The "between" which relates to birth and death already lies *in the Being* of Dasein. (Ibid, H. 374)

Authentic Dasein is constituted in the transcending of the moment, as it is in the transcending of the world of space. Inauthentic Dasein, conversely, is lost in the present with no understanding of its temporality. It cannot solve the problem of how it owns its past and finds its continuous identity with itself over time a mystery. The future is awaited in alienated helplessness because inauthentic Dasein has no way of escaping the endless series of "now" moments that make up its time.

I will now set out what can be taken to be a Heideggerian model of the self, although it is already clear that the term model may be inappropriate given the radically different interpretations provided by Heidegger. Heidegger's alternative to the Cartesian model of the self will resemble less a model and more a set of conditions which make existence as "self" possible. In the next section I will focus on these conditions.

Goldilocks Apparent

Hume remained perplexed as to the ground for the continuity of personal identity. His Goldilocks disappeared each time he looked for her, and finding nothing but the constantly changing flux of ideas and impressions he was forced to concede that justification for even this apparently most self-evident of all beliefs could not be found. It is clear from all that has been said so far that Heidegger takes an entirely different approach to the temporally continuous nature of selfhood.

> This question does not ask how Dasein gains such a unity of connectedness that the sequence of "Experiences" which has ensued and is still ensuing can subsequently be linked together; it asks rather in which of its own kinds of Being Dasein *loses itself in such a manner that it must, as it were, only subsequently pull itself together out of its dispersal and think up for itself a unity in which that "together" is embraced.* (Heidegger, 1987, H. 390)

In typical fashion Heidegger reverses the question of personal identity in exactly the same way that he reverses the problem of the "veil of the senses". The onus is not on those who wish to show the connection between Being and the world and Being and time but on those who maintain separatedness. Heidegger's self is not the Cartesian subject. "To define the 'I' ontologically as '*subject*' means to regard it as something always present-at-hand" (Ibid, H. 320), and thus in the inauthentic ways of everydayness. More accurately,

> *In saying "I", Dasein expresses itself as Being-in-the-world*

and

> In saying "I", I have in view the entity which in each case I am as an "I-am-in-a-world". (Ibid, H. 321)

Selfhood rather than the self is a more appropriate label for what we are describing here, denoting activity and process as opposed to the substance of the Cartesian subject.[35] The activity that is denoted is Dasein's involvement, or its meaning as care. It is through care (and therefore temporality) that selfhood can be understood. It is this activity expressed by the notion of care that constitutes selfhood. We have already seen that the meaning of care is authentic temporality and it now remains to show how selfhood is given in the care structure.

Whereas the traditional formulation of the problem of personal identity seeks, and fails, to identify the entity that is self, Heidegger's interpretations of everydayness seek to understand the process that is selfhood. Heidegger does not seek the objective, or the subjective, self, having demonstrated that these forms are derived from more primordial "ways of Being" and provide only limited opportunities to understand the Being of Dasein. It may appear that Heidegger's answer to the problem of personal identity is unsatisfactory because he does not answer the question "What am I?" However it should be clear by now that Heidegger's work questions the usefulness, and the possibility, of asking questions of this nature.[36] The value of such questions is limited by the subject/object structure, which such questions imply. Nowhere is this deficiency more clearly illustrated than in the nature of the individual consciousness itself in which, as observer and observed, subject and object must somehow co-exist with itself. The pre-supposition of the subject/object framework in which the traditional analysis takes place is that the self is an entity the Being of which is given by being present-at-hand. We have already seen that this is mistaken, and is the source of the Cartesian problem. In Heidegger's, terms if the Being of Dasein is to be defined it will be so as activity, as the "stretching along between birth and death". If this seems to say little it is only because we have misunderstood the traditional attempts of Cartesians to have been saying more than they actually could. All of the Cartesian attempts have tried to work within the subject/object structure (even those who have attempted to subvert some of the aspects of this structure) and merely wrestled with the problems it creates. In this they have not addressed the question of the meaning of Being at all. This is the question towards which all of Heidegger's efforts are directed.

Heidegger addresses the problem of selfhood in the section of *Being and Time* headed "Care and Selfhood" (H. 316-323) in which he says,

> *The constancy of the Self*, in the double sense of steadiness and steadfastness, is the *authentic* counter possibility to the non-Self-constancy which is characteristic of irresolute falling. Existentially, *"Self-constancy"* signifies nothing other than anticipatory resoluteness. (Ibid, H. 322)

This indicates that the solution to the problem of identity is only to be found through the understanding of authentic Dasein.

> Dasein *is authentically itself* in the primordial individualisation of the reticent resoluteness which exacts anxiety of itself. *As something that keeps silent*, authentic *Being*-one's-Self is just the sort of thing that one does not keep on saying "I"; but in its reticence it "*is*" that thrown entity as which it can authentically be. (Ibid, H. 322-3)

In saying this Heidegger not only dismisses the Cartesian subject, which is founded on constantly saying "I", but also goes some considerable way to set out his alternative, nebulous as this may appear. The Heideggerian self is what it "is", and is defined simply by the fact that it exists, and exists as being-in-the-world and as temporal. This is made explicit when Heidegger says:

> The ontological structure of that entity which, in each case I *myself* am, centres in the Self-subsistence of existence. Because the Self cannot be conceived either as substance or as subject but is grounded in existence, our analysis of the inauthentic Self, the "they", has been left wholly in tow of the preparatory Interpretation of Dasein. Now that Selfhood has been *explicitly* taken back into the structure of care, and therefore of temporality, the temporal Interpretation of Self-constancy and non-Self-constancy acquires an importance of its own. (Ibid, H. 332)

It is now apparent that authentic selfhood is qualitatively different from the substantial subject self of inauthentic Dasein. The modification of inauthentic existence, which is required if authentic possibility is to emerge, is the transformation of perspective which is brought by transcendence. Selfhood is "taken back" into the structure of temporality, and in this its form is revealed as temporal. Temporality is the form of authentic Dasein, and the shift in perspective, which transcendence brings, is the shift from the contents of everyday being to the form of authentic being. It is a new seeing of that which was already there, but which has been concealed by the way of being of everyday inauthentic Dasein. In effect Heidegger's analysis of temporality makes redundant questions regarding the nature of the self, and all that is required now is to make the earlier interpretations, and identifications, of Dasein and time conclusive in affirming the continuity of identity of the self over time.[37] Critically, at this point, we may argue that Heidegger's reasoning appears to be circular because of the apparent mutual dependence of Dasein and time, with each providing the ground for the other. Neither appears certain. But this is to ask a strictly un-Heideggerian question, and one characteristic of the kind of Cartesian epistemology that Heidegger has already rejected and replaced. As he says himself,

> We cannot ever "avoid" a "circular" proof in the existential analytic, because such an analytic does not do *any* proving *at all* by the rules of the "logic of consistency". What common sense wishes to eliminate in avoiding the "circle", on the supposition that it is measuring up to the loftiest regions of scientific investigation, is nothing less than the basic structure of care. (Ibid, H. 315)

Heidegger will not permit the separation of phenomena that are integral to one another. Rather than avoiding circularity we must leap into the circle, in which meaning, and therefore understanding, are only given within the context of existing. We cannot hope to understand selfhood if we attempt to deny the fundamental way of Being of Dasein. The Cartesian attempt to do this, in stripping away all of my involvements, in a vain effort to centre on what I am, removes all possibility of success from the Cartesian project in respect of theories of the self. If the meaning of Dasein is care, and care is grounded in temporality, then, to seek an understanding of the self outside the circle of temporality will be misguided and fruitless. We simply do not have a perspective outside our own temporality from which to begin the traditional Cartesian analysis. Moreover, viewed from the Heideggerian perspective, the attempts of Cartesians, like Hume, to show the continuity of personal identity over time, is an attempt to prove something, the denial of which is fundamental to the approach itself, that is the unity of the self and temporality. This means that not only will the search end in confusion, but an alternative approach, which affirms unity and denies separation, will be rejected because it undermines the entire methodological edifice. Just as the Cartesians must separate the subject from time so the Heideggerians cannot deliver a Cartesian subject.[38] Hume's perplexity results from trying to see how a self-constant self-subsistent entity, (himself), can exist in time which is by its nature transitory and inconstant. This is an equation that can never balance. Heidegger re-interprets the phenomena and shows that self-constancy is grounded in temporality, and that temporality exists as a consequence of this kind of Being. The continuity of personal identity is a problem, but it is not a problem of understanding how the self is set in time, but more a problem of the interpretation of Being itself. This interpretation cannot be divorced from the phenomenon of temporality, and leads directly to this phenomenon.

If objections to Heidegger's model of selfhood are to be sustained they cannot be sustained by using a methodology which Heidegger has already shown to be inadequate in providing an interpretation of experience of the world and of the self. The resistance of the problems of knowledge and personal identity to various Cartesian attempts to solve them is sufficient to call into question both the methodology and the tradition that poses these questions in the first place. It is important to remember at this stage that Heidegger has not only demonstrated the inadequacy of Cartesian epistemology (including clock time), but has shown how its notions arise from necessary, but inauthentic, interpretations of everydayness. The problems of knowledge and identity are derived from the inauthentic interpretation of everyday experience. As "problems" they cannot be "solved" by inauthentic methodology, and they cannot be sustained as problematic in the context of authentic interpretations of phenomena like the world, the self, death, and temporality. Hence their apparent disappearance.

Heidegger's work does not solve the problem of the continuity of personal identity over time; it shows how the problem itself is derived from a misdirection of philosophical effort into the search for essence and a consequent misunderstanding of the meaning of Being. A similar defence can be raised to the charge that Dasein has simply been transmuted into the subject self. Although Heidegger's terms "Self" and "Dasein" are interchangeable in some of the sections quoted above, this does not mean that Dasein is the self in Cartesian terms. Heidegger has not found Goldilocks; he has shown that the little girl and the three bears can only be understood within the hermeneutic circle of their strange story; neither can exist without the other. When Heidegger uses Dasein and Self interchangeably he does so on the understanding that he has already rejected the substantial self of the Cartesian tradition. The Self is Dasein, but Dasein is not the self. Selfhood cannot be co-terminous with the substantial self of Descartes because of its projecting and having-been. These must remain beyond the substantial self of everyday inauthenticity, and yet provide the ground for everyday selfhood, as care, by embodying temporality.

If we accept that Dasein is not made up simply of the sum of its momentary experiences, the constantly passing series of "now" moments, then the past of Dasein is not simply those moments which have passed and the future is not simply those moments which have yet to come, and when Heidegger says of Dasein, "It stretches *itself* along in such a way that its own Being is constituted in advance as a stretching along" he means that "the 'between' which relates to birth and death already lies *in the Being* of Dasein".[39] Dasein is not made temporal, and does not have a history, because things happen to Dasein in temporal sequence. Rather Dasein is itself temporal and

> As long as Dasein factically exists, both the "ends" and their "between" *are*, and they *are* in the only way which is possible on the basis of Dasein's Being as *care*.

Hence, "As care, Dasein *is* the 'between'" (Ibid, H. 374). Just as the world has its worldhood through the involvement with Dasein so history, as a possibility, is founded on the temporality of Dasein. Dasein does not just 'stand in history', Dasein is primarily historical. "Dasein factically has its 'history' and can have something of the sort because the Being of this entity is constituted by historicality" (Ibid, H.382). History itself, beginning with the history of Dasein, is only possible on the foundation that Dasein itself is temporal in its Being. The question of the continuity of personal identity is a question that first removes the ground on which it stands, since we are only able to look back because we are historical, so,

> Our going back to "the past" does not first get its start from the acquisition, sifting and securing of such material; these activities presuppose *historical Being towards* the Dasein that has-been-there - that is to say, they presuppose the historicality of the historian's existence. (Ibid, H. 394)

In the question of the identity of the self, the self is its own historian and therefore historical itself. This also raises questions about how we understand the temporal sequence itself; past, present and future are only sequential in the everyday experience of inauthentic Dasein in which moments come and go. We have now seen that this analysis is grounded on an interpretation of the self as an entity present-at-hand which fails to capture an understanding of Dasein as a whole. Authentically (ontologically) the past is not simply earlier than the present and the future is not simply later;

> The movement of historizing in which something "happens to something" is not to be grasped in terms of motion as change of location. (Ibid, H. 389)

Dasein's Being is constituted by the stretching along.

Finally Heidegger sums up the conclusive response to the question of personal identity, taking into account all that he has said so far about what Dasein is not, and how it can be understood.

> *Only as an entity which, in its Being, is essentially **futural** so that it is free for its death and can let itself be thrown back upon its factical "there" by shattering itself against death - that is to say, only an entity which, as futural, is equiprimordially in the process of **having-been**, can, by handing down to itself the possibility it has inherited, take over its own thrownness and be **in the moment of vision** for "its time". Only authentic temporality, which is at the same time finite, makes possible something like fate - that is to say, authentic historicality.* (Ibid, H.385)

This is the definitive statement of Heidegger's notion of authentic selfhood, but whether Descartes, Hume, Kant, or even Sartre would have recognised it as such is doubtful. I will now sum up Heidegger's replacement of the Cartesian model of the self before going on, in the final chapter of this book, to consider how far this can provide a basis for being-with-Others as an alternative to Stirnerian egoism, and to briefly set out some of the criticisms that may be levelled at the Heideggerian model of selfhood.

Heidegger's Dasein - a Being in Time

In the preceding two chapters we have seen how Heidegger has shown that Dasein cannot be understood apart from the context of the world and temporality. Authentic Dasein is temporal being in the world, as such it defies questions as to how Dasein may know the world and how Dasein may know itself.[40] In the discussion of Dasein's being-in-the-world Heidegger shows how the spatiality of Dasein can be understood and in the discussion of temporality we see how temporality grounds the Being of Dasein and *vice versa*. With this analysis of space and of time Heidegger has given the structure within which Dasein *is* as existing. Furthermore he has demonstrated how the problems of knowledge and identity over time themselves arise from interpretations of Dasein, which though not fundamental, and to that extent inadequate (inauthentic), are necessary for the everyday conduct of Being.

Heidegger's work in *Being and Time* and elsewhere during this period provides an alternative to the Cartesian model of the self, an alternative which does not encounter, or pose for itself, the intractable problems of knowledge and identity, which successive, and often imaginatively innovative, Cartesians fail to solve. On this basis we may at least suggest that the Heideggerian alternative is better. It is a theory that provides a more consistent (less problematic) explanation of existence and experience, and consequently a notion of selfhood appropriate both to everyday experience and the deeper understanding of this experience. The Being of Dasein is no longer divorced from the Being of entities in the world nor from itself at different times. There is no fundamental separation between the "me" and the "not-me" nor between the me-now and the me-not-now. In Heideggerian terms the meaning of the Being of Dasein is Care, Care is grounded in temporality, and selfhood is implicit in Care. In complete distinction from the Cartesian self, including the self of Stirner's Unique One, the Heideggerian self is not distinct but transcendent, or more accurately, transcending. Dasein exists as thrown and projecting being-in-the-world and not as self subsistent thinking being. What this means for positions such as that taken by Stirner should already be clear but will be made explicit in the next, concluding, chapter.

Notes

1. See Heidegger, 1987, H. 61 for an expression of the sheer inescapability of the world for Dasein.
2. See Heidegger, 1987, H. 231-235 and Heidegger, 1982, pp. 227-229.
3. See, Poggeler, "Being as Appropriation", pp. 84-86, and Dreyfus, "Heidegger's History of the Being of Equipment", both in *Heidegger and Modern Philosophy*, 1968, Ed. Murray.
4. See also Heidegger's, *History of the Concept of Time* (1985).
5. See Heidegger's, *Kant and the Problem with Metaphysics* (1990), especially Part One.
6. See, Nicholson, "Ekstatic Temporality in 'Sein und Zeit'", on Care and Temporality.
7. For expositions of Heidegger's analysis of death see, Macquarrie, 1968, pp. 28-32, and Zimmerman, 1986, pp. 69-100.
8. Heidegger says, "Let the term '*dying*' stand for that *way of Being* in which Dasein *is towards* its death" (1987, H.247).

9. For a graphic and vivid description of the death of another and its sheer inaccessibility few accounts could surpass Simone De Beauvoir's account of her mother's death in *A Very Easy Death* (1987).
10. I will return to this potential criticism of Heidegger in the concluding chapter. Also see Ridley Scott's film *Blade Runner*, particularly the scene in which the replicant Roy Batty saves the life of Dekkard in a final heroic gesture before dying, and Zimmerman's discussion of heroism in Heidegger in *Eclipse of the Self*, (1986, pp. 81-93). There are also parallels with Nietzsche in this area, see, Havas, "Who is Heidegger's Nietzsche?".
11. Heidegger, 1987, H. 269.
12. See Spiegelberg, 1960, Vol.I, pp. 331-333 for a discussion of the importance of this distinction in Heidegger's work.
13. Heidegger says that, "The temporality of fear is a forgetting which awaits and makes present" (1987, H. 342), which is exactly what Hume is doing when he is perplexed by the contradiction between his impression of diversity and his search for identity.
14. Richardson, 1986, Chapter Three, Section One and Section Three, parts (d) and (e).
15. Heidegger, 1987, H. 261.
16. There is an obvious parallel between Heidegger's analysis of death and the taking over of this phenomenon by authentic Dasein, with Hegel's discussion of the transition to self consciousness set out in his *Phenomenology of Spirit*, when Hegel says, "The individual who has not risked his life may well be recognised as a person, but he has not attained to the truth of this recognition as an independent self consciousness" (Hegel, 1977, p.114). This sounds like a cruder version of Heidegger's taking over death as the ownmost and unavoidable possibility of Dasein. Both engender the acceptance of finitude as a fundamental and constitutive characteristic of Being. Heidegger discusses this part of Hegel's work in his own *Hegel's Concept of Experience* (1970) especially in the second part, "Self Consciousness".
17. Heidegger, 1987, H. 266.
18. See Richardson, 1986, Chapter Three, Part One, for a discussion of Dasein's being-guilty. Also, Blattner, "Existential Temporality in *Being and Time*", pp.110-112.
19. For an exposition of Heidegger's use of the notion of conscience see, Waterhouse, 1981, pp. 98-103.
20. This will clearly have implications for ethical theory, implications which go far beyond the scope of this thesis. Richardson recognises this in *Existential Epistemology*, pp. 177-179, and it is discussed further by Bernasconi, "Deconstruction and the possibility of ethics" and, Derrida, "Violence and Metaphysics". There are further and obvious connections between this line of discussion in Heidegger's work and Stirner's egoism, and I will return to this aspect in Chapter Nine.
21. Again there is a parallel here between Heidegger on inauthentic Dasein and Marx on "Estranged Labour" in his *Early Writings* (1981).
22. Heidegger, 1987, H. 277.

23. Once again Heidegger will allow no moral overtone to be given, even to this heavily loaded term.
24. Ibid, H. 296.
25. Zimmerman, in characteristic Heideggerian fashion says, "An ecstatic Dasein stretches itself out towards the future in terms of the still determinative past. This ecstatic self-stretching is the temporal transcendence which constitutes the clearing in which beings can be manifest" (1986, p. 105).
26. Heidegger, 1987, H. 299.
27. Heidegger says, "That *Present* which is held in authentic temporality and which thus is *authentic* itself we call the '*moment of vision*'" (1987, H. 338).
28. See also, Guignon, "History and Commitment in the early Heidegger", Zimmerman, (1986, p. 100), on Temporality and Selfhood, and Nicholson, "Ekstatic Temporality in 'Sein und Zeit'".
29. For parallel discussions elsewhere in Heidegger's work see *The Basic Problems of Phenomenology* (1982) Part Two, where temporality is discussed in the context of the question of ontological difference, and *A History of the Concept of Time* (1985).
30. Heidegger says, "Temporality 'is' not an entity at all" (1987, H. 328).
31. This does not mean that nothing could have been before Dasein existed. See Guignon, "History and Commitment in the early Heidegger", for a discussion of this issue. There is, however, a sense in which nothing *exists* without Dasein, but this is because of the way in which Heidegger uses the term "existing" to denote the active standing out of Dasein in the world. In this way only Dasein can exist and consequently can only understand the world from the point of view of this existing. So, as Macquarrie says, "The understanding of Being which is already given with human existence, as itself kind of being, allows the enquiry to get started, but finally existence itself can only be understood in the light of Being" (Macquarrie, 1968, p. 9). See also Fell, "The Familiar and the Strange: On the Limits of Praxis in the Early Heidegger", for a discussion of the distinction between "nature" and "world".
32. Heidegger, 1987, Division Two, Part IV, "Temporality and Everydayness".
33. See Heidegger, 1987, H. 411-428, for Heidegger's setting out of the relation between clock time, or public time, and authentic temporality. Also see Barash, 1988, for a more extended discussion of this issue.
34. The feature of action and Being that is derived from the temporality of being-in-the-world Heidegger calls "datability" (1987, H. 407). It is because our involvement has temporal structure (beginning, middle and end) that we are able to conceive of our being-in-the-world as taking place in time. Our temporally structured activity allows us to date and time our being-in-the-world in such a way that clock time is made possible by the temporal structure of Dasein as existing and through datability. Heidegger is giving us a metaphysics of time as the form of Being.
35. Zimmerman says, "I come to know myself not so much by abstract self reflection as by taking on roles in the various social groups into which I am born. I learn about what it means to be human from the very activity of being human" (1986, p. 30).
36. Poggeler, "Being as Appropriation".

37. This identity will not only absolve Heidegger of the need to prove continuing personal identity over time but also show how the question could be asked in the first place.
38. Richardson, 1986, pp. 196-203.
39. Heidegger, 1987, H. 374.
40. Conversely it poses question about how Dasein can come to know itself and the world.

9
Conclusion - How to Argue with an Egoist

The aim of this book has been to investigate the formulation of a theory of the self. The structure of this book is made up of a series of critical examinations of theories of the self, theories implicit and explicit in the work of Stirner, Laing, Descartes, Hume, Kant, Sartre, and finally, Heidegger. The method that I have used is to focus on two problems, the problem of knowledge of the not-self, (external objects, other selves etc.) and the problem of the continuity of the self over time (the problem of personal identity). I have taken these problems as a means of approaching the fundamental issues of the spatiality and temporality of the self. As a consequence some conclusions with regard to notions of space and time have also emerged.

The argument which I have developed as the work has progressed is that, criticism of a tradition which begins with Descartes, and runs through the work of Hume, Kant, and Sartre, is not only effective against the specific positions taken by these philosophers, but cumulatively points towards the need to question the underlying common assumptions on which their work rests, and thereby develops into a critique of the whole tradition which they represent. It is my contention that the writers of this tradition cannot adequately answer the problems of knowledge and personal identity. I have used the early work (1925-1929) of Martin Heidegger to show why they fail, and then followed his work through as he demonstrates how and why their position arises. The effect of Heidegger's criticism of these other writers is to envelop and undermine their positions, which are revealed as derived from an underlying, more primordial, ontological, structure of the self. It is clear that, while each of the first four mainstream philosophers I have examined have made significant contributions to the debate about the nature of the self, their combined work represents, not only a historical, but also a philosophical continuum. None of them has succeeded in satisfactorily solving the problems of knowledge and identity, and to this extent no satisfactory theory of the self emerges from their work. The success of their work is indicated by the extent to which Heidegger uses it to develop his own position, their failure by the effectiveness of his criticism in undermining their positions.

In order to determine whether or not the aim of this book has been attained, it is necessary first to return to the dispute set out in Chapters Two and Three, between Max Stirner and R.D. Laing, to focus on the philosophical underpinnings of these two less than mainstream disputants, and to see what consequences the later critical examinations of these underpinnings have on their respective cases. In other words how do the critical examinations of Descartes, Hume, Kant, Sartre and Heidegger affect an evaluation of the positions of Stirner and Laing? Following that I will reflect on Heidegger's position in relation to the tradition and the relative strengths of his theory of the self in comparison with the theories offered by the other philosophers I have examined. Finally, I will briefly compare the positions of Stirner and Heidegger relative to the issue of individuality.

Stirner and Laing Revisited

At the end of Chapter Three it was at least clear that the theories of the self put forward by Max Stirner and R.D. Laing were radically different. Against Stirner's proud (almost fanatical) individualism of "the Owner" and "the Unique One", we have Laing's individual, healthy only if integrated into the society of others, and spiralling down to destruction when isolated in the way that Stirner demands and revels in.

While taking Laing's work in *The Divided Self* as *prima facie* indication that Stirner's position could be rejected there was insufficient in Laing to reject Stirner outright. A close examination of the philosophical underpinnings of the positions of both Stirner and Laing was required. Moreover, even before engaging the debate at the philosophical level, I expressed some reservations about Laing's position, as against Stirner's individualism and egoism, when it began to appear that Laing's ideas about the self might add up to exactly the kind of disguised normative position which Stirner is exposing and damning in *The Ego and Its Own*, (a possibility recognised by Laing and one which he explicitly wishes to avoid). If we are, in the end, to reject Stirner's position it is crucial that this rejection is not simply based on ground that the Stirnerian fundamentally denies. If, as seems obvious, Stirner sets out, and rejoices in, an isolationist view of the self, and rejects the fundamentally relational nature of Laing's self, then the theory of the relational self must be further supported against Stirner's egoism. Clearly, for Stirner, the Unique One must remain unique and separated. Equally the egoist cannot just be characterised as 'mad' by the psychiatrist, when the egoist denies the ground on which the psychiatrist stands. It is because of this that an examination of the fundamental ontology underlying the positions of Stirner and Laing must be used to discover the real basis of their difference, and to furnish the grounds on which to choose between them.

On the basis of his singular subjectivism I have taken Stirner's position to be basically Cartesian and used not only Descartes, but also Hume, Kant and Sartre's existentialism to illustrate possible ontological positions which might support his view of the self. For Laing, who is not primarily a philosopher, but who equally clearly holds a very different view of the self from Stirner, I have used the early work of Heidegger, in particular his *Being and Time*, to support a relational theory of the self.[1] This course is further, if indirectly, indicated by Laing both by the language he uses, and the general structure of his argument with regard to the self. At a deeper level the problems of knowledge and personal identity are expressed as the questions of the spatiality and temporality of the self. The problem of knowledge is the problem of the relation of the subject to entities that are not-itself. The nature of this relationship, or more often its possibility, is concerned with the existence in space of discrete entities, which, although they must remain discrete and therefore in some way separate, must also interact. The model of subject consciousness, adopted in one way or another by Hume, Kant, Sartre, and by implication, Stirner, makes the relationship between this subject and other discrete entities problematic. By emphasising the singularity of the subject and its self-subsistence the subject is disabled from relation to entities "beyond" itself. All I have are my perceptions, and I have no way of knowing whether these subjective phenomena accurately represent "objective" reality, even to the extent that I find it difficult to prove that there is an "objective" reality at all. The representational model of perception, which grows out of this kind of subjectivity, makes the spatiality of the world a problem because it provides no route to a pre-supposed spatial world existing independently of the subject.

The problem of the continuity of personal identity over time provides the focus for the parallel argument in respect of temporality. Simply, the traditional model does not provide ground for the affirmation of identity over time, and therefore no ground for the relation of the self to itself at another time. In the same way that the existence of objective space is called into question by the problem of knowledge, so the existence of objective time is called into doubt by a methodology that cannot connect apparently successive moments in time. This is witnessed by its failure to connect entities not with other entities, but with precisely identical entities at another time.

It is central to this work that the attempts by Descartes, Hume, Kant and Sartre to provide satisfactory solutions to these problems are ultimately unsuccessful, and this is what I have argued in Chapters Four, Five and Six. By "satisfactory" I take to mean a theory that is consistent within itself and with all the aspects of my everyday experience, and which does not generate problems or paradoxes with regard to this experience. The failure of these Cartesians is rooted in their attachment to the notion of fundamental subjectivity and a dualistic separation of the world into subject and object. At an even deeper level it is clear that "thinghood" is central to their enquiries about the nature of the self, a position radically undermined by Heidegger in his work on phenomenological ontology.

It is my initial conclusion, following the examination of the works of Descartes, Hume, Kant, Sartre and Heidegger, that only Heidegger develops an ontology that satisfactorily explains and interprets both the spatiality and temporality of the self (as set out respectively in Chapters Seven and Eight). None of the others are successful in satisfactorily, or completely, providing such an ontology. Although each makes a contribution to the debate, they eventually fail in different degrees, and succeed more or less according to how closely they approach the Heideggerian position. With regard therefore to the initial dispute between Stirner and Laing, it appears that Laing's work can be grounded in such a way that the criticisms it implies of Stirner's egoism are very much more than just mud slinging. Stirner's egoist appears to be not simply "mad", as judged by a concealed normative standard of sanity, but as representing an ontologically incomplete and inadequate notion of selfhood. Isolated subjectivity, gloriously promoted by Stirner, does not adequately reflect Being as it is experienced, so his view of the self is mistaken.[2] In this light Laing's work with patients is aimed at restoring individuals to the possibilities of their being, and it applies an idea of authentic selfhood as liberating, and not, as Stirner would claim, as entrapment in structures which fetter and distort the individuality of the self. I will now summarise the failure of Stirner's position to deliver a notion of the self in space and time and then go on to develop an understanding of the crucial differences between these positions and that taken by Heidegger.

Heidegger and the Tradition

In Chapters Four, Five and Six I have argued that the positions of, Descartes, Hume, Kant, and the early Sartre, fail to provide the basis for an adequate theory of the self, as a direct consequence of their failure to solve the problems of knowledge and personal identity. This failure is openly discussed by Hume, in the Appendix to the *Treatise*, and by Sartre in "The Reef of Solipsism" (Sartre, 1956, pp. 223-233). The aim of my investigations in respect of these philosophers has been to show that, if they founder on this reef, then their theories of the self will lead to the egoism of Stirner. While each one of the four progresses the debate, adding wider and more subtle insights, none of the four can effectively or completely counter Stirner's extreme subjectivism and egoism.

Heidegger has claimed to do more than reject the Cartesian position in all its guises. He wishes to demonstrate not only that the premise of the "thinghood" of individual existence and the possibility of its disconnection from the world is an error, but also that these interpretations, and the conclusions and problems to which they lead, arise precisely out of, and because of, the nature of our being, a nature which these positions either do not suspect or fail to articulate clearly or fully.[3] Heidegger wants to make this nature clear, and to give an alternative analysis of our everyday experience, and the everyday understandings, which arise from this experience. We are taken to task by Heidegger less for accepting the dualist's descriptions, and more for presuming that these descriptions are complete, and that the problems they present are insoluble. Heidegger does not dismiss the subject/object model; he wishes to show that it is itself derived from the more primordial relations of Being-in-the-world and Being-temporal which characterise selfhood at a more fundamental level. Heidegger wants to swallow the Cartesian position whole, without being poisoned by it.

Heidegger does not reject Cartesian, or specifically Kantian, methodology. The understandings generated from these premises have some, if derivative and limited, validity.[4] The issue between Heidegger and the tradition centres on the status, or primordiality, of the premises of the tradition, in particular the possible separation of self from world, and the singularity and self-subsistence of the self. It is Heidegger's contention that the understandings of the self and the world which arise in the development of Cartesian and post-Cartesian metaphysics, do so as a result of interpretations of everyday experience, which are preoccupied with the details of this experience. They therefore remain embedded in this experience, and consequently cannot take the analysis into the ground of this experience. They are understandings that grow out of premises which are not fundamental and which lead to incomplete and inadequate interpretations of self and world. Heidegger is saying that these are exactly the positions we would expect to arise, and which must arise in the first instance from the way of being of everyday Dasein, preoccupied, as it must be with the task in hand and the kind of engagements consequent upon being-in-the-world. In this way Cartesian and post-Cartesian, metaphysics is an exemplary expression of the way of being of "the they", and this is one of the possible ways of being of Dasein. However, it is authentic Dasein, as that which exists as possible ways of being, which first makes possible the ways of being of "the they". The failure of the tradition therefore is a failure to recognise the necessary foundation, which underlies it own presumptions. Heidegger's approach is to interpret everyday ways of being and to ask how it is possible for these to arise, and what kind of being is it that can exist in this way? Heidegger is asking altogether different questions to those posed by the tradition. But he is nevertheless able to demonstrate how and why these questions arise. The problems of knowledge and personal identity can arise only because Dasein exists as thrown and projecting being in the world, despite the fact that the tradition in which they arise cannot acknowledge the foundation from which they spring.[5]

The difficulty faced by Laing's patients is the difficulty they have in being-with. They struggle with their relatedness to the world, and especially to others like them. Heidegger's ontology shows that this relatedness is not simply socially or morally desirable but fundamental to, and constitutive of, the way of being of humans (as Dasein), and therefore constitutive of human society. Laing's patients, as manifestly unwell, seem only able to understand themselves as "things" and stumble when they seek relatedness to other "things". Similarly, Others persist in understanding them only as "things". The societal context is structured against them, and Laing's patients are caught in the trap of trying to live contrary to a way of being which they cannot escape, that is, relation to Others.[6] They attempt to deny their relation to the world and to others, in order to protect themselves and, in so doing, retreat into what they suppose to be the safety of subjective isolation. However, in this way they can only create the pretence of isolation, and a pretence that is diametrically at odds with their being-in-the-world. This contradiction is, in the end, not sustainable, and their sense of self collapses. Their progressive, and forced, retreat from connectedness, a connectedness that is made problematic by the initial presumption of subjective isolation, deepens the contradiction, and finally precipitates them into self destruction. Laing is attempting to bring his patients back to their essential being-in-the-world from their being as 'the they' and to help them to understand this constitutive characteristic of their being. In short Laing's thesis is that each individual Dasein must take over its own being-in-the-world and being-temporal as constitutive of what it is to be (including being-with-Others), and this endeavour is fully supported by Heidegger's analysis of Dasein in *Being and Time*. Laing's work is a commentary not simply on individual psychological breakdown, but on the kind of social structures, (the ways in which being is with Others), which lead to the portrayal of those who stand out against the way of being of "the they" as dysfunctional, or just plain mad. The ontology implied by Laing's work, and made explicit by Heidegger, is applicable not only inwardly, towards individual Dasein, but also outwardly, towards the view taken by each individual of others like themselves. This is because both Laing and Heidegger are convinced that isolated individuality is incomplete without the context of Others. Authenticity, for Laing, must be both an understanding of the nature of self and the nature of others. Being is, above all, social.

Stirner, on the other hand, appears to revel in an understanding of his Being which is radically inauthentic. His isolation from the world is almost complete and he resists every attempt to connect his interests to those of anyone else. "Away with any cause which is not wholly and entirely my cause".[7] Heidegger and Laing focus exclusively on being-with, Stirner only has eyes for himself, his relentless rejection of communitarian, or any other-regarding, values and his determined pursuit of self-interest, makes the efforts of Laing and Heidegger seem no more than attempts to deceive, and to rob Stirner of his individuality. Stirner resists the movement from self to other, doggedly clinging to his own "uniqueness" and claiming "ownership" as the only thing worth fighting for. Stirner's understanding of selfhood is referenced wholly inwards.

> Why will you not take courage now to really make *yourselves* the central point and the main thing altogether?

And,

> Therefore turn to yourselves rather than to your gods or idols. Bring out from yourselves what is in you, bring it to the light, bring yourselves to revelation. (Stirner, 1982, p.161)

Heidegger's work shows that Stirner's implied notion of the self (as isolated, self-creating and creative) is mistaken. That is, it takes an aspect of selfhood, (subjectivity), to be not only essential to, but exclusively constitutive of, selfhood. Heidegger shows that this is not the case and that selfhood, as represented by Dasein, is constituted by relation to the world, in the sense that it is the relating itself, the relating to its environment as being-in-the-world, and to itself as being-temporal. The ontology required to support Stirner's egoism is not sustainable. In fact, the ontology described by Heidegger contradicts any possible ontology that would support Stirner's position.

Stirner's egoism is an exhortation to self-realisation. It says, "be what you can become!" and, as such, it is self contradictory because it also exhorts the relational individual to become isolated. It appears that we cannot be the kind of Being which Stirner's egoism impels us towards without violating the central tenets of authentic being, in particular being-with-others. If this is so, then Stirner's egoism is self contradictory, because Stirner, a being in-the-world and a temporal being, attempts to become isolated and self subsistent.[8]

Stirner is seeking to compress his being to the inauthentic, preoccupied with the present, and locked into inauthentic relation to entities, including Others, in the world. By insisting that his own ego is paramount Stirner insists on the interpretation of himself as "thing" - most important of all "things", but "thing" all the same. In Heideggerian terms the egoist's position can only arise from an interpretation of being which is preoccupied with the details of everyday experience, and which therefore alienates the individual self from Others, and its own possibility for authentic being.[9] Stirner's egoism is also an attempt to impose a mistaken notion of selfhood onto Others and to transmit this notion into the world by prescribing a particular way of being towards Others, that is egoism, a way of being which treats others as essentially separated and therefore worthless, except as a means to the end of the egoist. Stirner's egoism therefore strikes at the very heart of authentic being-with-others. It is now clear that it is only in not-being that Dasein can achieve the glorious isolation celebrated by Stirner; only by no longer having-a-world can Dasein become an "Owner". The contradiction is complete. This is the fatal contradiction in Stirner's egoism, and Laing's patients are the final tragic outcome of the same ontological errors, which ground this position.

To Choose or Not to Choose?

Heidegger's work shows that Stirner's egoism is mistaken and self defeating. Stirner's egoism draws attention to the individuality of the being of Dasein at the cost of "forgetting", or concealing, being-in-the-world and being-temporal. The tradition, of which Stirner is the most extreme example, misunderstands being and divides Dasein from the world of entities and other Dasein. A satisfactory theory of the self cannot be found within the tradition because of the way in which the tradition rests on the fracture between the individual and the world. Every attempt to derive a theory of the self beginning with the individual subject is frustrated, because, if such an attempt were ever to succeed the tradition itself would be subverted, and its premise, the singular subject, would be called into question. The co-existence of relation and subjectivity is rendered problematic by the tradition.

This is most evident in Sartre's existentialism. In his discussion of the existence of the Other in "The Look"[10] he begins with the premise of the *cogito*,[11] which isolates consciousness from the world, but concludes with a profound unity of being, with the Other welling up within his own subjectivity, a welling up which directly violates the self subsistence given, and required by, the *cogito*. Whichever way it is re-interpreted, the *cogito* admits no such unity of being and herein lies the contradiction at the heart of Sartre's position.

In exchange for these problems Heidegger offers a new analysis of human being through the analysis of Dasein. Dasein is the activity of being, the process of existing, and resists all attempts to characterise it as the subject. Heidegger has tried to make the self of Dasein immune from the problems encountered by the subject and has been successful, at least in respect of the problems of knowledge and personal identity. From Heidegger we gain a new understanding of the genesis of these problems and a perspective that liberates us from seeing them as problems at all.

> I now no longer have as a problem the being in its own self in regard to the peculiar mode of being belonging to it, but instead the being *as standing opposite, as standing over against.* (Heidegger, 1982, p.156-7)

What is problematic is the kind of approach that formulates the questions as problematic.

Heidegger's alternative characterises individual Dasein as being-in-the-world and being-temporal, and these relational facets of Dasein are not options which Dasein can choose, or not, to provide itself with, but are constitutive of its being.[12] Without the connection between Dasein and entities, not only in the present, but temporally, there is no Dasein. Dasein is contextual, and not in the sense that it is one object among others, but in the sense that it is structured as context. The attempt to withdraw Dasein from its involvements misses the target because it denies Dasein's possibility for authentic being, which is, in part, constituted as being-with-others. This means that social behaviour of some sort is implicit in the being of Dasein, and, individual Dasein, in failing to recognise, or seeking to avoid, this will deny its possibility for authentic being, the possibility which grounds all of the possibilities of Dasein. The form of the Being of Dasein is social.

The terms "authentic" and "inauthentic" are key operators in Heidegger's ontology and we must remember that he gives no normative values to this pair of terms. Heidegger claims to be concerned only with ontology and not with ethics. There is no way in which Heidegger means to say that authentic is in any way better than inauthentic, no statement of value is given. He has given a, more or less, clear exposition of the nature of (human) Dasein and of what it is to be, and this would seem to be an appropriate starting point for a discussion as to how we might behave towards one another. We have, at least, the building blocks in the understanding of the nature of individual Dasein. But it is at the point of the commencement of ethical theorisation, that the most serious problem with Heidegger's ontology comes to the fore.

In our understanding of individual Dasein selfhood turns out to be radically different from the entity we anticipated finding at the beginning of the enquiry. There is a strong sense in which Dasein is not individual at all, and certainly not in the sense of an isolated, or even isolable, entity. Dasein is formally and inescapably connected to the world, in that it cannot choose to be not related to Others, however hard it might try to conceal this ontological connection. It might even appear that Dasein must comport itself towards others as it would towards itself, and, moreover it might seem that this imperative is not only ethical but ontologically grounded. With Heidegger's ontology there is apparently no more room for argument, I must be what I already am. However Heidegger's ontology generates only formal imperatives, it can provide no guidance for authentic Dasein in its relation towards Others. Heidegger's Dasein is in a world and temporal. In this sense it is social (as ontologically relational), but not necessarily ethical. We are not relieved of the anguish of having to choose how to act by the illumination of fundamental ontology provided by Heidegger, it is only confirmed that we must choose.[13]

Heidegger has disabled Stirner's egoistic position, but in defeating the egoist Heidegger has not provided a new arbiter between moral systems. Heidegger's "ethic", if we were to call it that, would be something like, "be what you are!" and this offers little in answer to the question, what should I do?

Ironically, considerable and significant similarities between the positions of Heidegger and Stirner now begin to emerge. Although Heidegger denies any ethical imperative in his work, his repeated use of ethically loaded terms, like care, resoluteness and authenticity, and the strongly implicit presumption that we should strive to rise above and overcome the ways of being of "the they" and become authentic, make this denial difficult to accept. In fact by refusing to engage in ethical debate Heidegger is more closely amoral even than Stirner, who is really more anti-moral than amoral because he so loudly rejects the claims of morality. Both philosophies are philosophies of self-realisation and self-creation and, in the sense that they prescribe, explicitly or implicitly; ways of being towards others, both are ethical positions in spite of their denials. Both exhort the individual to self realisation despite their widely differing ontological foundations.

The consequences of Heidegger's work, for ethics, are surprising. It appears at first that he has provided the ground for ethics through a new and clear understanding of what it is to be. In understanding the authentic possibility of Dasein, other-regarding becomes not a choice we can make, but a choice we have to make. As Sartre says, not choosing is a choice in itself.[14] The sharp ontological distinction we have got used to making between ourselves and others within the Cartesian tradition is impossible once we reject this tradition and embrace Heideggerian ontology. *Mitsein*, being-with-Others is part of the way of being of authentic Dasein, but the further the analysis is pursued, the more it seems that the Heideggerian move does no more than make ethics a formality. As the ground for ethics emerges out of Heideggerian ontology so it becomes clear that this ethic, and the ontology it rests on, is formal and empty,[15] and this is exemplified in its failure to engage in ethical discussion, and in its emerging similarity with Stirnerian egoism. The spectatorial perspective, which Heidegger undermines, is the perspective of free (Stirnerian) human being choosing between possible alternative courses of action, and Heidegger offers nothing to guide this choice beyond the formal confirmation that it must be made. In this sense Heidegger's claim to offer no ethic is justified. In destroying Stirner's egoism, and subverting the tradition, Heidegger presents the pure form of being, devoid of content, and can therefore provide no further ethical guidance, beyond the formal necessity of relating to others. Heidegger therefore provides the starting point from which ethical theorising must begin but no guidance as to the direction it should take. In terms of its value as a philosophical position this constitutes a serious defect in Heidegger's position and one that may eventually devalue what he has to say about Being. Heidegger's work is not the answer to all of our philosophical problems. However, as I indicated earlier, it is all too easy to take Heidegger to be saying more than he actually is saying. In fact Heidegger can make no ethical pronouncements based on his work in *Being and Time*, not because he denies that he is "doing ethics" but because it is not possible to "do ethics" from this point of view.

In the final concluding section I will briefly look at the consequences of this irony and examine how, and why, it has arisen as a consequence of the nature of Heidegger's notion of selfhood. This will amount to a brief re-assessment of the notion of individuality in Heidegger's work, and will cast Stirner's apparently hopeless position in a more optimistic, if not a less problematic, light.

Heideggerian Heroes

Heidegger provides the ontological ground on which Stirner's egoism can be refuted as theory of the self, but then fails to provide any ethical direction, and falls back towards the empty ethical formalism at the heart of Stirner's position. In order to understand the reasons for this irony an important feature of Heidegger's analysis needs to be recognised. Heidegger's rejection of the traditional approach is essentially a rejection of the question of content of Being (what is it?), in favour of the formal question of being (what is its meaning? or what makes it possible?). Not only is the former unanswerable in the tradition which poses it, but the attempts to answer it distract attention from what Heidegger sees as the more primordial analysis of the meaning (form) of being. This leads Heidegger to an understanding of the being of Dasein in terms of "ways of being" as opposed to any kind of subject. Heidegger's approach produces a radical re-interpretation and re-application of the phenomenological method of his early mentor Husserl, in which Heidegger rejects the premise that phenomenology has nothing to say about ontology and, instead, insists that phenomenology is the only means of access to ontological structures.[16] Heidegger affirms not only the possibility of phenomenological ontology but its necessity. This move is a move towards formal analysis, and, although Heidegger repeats Husserl's cry, "to the things themselves", his attention is drawn not to the things but to their form, their way of being. This is also the source of Heidegger's explanation of how the positions of his precursors arise. The works of Descartes, Hume, Kant and even Sartre, are not simply rejected as wrong by Heidegger but are undermined and characterised as incomplete or misguided, a telling of partial truth. Descartes, Hume, Kant and Sartre are asking the wrong questions.

Heidegger begins his investigation with an investigation of the everyday and, in particular, with an investigation into the everyday experience of Dasein. This experience is characterised, even constituted, by the continual encounter with entities in the world that makes up the experience of Dasein. However, unlike all his predecessors, Heidegger will not concern himself with the contents of these experiences, he will not ask questions about the conformity between the phenomenal experience and the posited objects of this experience.[17] Heidegger is concerned with the fact of experience and how it is made possible. He asks the formal question of experience and seeks the structures which underlie the phenomenon of experience itself, hoping thus to undermine disputes concerned with the contents of actual experiences. This is the way that Heidegger avoids the problem of knowledge. Moreover Heidegger does not simply reject the subject centred phenomenalism of the tradition, he explains how this way of being arises on the foundation of, what he calls, more primordial structures of Being. For Heidegger, as for the traditional phenomenology of Kant and Husserl, phenomena are all that we can experience, (to the things themselves!), furthermore phenomena conceal the nature of the reality on which they rest. In the tradition this model is nowhere better described than by Kant and it leads him to the "thing in itself", existing but inaccessible to experience, hidden by phenomena. Heidegger is close to Kant on this point and is in sympathy with the interpretation of the Kantian argument which says that the phenomenal object and the thing-in-itself are not two different objects but one and the same, understood by sensibility and by reason.[18] Heidegger takes the argument a stage further by refusing to posit the existence of the thing-in-itself at all and by returning to the everyday (phenomenal) world. He understands phenomena as concealing, but not as concealing in the way of being-in-front-of. It is more a question of where we are standing than what is in the way, more about the actual questions we are asking. It is our preoccupation with the contents of phenomena which conceals and it is only when our attention is drawn to more formal questions about experience that the form of experience is revealed. In this way we can re-interpret everyday experience with new eyes. Phenomena alone cannot conceal, and to understand them as so doing is to fall into yet another variety of the subject/object trap. The experience of phenomena is inextricable from the experiencing entity, and it is only in the *relation* of experience that concealment can take place. In essence Heidegger demonstrates that the apperception of unity is the unity of apperception, but only because the latter is the pre-existing ground which implies the former. That is, the apperception of unity is only possible because of the fundamental unity of apperception that is Dasein. Kant fails to recognise this and cannot progress from the apperception of unity to the unity of apperception, and from there to a notion of selfhood as transcendence.

The formalism of Heidegger's approach is exemplified by the methodology that he uses to interpret everydayness. Heidegger calls our attention not directly to the things themselves, but to entities in their absence, malfunctioning, or in the way (obtrusive, conspicuous, obstinate).[19] In addition to avoiding the objectification of these entities as objects of perception, and, calling attention to the contextual functionality of entities we find in the world (ready-to-handness), this, at first rather strange way of looking at entities by not looking at them, calls our attention to their form. We understand the screwdriver that is missing as the form of lacking screwdriverness within the context of our activity in the world. We know what we need by understanding what we need it for. Entities are understood functionally, and we thereby recognise their essential interconnectedness to other entities and to Dasein, which by its own activity (projecting) makes them ready-to-hand. It is easy to see how, by this route; Heidegger is able to arrive at the conclusion to Division I of *Being and Time* and to determine that the Being of everyday Dasein is Care. Care is the fact of involvement or engagement, with entities in the world, the form of the being of everyday Dasein. Nothing is said about the details of this involvement. The ethical overtones of the word "care" are explicitly rejected to make it clear that no particular styles, or ways of involvement, are favoured. Indeed the asking of such questions is characterised critically, as a return to the preoccupation with the contents of particular experiences and the conspiratorial concealment of fundamental ontology undertaken by "the they". Care is a formal notion if it is anything at all, it says nothing more or less than that this is the form that the being of Dasein must take, however much this form is concealed, sometimes deliberately, and even necessarily, in the everyday engagement of Dasein in the world. The notion of Care is therefore formally amoral, despite Heidegger's attempt to avoid this interpretation.[20]

In Division II of *Being and Time* Heidegger provides three more key interpretations leading to the setting out of the meaning of the being of authentic Dasein. These are the interpretations of death, conscience and resoluteness. I will now demonstrate not only how these interpretations provide formal notions of these three phenomena and lead to an heroic notion of selfhood, but also how they echo Stirner's position.

The interpretation of death begins with the apparent rejection of all phenomenal experience of death. I cannot experience my own death since this phenomenon is precisely that which denies me the possibility of any further experience. Neither is the experience of the death of another a suitable point of entry into the analysis because it is the impossibility of my own being which is here under scrutiny. Death can only be understood as my possibility, ownmost, uttermost, and not to be outstripped. In essence Dasein exists as that which dies, but not simply in the sense of an ending, as would an animal, but because Dasein exists as projecting, as possibilities. The death of Dasein is the loss of possibility. Dasein is being-towards-death whichever way it chooses to interpret death, and irrespective of its mode of death. Dying is one of the ways of being of Dasein, a way of being which Dasein must understand and which constitutes Dasein. Interpreted in this way death (as dying) is no longer an event in the future, not something that will simply *happen to* Dasein, but part of Dasein from the moment it first exists. The transposition in Heidegger's analysis from death to dying is the move from content to form. The mode of death, its timeliness or otherwise are not relevant to this interpretation, even though they constitute the everyday preoccupation with death. Heidegger has given us a notion of dying as a constitutive characteristic of Dasein. Authentic Dasein is then called upon to take this ultimate possibility to itself and to abjure the inauthentic interpretations of death put forward by "the they", interpretations which alienate Dasein from its ultimate, and therefore all other, possibilities. Authentic Dasein understands itself as dying and therefore as finite, but this understanding is no more than an understanding of the form of its being and leaves authentic Dasein facing up to its end whatever it may be, and whenever it may come. Dasein must have the courage to take over its own being, and this is expressed in no uncertain terms in Heidegger's essay "What is Metaphysics?"

> The dread by the courageous cannot be contrasted with the joy or even the comfortable enjoyment of a peaceable life. It stands - on the hither side of all such contrasts - in secret union with the serenity and gentleness of creative longing. ("What is Metaphysics?", in, Heidegger, 1968, p. 374)

> Dread is there, but sleeping. All *Da-sein* quivers with its breathing: the pulsation is slightest in beings that are timorous,... it is readiest in the reserved, and surest of all in the courageous. (Ibid, p. 373)

> The clear courage for essential dread (*angst*) guarantees that most mysterious of all possibilities: the experience of Being. (Ibid, p. 386)

The very language used by Heidegger in this essay invites comparison with Stirner at his most passionate.

> I am the *owner* of my might, and I am so when I know myself as *unique*. In the *unique one* the owner himself returns in to his creative nothing of which he is born. Every higher essence above me, be it God, be it man, weakens the feeling of my uniqueness, and pales only before the sun of this consciousness (Stirner, 1982, p.366),

> Therefore turn to yourselves rather than to your gods or idols. Bring out from yourselves what is in you, bring it to the light, bring yourselves to revelation. (Ibid, p. 161)

Even more evocative of Heidegger, "Why will you not take courage now to really make *yourselves* the central point and the main thing altogether" (Ibid, p. 161). Heroic stuff indeed and not so very different from each of these philosophers,[21] but not necessarily useful in describing a notion of selfhood since it appears that it does not matter how or when we die but how we face death.[22] Although it is clear that every Dasein must have an actual death, describable in terms of its mode and timing, there is no necessary connection here between the details of the event and the formal notion of dying. Any contents may fill up the form of Dasein's dying, leaving death itself no more than a formal requirement. What is important, or so it seems, is not how or when we die but how we view our dying. The divorce between form and content is absolute and complete. Although it appeared that Heidegger's ontology fatally undermined Stirner's position, it is now becoming clear that their notions of selfhood may not be so far apart after all.

A similar pattern is presented in Heidegger's interpretation of conscience. The everyday phenomenon of conscience is identified as a voice from beyond Dasein, telling Dasein what to do, passing opinions on the past actions and future intentions of Dasein. Heidegger rejects this interpretation in favour of a wholly formal notion of conscience in which the authentic conscience is manifest to Dasein as reticence and is authentically recognised as the voice of Dasein calling to itself. At this point Heidegger appears to be at his most oblique, conscience is not "heard" at all, even though its origin is internal to Dasein, but in this way it is most authentically understood. Once again it is the form, or possibility of *having a conscience*, which interests Heidegger, as opposed to any explicit manifestation of a particular conscience. His focus is on the kind of being which can have the experience of conscience rather than on particular examples of the phenomenon. Authentic conscience is expressed by reticence because reticence is the absence of explicit phenomenal contents and therefore draws attention only to the form of conscience, or the possibility of having a conscience. Heidegger makes no judgements about particular experiences of conscience (in fact he rejects such judgements), but simply forces recognition that the fact of conscience implicates Dasein in its being. This is the being-guilty of Dasein, but like dying, it is no more than the form of the being of Dasein. Once again, as with death, there must be everyday experience of conscience, but, once again, this requirement is merely formal and does not connect, in terms of its contents, with the everyday experience of conscience. The specific words of my everyday conscience are irrelevant to ontological inquiry, mere distraction. Once again we can draw a parallel with Stirner who rejects all calls from beyond his own self, which appear to be telling him what to do. For Stirner the only valid notion of conscience would be a call from his unique self to the self lost and fettered in the chains of morality. Stirner's conscience can only call him forth to be an Owner, to take over all that he is himself.[23] In both Heidegger and Stirner conscience is the exhortation to the self, from the self, to take up its own self realisation.

Finally, in the progress towards authentic Dasein, Heidegger develops the notion of resoluteness as the authentic orientation of Dasein towards the ontological truth of its own being. However, once again, the cry "be resolute!" has no content, and the emptiness persists even though Heidegger is explicit when he says, "Resoluteness 'exists' only as resolution".[24] This apparent connection between the form and content of resoluteness falls because Heidegger will not specify any particular resolution or favour one kind of resolute action over another. It looks as if we understand our potentiality-for-being-authentic simply by being resolute, by wanting to have a conscience, by anticipating death. Authentic Dasein takes the form of anticipatory resoluteness, but Heidegger will say nothing about the contents of authentic Dasein, perhaps because to do so would be to engage in a peculiarly inauthentic discourse of the type he rejects.

Heidegger will issue no moral prescriptions beyond the pure formalism of "be yourself", "be resolute", in short "be a hero". This deliberate failure of Heideggerian ontology to engage with the specific contents of the being of Dasein leaves a vacuum at the core of Dasein, a vacuum into which the passionate egoism of Stirner will rush.[25] Heidegger's hero is Stirner's Owner in that resolute authentic Dasein is the end product of Dasein's self realisation and liberation from the ways of being of "the they", just as the Owner is the ultimate self realisation of the Stirnerian ego when the attempted deceptions of the moral, and of society, are swept away. Heidegger and Stirner both have self realisation in common at the core of their notion of selfhood. The works of both are expressions of the same preferred form of being.

This is the single significant, and probably damning, consequence of Heidegger's ontology. Heidegger refuses to endorse any particular ethical values; his work is an attempt to go beyond good and evil, as is that of Stirner. For different reasons both fail or refuse to answer the question, "What ought I be like?" and despite everything that Heidegger says this remains an important question, which requires an answer. Without an answer we will be unable to distinguish between the philanthropist and the serial murderer, both may be realising their authentic-potentiality-for-being, and for both the actual contents of their actions will be irrelevant to our ontological judgements about their relative authenticity.[26]

In the end Heidegger's ontology fails everyday Dasein. Heroism is common to both Stirner's and Heidegger's notion of selfhood because both pursue formal projects and arrive at a purely formal notion of heroic selfhood - authentic Dasein and the Owner. Neither is prepared to discuss the relative merits and demerits of particular actions contemplated or carried out by individuals, except in respect of their formal ontological relevance. The heroic self underpins the positions of both Heidegger and Stirner, the difference is that Stirner makes this explicit while Heidegger attempts to deny it, however, even in the very act of denial we have seen how Heidegger must affirm the heroism of Dasein. Although it appears that Heidegger's work fatally undermines Stirner's position this is not so in the end, Stirner's Owner re-emerges in authentic Dasein. The same project is common to both and leads to the same conclusion. Heidegger's story has a hero, the hero is Dasein.

The formalism of Heidegger's authentic Dasein (and the Stirnerian Owner) tell us more than that we should be ourselves, they tell us that we should expect to be told no more, and to carry the responsibility for what we do alone. They tell us not to seek the comfortable excuse of overarching moral principle. The empty formalism of both Heidegger's and Stirner's notions of the self seems to leave a vacuum at the very point at which we seek most guidance. How are we to be in the world once we become authentic, an "Owner"? In Heideggerian, and Stirnerian, spirit we can ask in answer to this question, what kind of Being could ask such a question? The only answer to this must be, a Being that is free to choose. The vacuum is the space for free choice. The philosophies of Stirner and Heidegger share a celebration of human freedom in their different ways and this is their greatest achievement. All that ontology will ever tell us is, "Be yourself", and perhaps self realisation is the only good worth having?

Notes

1. Laing explicitly recognises the influence of Heidegger's work on his own, for example, Laing, 1965, p.52, and p.125, p.132.
2. In Heideggerian terms Stirner's Unique One is an example of Being which does not seek authenticity and which attempts to deny its very possibility. The Unique One is trying to be wholly and solely preoccupied with present concerns and to live only as fallen.

3. Heidegger, 1987, notably, H. 22-25, 89-101, 204-206.
4. Marx, W, 1971, pp. 86-90.
5. Richardson, 1986, Part Two.
6. Laing, 1965, "The Case of Peter", pp. 120-133, and "Mrs R." pp. 54-58.
7. Stirner, 1982, p. 5.
8. Without doubt Stirner's egoism is also a sort of ethical position, that is, it prescribes behaviour towards others, albeit in a way which is dismissive of the claims of others against the individually determined ego. As morality Stirner's egoism is anti-morality. I will return to this aspect of Stirner's egoism in the next section.
9. "Man is never first and foremost on the hither side of the world as a 'subject', whether this is taken as 'I' or 'We'. Nor is he ever simply a mere subject, which always simultaneously is related to objects so that his essence lies in the subject-object relation. Rather before all this, man in his essence is ek-sistent into the openness of being, into the open region that clears the 'between' within which a relation' of subject to object can 'be'" (Heidegger, 1994, p.252).
10. Sartre, 1956, pp. 252-302.
11. "...the only point of departure possible is the Cartesian *cogito*" (Sartre, 1956, p.251).
12. Heidegger, 1987, H. 57-59.
13. I will return to Heidegger's formalism in the next section. Also see, Bernasconi, "Deconstruction and the possibility of Ethics" and, Havas, "Who is Heidegger's Nietzsche?".
14. Sartre, 1991, pp. 28-31.
15. Waterhouse calls this, "The Vacuity of Heidegger's Authenticity", Waterhouse, 1981, pp. 177-192, and argues in "A Critique of Authenticity", that Sartre's despair at the end of *Being and Nothingness* is more realistic than the heroism implied in Heidegger's notion of authentic Dasein.
16. Spiegelberg, 1960, Vol. I, p. 347 and see Waterhouse, 1981, pp. 35-48.
17. Heidegger avoids both sides of the question, he seeks neither to conformity of knowledge to objects, like Hume, nor objects to knowledge, like Kant.
18. Heidegger, 1990, p. 21 and 1982, Chapter Three.
19. Heidegger, 1987, H. 73-76.
20. Rorty in "Overcoming the Tradition: Heidegger and Dewey", is critical of Heidegger's approach in this area and a counter argument to Rorty is given by Okrent, "The Truth of Being and the History of Philosophy".
21. There are also echoes here of Nietzsche when he says, "Every superior human being will instinctively aspire after a secret citadel where he is *set free* from the crowd, the many, the majority, where, as its exception, he may forget the rule 'man' - except in the one case in which, as a man of knowledge in the great and exceptional sense, he will be impelled by an even stronger instinct to make straight for this rule" (Nietzsche, 1973, §26 p. 39), and Havas suggests that, "Heidegger might be considered to be one of Nietzsche's most pitiless readers" ("Who is Heidegger's Nietzsche?" p. 243).
22. Ridley Scott's film *Blade Runner* demonstrates this point brilliantly when the replicant Roy Batty performs an heroic gesture in saving the life of Dekkard, his relentless pursuer and would-be executioner, as the last act of a life which until

then has been ungrounded. In being a hero Roy Batty has finally learned to be a "human", or in Heidegger's terms, he has achieved authentic selfhood.
23. Again Ridley Scott's character, Roy Batty, shortly before dying, takes over his own past as having been a replicant and in so doing recaptures all the moments of his life, as he says, "all these moments will be lost in time, like tears in rain".
24. Heidegger, 1987, H. 298.
25. This is what Waterhouse calls the "vacuity" of Heidegger's authenticity. (1981, pp. 177-192), and it is a danger recognised by Nietzsche when he says, "He who fights monsters should look to it that he himself does not become a monster. And when you gaze long into an abyss the abyss also gazes into you" (Nietzsche, 1973 §146, p. 84).
26. See Raskolnikov's rationalisation of his murder of the old pawnbroker in *Crime and Punishment* and Grossman's discussion of this in his biography *Dostoyevsky*, pp. 359-361.

Bibliography

Barash, J.A. (1988), *Martin Heidegger and the Problem of Historical Meaning*, Martinus Nijhoff, The Hague.
Bennett, J. (1971), *Locke, Berkeley, Hume - Central Themes*, Clarendon, Oxford.
Berkeley, G. (1975), *The Principles of Human Knowledge*, Collins/Fontana, London.
Bernasconi, R. (1987), "Deconstruction and the Possibility of Ethics", *Deconstruction and Philosophy - The Texts of Jacques Derrida*, Ed. Sallis, J., University of Chicago Press.
Blattner, W. (1992), "Existential Temporality in Being and Time", *Heidegger: A Critical Reader*, Ed. Dreyfus, H.L. and Hall, H., Blackwell, Oxford.
Bradley, F.H. (1988), *Ethical Studies*, Clarendon, Oxford.
Brandom, R. (1992), "Heidegger's Categories in Being and Time", *Heidegger: A Critical Reader*, Ed. Dreyfus, H.L. and Hall, H., Blackwell, Oxford.
Bricke, J.(1980), *Hume's Philosophy of Mind*, Edinburgh University Press.
Camus, A. (1983), *The Outsider*, Penguin, Harmondsworth.
Cassirer, H.W. (1954), *Kant's First Critique*, Allen and Unwin, London.
Caws, P. (1979), *Sartre,* Routledge and Kegan Paul, London.
Clark, J.P. (1976), *Max Stirner's Egoism*, Freedom Press, London.
Cooper, D. E. (1990), *Existentialism. A Reconstruction*, Blackwell, Oxford.
De Beauvoir, S.(1987), *A Very Easy Death*, Penguin, Harmondsworth.
Derrida, J. (1978), "Violence and Metaphysics", *Writing and Difference*, University of Chicago Press.
Descartes, R. (1954), *Philosophical Writings*, Nelson University Paperbacks, London.
Descartes, R. (1986), *Meditations on First Philosophy*, Cambridge University Press.
Descartes, R. (1988), *Selected Philosophical Writing*, Cambridge University Press.
Descartes, R. (1991), *The Philosophical Writings of Descartes Vol. III*, Cambridge University Press. 1991
Dick, P.K. (1972), *Blade Runner*, Grafton, London.
Dostoyevsky, F.M. (1973), *Crime and Punishment*, Penguin, Harmondsworth.

Dreyfus, H. (1992), "Heidegger's History of the Being of Equipment", *Heidegger: A Critical Reader*, Ed. Dreyfus, H.L. and Hall, H., Blackwell, Oxford.

Dreyfus, H. and Haugeland, J.(1978), "Husserl and Heidegger: Philosophy's Last Stand", *Heidegger and Modern Philosophy*, Ed. Murray, M., Yale University Press.

Ewing, A. (1938), *A short commentary on Kant's Critique of Pure Reason*, Methuen, London.

Fell, J.P. (1979), *Heidegger and Sartre*, Columbia University Press, New York.

Fell, J.P. (1992), "The Familiar and the Strange: On the Limits of Praxis in the Early Heidegger", *Heidegger: A Critical Reader*, Ed. Dreyfus, H.L. and Hall, H., Blackwell, Oxford.

Foucault, M. (1988), "Technologies of the Self", *A Seminar with Michel Foucault*, Ed. Martin, L., Gutman, H., Hutton, P.H., University of Massachusetts Press.

Garrett, B. (1998), *Personal Identity and Self Consciousness*, Routledge, London and New York.

Gelven, M. (1970), *A Commentary on Heidegger's Being and Time*, Harper and Row, New York.

Glover, J. (1988), *The Philosophy and Psychology of Personal Identity*, Allen Lane, London.

Greene, M. (1983), *Sartre*, University Press of America, Washington, D.C.

Grossman, L. (1974), *Dostoyevsky*, Allen Lane, London.

Guignon, C.B. (1983), *Heidegger and the problem of knowledge*, Hackett Publishing Co., Indianapolis.

Guignon, C.B. (1992), "History and Commitment in the Early Heidegger", *Heidegger: A Critical Reader*, Ed. Dreyfus, H.L. and Hall, H., Blackwell, Oxford.

Haar, M. (1992), "Attunement and Thinking", *Heidegger: A Critical Reader*, Ed. Dreyfus, H.L. and Hall, H., Blackwell, Oxford.

Habermas, J. (1987), *The Philosophical Discourse of Modernity*, Polity Press, Cambridge.

Harries, K. (1978), "Fundamental Ontology and the Search for Man's Place", *Heidegger and Modern Philosophy*, Ed. Murray, M., Yale University Press.

Haugeland, J. (1992), "Dasein's Disclosedness", *Heidegger: A Critical Reader*, Ed. Dreyfus, H.L. and Hall, H., Blackwell, Oxford.

Havas, R.E. (1992), "Who is Heidegger's Nietzsche?", *Heidegger: A Critical Reader*, Ed. Dreyfus, H.L. and Hall, H., Blackwell, Oxford.

Hegel, G.W.F. (1977), *The Phenomenology of Spirit*, Clarendon, Oxford.

Heidegger, M. (1962), *Kant and the Problem of Metaphysics*, Indiana University Press, Bloomington.
Heidegger, M. (1968), "What is Metaphysics?", *Existence and Being*, Vision Press, London.
Heidegger, M. (1969), *The Essence of Reasons*, Northwest University Press, Evanston.
Heidegger, M. (1970), *Hegel's Concept of Experience*, Harper and Row, New York.
Heidegger, M. (1982), *The Basic Problems of Phenomenology*, Indiana University Press, Bloomington.
Heidegger, M. (1985), *History of the Concept of Time*, Indiana University Press, Bloomington.
Heidegger, M. (1987), *Being and Time*, Blackwell, Oxford.
Heidegger, M. (1990), *Kant and the Problem of Metaphysics*, Indiana University Press, Bloomington.
Heidegger, M. (1994), "Letter on Humanism", *Basic Writings*, Ed. Krell, D.F., Routledge, London.
Hintikka, J. (1968), "Cogito, ergo, Sum: Inference or Performance", *Descartes:A Collection of Critical Essays*, Ed. Doney, W., Macmillan, London.
Hume, D. (1959), *A Treatise of Human Nature. Vol. I*, Everyman, London.
Hume, D. (1959), *A Treatise of Human Nature. Vol. II*, Everyman, London.
Hume, D. (1970), *Enquiries Concerning Human Understanding*, Clarendon, Oxford.
Kant, I. (1956), *Groundwork of the Metaphysic of Morals*, Harper and Row, New York.
Kant, I. (1977), *Prolegomena to any future metaphysics*, Hackett Publishing Co., Indianapolis.
Kant, I. (1992), *Critique of Pure Reason*, Macmillan, London.
Kemp, J. (1968), *The Philosophy of Kant*, Oxford University Press.
Kemp Smith, N. (1960),*The Philosophy of David Hume*, Macmillan, London.
Kenny, A. (1993), *Descartes:A Study of his Philosophy*, Thoemmes Press, Bristol.
Kirsner, D. (1976), *The Schizoid World of Jean-Paul Sartre and R.D. Laing*, University of Queensland Press, St Lucia, Queensland.
Laing, R.D. (1965), *The Divided Self*, Penguin, Harmondsworth.
Laing, R.D. (1967), *The Politics of Experience and The Bird of Paradise*, Penguin, Harmondsworth.
Laing, R.D. (1969), *Self and Others*, Penguin, Harmondsworth.
Locke, J. (1975), *An Essay Concerning Human Understanding*, Fontana/Collins, London.

Malcolm, N. (1968), "Descartes proof that his essence is thinking", *Descartes: A Collection of Critical Essays*, Ed. Doney, W., Macmillan, London.
Macquarrie, J.(1968), *Martin Heidegger*, John Knox Press, Richmond, Virginia.
Macquarrie, J. (1972), *Existentialism*, Penguin, Harmondsworth.
Marx, K. (1981), *Early Writings*, Penguin, Harmondsworth.
Marx, K. and Engels, F. (1965), *The German Ideology*, Lawrence and Wishart, London.
Marx, W. (1971), *Heidegger and the tradition*, Northwestern University Press, Evanston.
Matthews, H.E. (1982), "Strawson on Transcendental Idealism", *Kant and Pure Reason*, Ed. Walker, R.C.S., Oxford University Press.
McCulloch, G. (1994), *Using Sartre: An Analytical Introduction to Early Sartrean Themes*, Routledge, London and New York.
Meszaros, I. (1979), *The Work of Sartre, Vol. I: The Search for Freedom*, Harvester Press, Brighton.
Mill, J.S. (1962), "On Liberty", *Utilitarianism*, Ed Warnock, M., Collins/Fontana, London
Mill, J.S. (1962), "Utilitarianism", *Utilitarianism*, Ed. Warnock, M., Collins/Fontana, London.
Modell, A.H. (1993), *The Private Self*, Harvard University Press, Massachusetts.
Mulhall, S. (1996), *Heidegger and Being and Time*, Routledge, London.
Natanson, M. (1973), *A Critique of Jean-Paul Sartre's Ontology*, Martinus Nijhoff, The Hague.
Nicholson, G. (1986), "Ekstatic Temporality in Sein und Zeit", *A Companion to Martin Heidegger's Being and Time*, Ed. Kockelmans, J.J., University Press of America, Washington D.C.
Nietzsche, F. (1973), *Beyond Good and Evil*, Penguin, Harmondsworth.
Nietzsche, F. (1986), *Daybreak*, Cambridge University Press.
Norman, R.J. (1976), *Hegel's Phenomenology*, Sussex University Press.
Okrent, M. (1988), *Heidegger's Pragmatism - Understanding Being and the Critique of Metaphysics*, Cornell University Press, Ithaca & London.
Okrent, M. (1992), "The Truth of Being and the History of Philosophy", *Heidegger: A Critical Reader*, Ed. Dreyfus, H.L. and Hall, H., Blackwell, Oxford.
Olafson, F.A. (1987), *Heidegger and the Philosophy of Mind*, Yale University Press.
Parfit, D. (1984), *Reasons and Persons*, Clarendon, Oxford.
Pascal, B. (1961), *Pensées*, Penguin, Harmondsworth.

Paterson, R.W.K. (1971), *The Nihilist Egoist - Max Stirner*, Oxford University Press.
Paton, H.J. (1936), *Kant's Metaphysics of Experience* (Two Vols.), Allen and Unwin, London.
Paton, H.J. (1963), *The Categorical Imperative*, Hutchinson, London.
Penelhum, T. (1968), "Hume on Personal Identity", *Hume:A Collection of Critical Essays*, Ed. Chappell, V.C., Macmillan, London.
Penelhum, T. (1975), *Hume*, Macmillan, London.
Plato (1971), *Gorgias*, Penguin, Harmondsworth.
Poggeler, O. (1978), "Being as Appropriation", *Heidegger and Modern Philosophy*, Ed. Murray, M.,Yale University Press.
Popkin, R.H. (1968), "David Hume: His Pyrrhonism and His Critique of Pyrrhonism", *Hume: A Collection of Critical Essays*, Ed. Chappell, V.C., Macmillan, London.
Richardson, J. (1986), *Existential Epistemology - A Heideggerian Critique of the Cartesian Project*, Clarendon, Oxford.
Ricoeur, P. (1992), *Oneself and Another*, University of Chicago Press, Chicago and London.
Rorty, R.(1978), "Overcoming the tradition - Heidegger and Dewey", *Heidegger and Modern Philosophy*, Ed. Murray, M.,Yale University Press.
Rorty, R. (1992), "Heidegger, Contingency and Pragmatism", *Heidegger: A Critical Reader,* Ed. Dreyfus, H.L. and Hall, H., Blackwell, Oxford.
Ryle, G. (1949), *The Concept of Mind*, Hutchinson, London.
Sartre, J-P. (1956), *Being and Nothingness*, Philosophical Library of New York.
Sartre, J-P. (1956), *Words*, Penguin, Harmondsworth.
Sartre, J-P. (1957), *The Transcendence of the Ego*, Noonday Press, London.
Sartre, J-P. (1963), *The Age of Reason*, Penguin, Harmondsworth.
Sartre, J-P. (1965), *Nausea*, Penguin, Harmondsworth.
Sartre, J-P. (1966), *The Reprieve*, Penguin, Harmondsworth.
Sartre, J-P. (1968), "Cartesian Freedom", *Literary and Philosophical Essays*, Hutchinson, London.
Sartre, J-P. (1984), *Iron in the Soul*, Penguin, Harmondsworth.
Sartre, J-P. (1991), *Existentialism and Humanism*, Methuen, London.
Sayers, S.P. (1985), *Reality and Reason:Dialectic and the Theory of Knowledge*, Blackwell, Oxford.
Schatzki, T.R. (1992), "Early Heidegger on Being, the Clearing and Realism", *Heidegger: A Critical Reader*, Ed. Dreyfus, H.L. and Hall, H., Blackwell, Oxford.
Scott, R. (Dir.) (1982), *Blade Runner* (film).

Scruton, R. (1982), *Kant*, Oxford University Press.
Searle, J.R. (1992), *The Rediscovery of the Mind*, MIT Press, Cambridge, Mass.
Solomon, R. (1988), *Continental Philosophy since 1750 - The Rise and Fall of the Self*, Oxford University Press.
Spiegelberg, H. (1960), *The Phenomenological Movement - a Historical Introduction. Vol. I*, Martinus Nijhoff, The Hague.
Stirner, M. (1982), *The Ego and Its Own*, Rebel Press, London.
Strawson, P.F. (1964), *Individuals*, Methuen, London.
Strawson, P.F. (1993), *The Bounds of Sense - An Essay on Kant's Critique of Pure Reason*, Routledge, London.
Stroud, B. (1982), "Transcendental Arguments", *Kant and Pure Reason*, Ed. Walker, R.C.S., Oxford University Press.
Taylor, C. (1989), *Sources of the Self – The Making of Modern Identity*, Cambridge University Press.
Walsh, W.H. (1975), *Kant's Criticism of Metaphysics*, Edinburgh University Press.
Walsh, W.H. (1982), "Self Knowledge", *Kant and Pure Reason*, Ed. Walker, R.C.S., Oxford University Press.
Warnock, M. (1966), *The Philosophy of Sartre*, Hutchinson, London.
Waterhouse, R. (1977), "Husserl and Phenomenology", *Radical Philosophy 16*.
Waterhouse, R. (1978), "A Critique of Authenticity", *Radical Philosophy 20*.
Waterhouse, R. (1980), "Heidegger's 'Being and Time'", *Radical Philosophy 26*.
Waterhouse, R. (1980), "Heidegger's Early Development", *Radical Philosophy 25*
Waterhouse, R. (1981), "Heidegger: An Assessment", *Radical Philosophy 27*.
Waterhouse, R. (1981), *A Heidegger Critique*, Harvester Press, Brighton.
Williams, B. (1968), "The certainty of the *cogito*", *Descartes: A Collection of Critical Essays*,Ed. Doney, W., Macmillan, London.
Williams, B. (1978), *Descartes: The Project of Pure Enquiry*, Penguin, Harmondsworth.
Williams, T.C. (1987), *The Unity of Kant's Critique of Pure Reason*, Edwin Mellen Press, Lewiston/Queenston.
Wilson, M.D. (1978), *Descartes*, Routledge and Kegan Paul, London.
Zimmerman, M.E. (1986), *Eclipse of the Self - The Development of Heidegger's Concept of Authenticity*, Ohio University Press.

Index

a priori, 61-65, 79, 80, 86, 87, 90, 104
absence, 12, 26, 27, 123, 125, 126, 128, 131, 147, 157, 188, 190
abstraction, 12, 17, 76, 80
anticipation, 155, 156, 159-161
anxiety, 152-156, 158-160, 164, 167
appearance, 29, 61-64, 68, 73-80, 87, 89, 140, 148, 149, 158
Aristotle, 10
authentic, 3, 4, 37, 41, 123, 130, 132, 139, 144-146, 149, 152-169, 171, 173, 174, 179, 180, 182-185, 188-194

Batty, Roy, 173, 193, 194
being-for-itself, 91, 94
being-guilty, 10, 158, 160, 161, 173, 191
being-in-itself, 91, 92, 94, 160
being-in-the-world, 120, 124, 127, 130, 137, 139, 141, 142, 146, 149, 157, 159, 165, 166, 168, 171, 172, 174, 180-184
Berkeley, 59, 65-67, 88, 89
Blade Runner, 11, 173, 193

Camus, 5, 15, 21, 27, 41
Care, 90, 130, 141, 144, 146, 148, 149, 153, 155, 157, 158, 161, 163-167, 170, 172, 185, 188
Cartesian, 2, 3, 8, 9, 11, 18, 24, 35-37, 40, 44, 47, 48, 50, 57-59, 61, 63, 65, 66, 70, 72, 73, 76, 81-88, 91, 95, 99, 102, 104, 105, 107, 109-115, 118-121, 123, 124, 126, 133-143, 146, 147, 149, 165-172, 178, 180, 185, 193
cogito, 3, 9-12, 18, 24, 25, 36, 40, 44-47, 49, 58, 68, 86, 87, 91, 94, 95, 98, 104-111, 115, 118, 122, 135, 141, 183, 193
Concern, 127
conscience, 3, 9, 10, 149, 156-161, 173, 188, 190, 191
conspicuous, 125, 147, 188
corporeal, 6, 44, 52, 91, 114

Dasein, 3, 4, 10, 41, 59, 84, 90, 117, 119-124, 126-132, 137, 139-175, 180-193
De Beauvoir, 5, 173
death, 3, 11, 55, 149-161, 165, 167, 169-173, 188-191
Dekkard, 173, 193
Derrida, 5, 173
Descartes, 1-4, 7, 10, 11, 20-22, 36, 41, 43-51, 57-61, 65-69, 73-75, 77, 78, 80, 85, 87, 89, 91, 98, 114, 116, 118, 122, 123, 125, 133, 135, 139, 142, 160, 170, 171, 176-179, 187
determinism, 98
disconnection, 21, 26, 49, 180
Dostoyevsky, 15, 21, 27, 41, 194
dualism, 1-3, 11, 24, 29, 33, 35, 58, 59, 63, 67, 70, 73, 76, 78-80, 82-87, 100, 113

egoism, 1, 4, 11, 12, 15-21, 29, 33, 35, 40, 49, 116, 171, 173, 177, 179, 182, 183, 185, 186, 191, 193
empiricism, 51, 55, 57, 59, 64-66, 71-74, 77, 83, 126

epistemology, 2, 3, 8, 11, 24, 40, 59-61, 70, 73, 77, 79, 102, 115, 121, 123, 133, 137, 143, 145, 147, 168, 169, 173
equipment, 125-132, 144, 147-149, 163, 164, 172
ethics, 20, 35, 144, 173, 184, 185
everydayness, 5, 59, 111, 117-121, 134, 135, 137, 138, 142, 148, 151, 157, 166, 169, 188
Existentialism, 3, 11, 21, 30, 71 112, 113, 178, 183

facticity, 98, 100, 162
fallen, 155, 157, 160, 192
Foucault, 5, 8
freedom, 3, 13, 14, 17-19, 21, 28, 30-32, 34, 41, 47, 95, 97-101, 109, 111, 112, 115, 150, 156, 158, 192
futurity, 149-151, 153, 155, 161, 162

God, 12, 14, 15, 27, 30, 44, 46, 48, 49, 94, 158, 190
Goldilocks, 8, 49, 54, 59, 67, 73, 74, 76, 91-93, 112, 115, 146, 147, 166, 170

Hegel, 5, 10, 12-14, 21, 108, 110, 113, 142, 144, 173
Heidegger, 1, 3-10, 13, 21, 22, 40, 41, 59, 77-90, 110-113, 115-136, 138-162, 164-194
hermeneutics, 10, 119, 143
history, 138, 147, 148, 164, 170
Hume, 1-4, 7-9, 12, 41, 43, 50-61, 63-67, 70-74, 77, 78, 80-82, 84, 87, 89, 91, 92, 103, 105, 114, 116, 117, 123, 133-136, 138-147, 153, 160, 166, 169, 171, 173, 176-179, 187, 193

Husserl, 5, 10, 118, 119, 142-144, 186, 187

idealism, 65-70, 73, 88, 89
imagination, 48, 55, 66, 69, 80, 98, 145
inauthentic, 130, 132, 145, 148-160, 163-166, 168, 169, 171-173, 177, 182, 184
intention, 8, 9, 41, 96-98, 103, 165

Kant, 1-4, 6-8, 11, 12, 58, 60-93, 96, 100-102, 112-116, 123, 133-136, 138, 139, 142-145, 147-149, 160, 171, 172, 177-179, 187, 193
Kierkegaard, 5

Laing, 1, 2, 4, 21-41, 43, 44, 111, 176-179, 181-183, 192, 193
Locke, 11, 43, 49, 50, 57
limit, 74, 100, 155

madness, 8, 23, 26, 35-41
Marx, 5, 14, 21, 143-145, 173, 193
Mersault, 15, 21, 41
Mill, 16, 21
mineness, 16, 120
Mitsein, 40, 115, 185
moment of vision, 160, 171, 174

Nietzsche, 5, 10, 41, 42, 173, 193, 194
nihilism, 5, 9, 17
nothingness, 21, 30, 35, 87, 93, 108-113, 144
noumenal, 62, 67, 68, 71, 72, 74-76, 87-89, 117, 119

obstinate, 125, 147, 188
obtrusive, 125, 131, 147, 188

Other, 3, 15, 23, 24, 27, 29, 34, 39, 40, 91-93, 95, 101-111, 113, 115, 128, 130, 131, 177, 183
Owner, 1, 4, 13, 15, 17, 29, 30, 47, 87, 177, 183, 191-192

phenomenology, 3, 5, 13, 70, 111, 115-122, 126, 139, 140, 143, 148, 149, 173, 186, 187
Plato, 10
presence, 18, 27, 45, 59, 78, 83, 85, 86, 93, 101, 113, 125, 129, 153
present-at-hand, 125, 127, 129-132, 134-137, 140, 158, 161, 165-167, 171
primordial, 17, 35, 81, 83, 85, 88, 125, 146, 150, 163, 167, 176, 180, 186, 187
projection, 37, 79, 81, 97, 99, 138, 154, 162, 164
psychology, 7, 8, 71, 102, 107

Raskolnikov, 15, 21, 27, 41, 194
ready-to-hand, 125, 127-129, 130-132, 134, 136, 140, 155, 188
Reason, 2, 51, 60, 61, 63-65, 67, 70-74, 76, 77, 79, 80, 82, 86, 89, 112, 138, 139, 148
resoluteness, 160-163, 167, 185, 188, 191
responsibility, 15, 17, 21, 51, 100, 157-159, 192
Ricoeur, 8-10
Roquentin, 15, 21, 41

sanity, 8, 23, 36-40, 179
Sartre, 1-8, 11, 15, 21-23, 30, 35, 40, 41, 77, 87, 91-116, 118, 123, 136, 142, 144, 160, 171, 176-179, 183, 185, 187, 193

scepticism, 46, 49, 51, 59, 60, 64, 65, 69, 72, 73, 80, 83, 114, 137, 143
Schematism, 77, 79-82, 85, 148, 149
schizophrenia, 21, 23, 25, 28, 30, 34, 36, 37
science, 7, 11, 60, 64, 88, 129
self-consciousness, 13, 18, 28, 64, 93
self-realisation, 38, 182, 185
sensations, 51, 56, 61-65, 116, 135
Sensibility, 62-64, 79
shame, 101, 105-109
situation, 38, 96-98, 100, 101, 105, 107, 125
solicitude, 10, 131, 144
solipsism, 18, 69, 103-105, 108-110, 137
soul, 6, 7, 47, 48, 71, 130
Spinoza, 10
Stirner, 1, 2, 4, 11-22, 24, 28-44, 47, 49, 108, 110, 111, 116, 172, 173, 176-179, 182, 183, 185, 186, 189-193
synthetic, 61, 64, 87

temporality, 1, 3, 7-9, 43, 58, 62, 63, 80, 90, 114, 116, 139, 142, 146, 148, 149, 153, 156, 158-166, 168-174, 176, 178, 179
the they, 132, 144, 151-156, 158-160, 180, 181, 185, 188, 189, 191
thing-in-itself, 62, 68-71, 75-79, 87, 89, 134-136, 187
things-in-themselves, 61, 62, 65, 67-70, 73-75, 78, 79, 100, 115, 118, 121, 129, 131, 134, 136
thrown, 153-155, 158, 165, 167, 171, 172, 181

transcendental, 5, 13, 16, 29, 38, 61, 64, 65, 68-73, 75, 76, 79, 81-84, 86, 88, 89, 112, 134, 140, 148
Transcendental Deduction, 79, 112

uncoupling, 26, 31
Understanding, 11, 62, 64, 72, 77, 79, 81, 137, 140, 148, 163, 164

Unique One, 12, 15, 17, 18, 30-35, 39, 172, 177, 190, 192

veil of the senses, 1, 11, 43, 61, 65, 76, 79, 139, 166

Wittgenstein, 10
worldhood, 126, 127, 129, 130, 170

For Product Safety Concerns and Information please contact our EU
representative GPSR@taylorandfrancis.com
Taylor & Francis Verlag GmbH, Kaufingerstraße 24, 80331 München, Germany

www.ingramcontent.com/pod-product-compliance
Lightning Source LLC
Chambersburg PA
CBHW071355290426
44108CB00014B/1563